Bernardin de Saint-Pierre, John Parish

**A Voyage to the Isle of Mauritius, (or, Isle of France)**

The Isle of Bourbon, and the Cape of Good Hope

Bernardin de Saint-Pierre, John Parish

**A Voyage to the Isle of Mauritius, (or, Isle of France)**
*The Isle of Bourbon, and the Cape of Good Hope*

ISBN/EAN: 9783744720519

Printed in Europe, USA, Canada, Australia, Japan

Cover: Foto ©Andreas Hilbeck / pixelio.de

More available books at **www.hansebooks.com**

# VOYAGE

TO THE

## ISLAND of MAURITIUS,

(Or, ISLE OF FRANCE)

THE

## ISLE of BOURBON,

THE

## CAPE of GOOD-HOPE, &c.

With Observations and Reflections upon Nature, and Mankind.

By a FRENCH OFFICER.

---

Homo sum; humani nihil a me alienum puto.    TER.

---

TRANSLATED from the FRENCH
BY JOHN PARISH.

---

LONDON:
Printed for W. GRIFFIN, N° 6, *Catharine-Street*, STRAND.
MDCCLXXV.

# TO THE
## MOST NOBLE
## THE
# MARQUIS OF GRANBY.

*MY LORD,*

THE Permission I have obtained of inscribing this Translation to your Lordship, affords me a happy Opportunity of expressing my grateful respect to the Memory of your truly NOBLE FATHER, and my EXCELLENT PATRON---'tis in vain for me to attempt his Panegyric: All I could say, would be but as the feeble Eccho of a Nation's Voice, loud raised in Honour of his Virtues. The Task would also be a painful one: For while I wrote, Sorrow would be excited that so much Worth were lost to his COUNTRY, to his FAMILY, and to *me*.

# DEDICATION.

Having declined to speak of your Father's Virtues, I cannot my Lord, with propriety enumerate Your's: But thus far I may say, and with truth; that at so early a period of Life, they add Lustre to the high Rank you support.

Your Lordship's Patronage is more than a Compensation to the Author, for my inability to do Justice to his Work, and reflects an Honour upon me, of which I am very truly sensible.

I am, with the most perfect Respect,

MY LORD,

YOUR LORDSHIP's

most devoted and
most obedient
humble Servant,

*June* 1, 1775.

JOHN PARISH.

# The TRANSLATOR's
# PREFACE.

THE Reader is here prefented with a Tranflation of a Work, which the late Doctor Goldfmith admired for the accuracy and ingenuity of its Obfervations, and for the Spirit of Benevolence and Philantrohpy which breathes through the whole. He wifhed it to be done into Englifh, and had he lived, his correcting Hand would have rendered the Tranflation more worthy of the Author and of the Public favour, than in the ftate, in which it is now fubmitted it to their Candour.

The Syftem of Vegetation contained in the three laft Letters, is written in the Ori-

# PREFACE.

ginal as a Dialogue: In its present form, it is much shorter, and yet contains the meaning the Author would convey. A long Table of Sea Terms is omitted, as also another very long one of Contents, and a considerable Part of the Journal from Port l'Orient to the Isle of France, which appeared rather uninteresting. For the same Reason, and because of the difficulties attending the Translating of the Conchyology, which Science indeed the Author professes himself very little acquainted with, the Description of that Part of the Natural History is also omitted. By this means the Translation is reduced to one half the Bulk and Price of the Original.

Desirous to give the Reader every Information relative to an Island which (to say no more of it) has been the Object of the particular Attention of two Men so ingenious and so able as the Abbé de la Caille, and our Author; the Translator begs Leave to insert the following Extract from a late Publication, the Author of which, Dr. Campbell, speaking of the Isle of France, says, " incredible " as it may seem, yet it is certainly Matter of " Fact, that in the space of five Years he *(Mon-*

## PREFACE.

" *sieur de la Bourdonnais*) rendered this Country
" a *Paradise*, that had been a Desart for five
" thousand, and this in spite of the Inhabi-
" tants, and of the Company, who being
" originally prejudiced by them, behaved
" ill to him at his Return. He soon made
" the Cardinal de Fleury, however, sensible
" of the true state of things, and compelled
" the Company to acknowledge, though they
" did not reward, his Services. He after-
" wards returned, as all the World knows,
" into the Indies, and perfected the Work he
" had begun; and to him it is owing that
" *the Isle of France is at present one of the
" finest*," *as it was always one of the most
" Important and Improveable spots upon the
" Globe.*"

# AUTHOR's PREFACE.

THESE letters were written to my friends during my voyage. After my return, I put them in order and printed them, as a public testimony of my acknowledgement of the good offices I had received.

THE plan I have adopted is this; having given an account of the plants and animals natural to each country, and of the soil in it's unimproved state, I then speak of the characters and manners of the inhabitants.

## The Author's PREFACE.

WHAT I have said, will perhaps be deemed a satire, but I can say with truth, that in speaking of men, I have spoken of their good actions with alacrity, and of their faults with candor.

AFTER speaking of the Colonists, I enter upon a detail of the vegetables and animals with which they have peopled the country. The industry, the arts, and the commerce of these countries are all included in agriculture. It should seem that this art, so simple, would be productive of the most amiable manners; but the life led by the people of the Isle of France, is far from a primitive one.

DEATH has snatched from us Monsieur de Tolbach, Governor of the Cape, who had been very obliging to me. If the place allotted him in these memoirs cannot now serve as acknowledgements, it may at least be an useful example of conduct to those Frenchmen who may be appointed governors in India. If from my account, they may be induced to imitate his virtues, I shall then indeed do honour to them.

I AM next to apologize for having treated of some subjects that I am a stranger to. I have written upon plants and animals, but I am not a Naturalist. Natural History is not shut up in libraries; it has rather

## The Author's PREFACE.

ther seemed to me, a volume, to be read by the whole world. I have traced through the whole, the most evident proofs of a providence; and I have treated it, not as a system that is pleasing to my fancy, but as a sentiment with which my heart is filled.

I shall at least, I think, have been of use to mankind, if the faint sketch I have given of the miserable lot of the Negroe slaves, should save them from one stroke of the whip; and if the Europeans who so loudly exclaim against tyranny, and among whom are composed such beautiful treatises of morality, may hereby be induced to cease being in India the most barbarous of all tyrants.

I shall think I have done service to my country, if I prevent but one single man of worth from quitting it, and if I have determined him to cultivate one additional acre in some heath that yet never has felt the plough.

To be sensible of this love for his country, a man must first quit it. I am attached to mine, although neither by my fortune, nor the rank I hold in it: but the place where I first saw the light, is dear to me: There, I have felt, have loved, have spoken.

## The Author's PREFACE.

This soil, so generally adopted by strangers, is delightful to me: here, all that can be desirable, is in abundance; and France, by the temperature of it's climate, the excellence of it's vegetables, and the industry of its inhabitants, is to be preferred to either India.

In fine, I love this country, where my connections are numerous, where esteem is the most refined, friendship most intimate, and virtue most amiable.

VOYAGES

A

# VOYAGE, &c.

## LETTER I.

*L'Orient,* 4 *January,* 1768.

I AM juft arrived at L'Orient after having felt the moft fevere cold. The road was frozen from Paris to within ten leagues of Rennes. This city, which was burnt in 1720, has now a grandeur which it owes to its misfortune. There are feveral new buildings, two handfome fquares, a ftatue of Lewis the XVth. and alfo one of Lewis the XIVth. The infide of the Parliament-Houfe is handfomely decorated, but with rather too much uniformity. The pannels of the wainfcot are painted white, and have gilt moldings. Moft of the churches and public buildings are in this tafte. In other refpects, Rennes is but a difmal town. It is fituated at the confluence of the *Villaine* and the *Ifle*; two fmall rivers. Its fuburbs are formed of fome dirty houfes; the ftreets are ill paved. The common people drefs in a coarfe brown ftuff, which gives them very much an air of poverty.

I saw in Britany, a vaft deal of uncultivated land. Nothing grows upon it but broom, and a fhrub with yellow flowers, which appeared to me a compofition position of thorns. The country people call it *Lande* or *Jan* \*. They bruise it to feed their cattle with †. The broom serves only to heat their ovens; it might be turned to better account, and especially in a maritime country. The Romans made a cordage of it, which they preferred to hemp, for their shipping. I owe this observation to Pliny, who is known to have commanded the fleets of the Empire ‡.

Might not these lands be sown to good purpose with potatoes, a certain subsistence, which can neither suffer by inclement seasons, nor the storehouses of monopolizers.

Industry seems checked equally by an Aristocratic government, or in a *pays d'etats* §. The Peasant, who is without a representative in the assembly, is likewise without protection. In Britany he is ill clad, drinks nothing but water, and lives upon black bread.

The misery of mankind always increases in the same degree as their dependance. I have seen the

---

\*. In one word, *Furze*. *T*.  † This is practised in some parts of *England*. *T*.

‡ This broom, which the author saw in Britany, must be of the kind, a species of the Spanish Spartum, which it is well known was used by the Ancients instead of hemp. *T*.

§ Many provinces in France have a kind of Parliament, and are called *Pais d'Etats*. These Etats are nothing more than an assembly of the Noblesse of the province, who meet at least once in every three years, for little other purpose, than to raise money for the crown; and in raising, take care to pay nothing themselves. Such an Aristocratical assembly, is supposed by many politicians, to be more tyrannical, than a sole and absolute governor. The Reader will distinguish the *Etats* from the *Parlement*, which in France, is only a Supreme Court of Judicature; by which, indeed, the King's edicts are obliged to be registered, before they are regularly of authority. *T*.

peasant

peasant rich in Holland; at his ease in Prussia; in a tolerable comfortable state in Russia, and labouring under the greatest penury in Poland: I shall then certainly see the Negro, who is the Peasant of our colonies, in a deplorable state. I account thus for what I have said; in a republic there is no sovereign, in a monarchy, but one; but in an aristocracy, every peasant is subject to his particular tyrant.

LIBERTY is the parent of industry. The Swiss peasant is ingenious, the villain of Poland is without imagination. This stupor of the soul, which enables a man, even more than philosophy, to bear up against misfortune, seems to me to be a peculiar blessing. When Jupiter, says Homer, *reduces a man to the state of a slave, he takes from him one half of his understanding.*

EXCUSE these reflections. When I see mankind struggling with great miseries, I cannot help enquiring, what will remedy them, or from whence they arise.

IN Lower Britany, Nature appears as it were, dwindled. The hills, vallies, trees, men and animals are very small there.

THERE are in many places quarries of slate, and of black and red marble, and mines of lead, mixed with silver, which is very ductile. But the real riches of this country are its linens, its threads, and cattle. Industry revives with liberty, from the vicinity of the sea-ports. This is perhaps, the only good consequence of a maritime commerce, which is little else than an avarice, pointed out by law. Strange lot of man, that he should frequently deduce greater benefits from the indulgence of his passions, than from the exercise of his reason.

The peasant here is much at his ease; he looks upon himself at liberty, from the neighbourhood of an element, all the roads to which are open. Oppression cannot extend itself to any thing beyond his fortune: Is he hard pressed, he embarks himself, and on shipboard finds the oak of his own inclosures; the linens woven by his own family, and grain, the growth of his own fields: Houshold Gods by whom he has been abandoned! In the commander of the vessel, he frequently recognizes the Lord of his own village, and in their common misery sees him a man, whose fortune is more to be complained of than his own. At liberty to judge of his own situation, he becomes master of it; and seated on the yard-arm, decides in the fury of a storm upon that, which on shore, he durst not make an object of enquiry.

I have not yet seen Port L'Orient. Half a league before our arrival, we crossed a small arm of the sea in a ferry-boat: I could scarcely distinguish the town. A thick fog covered the horizon: This is occasioned by the vicinity of the sea; but the winter is the less severe on this account.

This observation holds good as well in the neighbourhood of pools and lakes, as of the sea. May not this be to favour the propagation of a multitude of insects, and water vermin that inhabit the sands of the shore? Whether this conjecture is right or not, the facility of living there, and the mild temperature, draw from the North an infinite number of sea and water-fowls.

Nature may well reserve for them some portion of the coast, and of mild air, when she has allotted to the fishes alone, above half the world.

I am, &c.

## LETTER II.

*L'Orient, January* 18, 1768.

L'ORIENT is a small town in Britany, which the commerce of the East Indies renders daily more flourishing. It is, like all other new towns, regular, the streets in strait lines, but unfinished. It is but indifferently fortified. There are some fine warehouses, the Hotel des Ventes, and a tower, whence one may see, wharfs which are but just begun, and ground plats whereon buildings are marked out.—It is situated at the bottom of a bay which receives the rivers *Blavet* and *Ponscorf*; they are navigable, and a vast many ships come down by them to L'Orient. The entrance of this bay is narrow, and defended by a work they call Port Louis, or Blavet. The citadel of which is too much raised, and must occasion the shot fired from it to be but of little effect. Its flanks, too narrow in themselves, have also Orillons, which are never of use, but for defending the ditch; and there is none here but the sea, which washes the foot of the ramparts.

PORT LOUIS is an old, and deserted city. 'Tis a Gentleman of an ancient family in the neighbourhood of an East-India Nabob. The people of fashion live at Port Louis; but the merchants, the muslin, and silk warehouses, the money, and the pretty women, are all at L'Orient. Their manners are the same here as in other commercial ports. Every man's purse is open: but he lends money in the gross only; the

the interest of a sum for the Indies is twenty-five or thirty per cent. per ann. The borrower is much worse off than he that lends; his profits are uncertain, his bonds are not so. The law authorises this lending of money by contracts, and they give the creditors a sort of claim upon the whole ship's cargo. A power which extends over the entire fortune of most of the seafaring people.

There are three ships ready to sail for the Isle of France, the Digue, the Condé, and the Marquis de Castries. There are others fitting out, and some more on the stocks. The noise of the carpenters and caulkers, the concourse of strangers, and the perpetual moving about of vessels in the road, excites in the people a thirst after every thing that is maritime: the idea of fortune, constantly accompanying that of the Indies, adds to the illusion. You would think yourself a thousand leagues from Paris. The people of the country no longer speak French; those in town, know no other master, than the East-India Company. The better sort of people talk of the Isle of France and Pondicherry, as if they were just by. You will suppose that counting-house disputes come here in the bales from India, for interest rather tends to separate men from each other, than to bring them together.

I am, &c.

## LETTER III.

*Port L'Orient, February* 20, 1771.

WE waited only a fair wind, to set sail. My passage is taken on board the Marquis de Castries, a ship of eight hundred tons, and one hundred and forty-six men, loaden with naval stores for Bengal. My birth is a little recess from the Great Cabin. There are fifteen passengers, most of whom are lodged in the Gun-room, the place where they put the cartouches, and ordnance stores. The Master Gunner has the care of this part, and lodges here, as do also the Secretary, Chaplain, and Surgeon. Over this is the Great Cabin, where the passengers dine with the Captain. Over this again is the * Council Chamber, and the Captain's Cabin; it is decorated on the outside with a gallery, and is the finest room in the ship. The officers cabins are before you come to these abovementioned, that they may with the more ease look to what is going forward upon deck.

The crew lodge on the Forecastle, and between decks, a dismal hole, where one can see nothing. The † Galliards are the length of the whole ship, which is level with the Great Cabin, and has a gangway before it, as the Cabin has. The Kitchen, or Cook-room, is under the Forecastle. The provisions and merchandizes in the Hold; and the Powder-room is under the Gun-room.

* Called in English, the Coach. *T.*

† Galliards; the ship must, from this description, have had a spare deck. *T.*

I HAVE given you a general sketch of the difpofition of our ship; but to defcribe the diforder of it, is impoffible. There is no getting along for the cafks of champagne, wine, trunks, chefts and boxes every where about. Sailors fwearing, cattle lowing, birds and poultry fcreaming upon the Poop; and, as it blows hard, we have the additional noife of the whiftling of the Ropes, and the cracking of the timbers and rigging as the fhip rolls about at anchor. Several other fhips lay near us, and we are deafened by the hallowing of their officers to us, through their fpeaking-trumpets.

WEARIED with this uproar, I got into a boat and went afhore at Port Louis.

THE wind was very high; we walked through the ftreets, but met nobody. From the walls of the citadel, I faw the Horizon very black, and the ifland of *Groi* covered with a thick fog; upon the fhore crouds of women chilled with cold and fear, and a centinel at the point of the Baftion, in aftonifhment at the hardinefs of the poor wretches, who were fifhing in the midft of the tempeft.

WE returned, buttoned up clofe, wet through, and holding on our hats with our hands. As we went along, the ftreets were covered with fifh; white and purple fkait, thornbacks, dog fifh, conger eels of a monftrous fize, large bafkets full of crabs and lobfters, heaps of oyfters, mufcles and cockles, codlings, foles, and turbots; in fhort, as miraculous a draught as that of the apoftles.

THESE good folks are not without faith; for when they fifh for pilchards, a prieft goes in the firft boat, and gives his benediction to the water. One might see among them the conjugal affection of old times; for as they came dropping in, their wives and children hung about their necks: it is among these hard working people, that some remains of virtue is to be found, as if man retained his morals no longer than while he was in a state between hope and fear.

THIS part of the coast abounds in fish: each species of which is, in general, larger than they are elsewhere; but their taste is inferior. I was assured, that the pilchard fishery brought in four millions of livres, annually, to the revenue of the province. It is rather singular, that there are no crawfish in the rivers of Britany; occasioned, perhaps, by the stillness of the water.

WE are now got once more to our inn; the noise of the wind and sea still buzzing in our ears. Two Parisians, the Sieurs B***, father and son, who were to have gone in our ship, without saying a word to us, ordered a chaise, and are gone to Paris.

LETTER

## LETTER IV.

*On board the* MARQUIS DE CASTRIES, *the 3d of* MARCH, *Eleven in the Morning.*

I HAVE but juſt time to ſay adieu; we are ſetting ſail. Pray take care of the letters incloſed; three are for Ruſſia, Pruſſia, and Poland. Wherever I have travelled, I left ſomebody whom I regret.

BUT our anchor is a peek. I hear the noiſe of the Boatſwain's whiſtle, the capſtern, and the ſailors heaving anchor. The laſt gun is juſt fired. We are under ſail, and the ſhore, the ramparts and roofs of Port Louis begin to diſappear. Adieu, ye friends, who are dearer to me than the treaſures of India. Adieu! Adieu!

JOURNAL.

# JOURNAL.

## MARCH, 1768.

WE sailed on the third at a quarter past eleven in the morning, the wind at N. E. the tide not being high enough, we were very near touching upon a rock, to the right of the Channel. When we were abreast of the island of *Groi*, we lay to for some of the passengers and officers.

The 4th, the weather was fine; but the wind began to rise, and the sea to run high in the evening.

The 5th, a violent storm arose; the ship was on her way under her courses. I was terribly sea-sick. At half past ten in the morning, being in bed, I felt a great shock; somebody cried out, that the ship had struck. I went upon deck, where I found all the people in consternation. A wave struck us on the starboard-side and carried away the yawl, with the mate and three men. One of them only remained, entangled in the shrouds of the main mast, from whence he was taken, with his shoulder and hand shattered to pieces. It was impossible to save the others; they were seen no more.

This misfortune happened by the vessels not answering the helm. Her poop was too low in the water, to suffer the rudder to act properly upon her. The bad weather lasted all day, and the motion of the ship killed most of the poultry. I had a dog on board, that panted incessantly with uneasiness. The only

only animals that seemed insensible, were some sparrows and canary birds, accustomed to a perpetual motion. These birds are carried to India as curiosities.

I, as well as the other passengers was exceedingly sick. There is no remedy for this evil, which occasions the most dreadful reachings. It is good however, to take some dry food, and above all acid fruits.

The 6th, the weather being fine, we offered up our prayers for the souls of the poor sailors we lost in the late storm. The sea, in breaking upon the vessel, had split the beam that goes round the hatchway, although it was ten inches thick.

The 7th, we reckoned ourselves to be in the latitude of Cape Finistere, where gusts of wind, and a great sea, as at all other capes, are very common.

The 8th, a beautiful sea and fair wind. We saw flying about, some white birds with black borders round their wings; they call them Manches de Velours *(Velvet Sleeves)*

The 9th and 10th, the air began to be sensibly hotter, and the sky more pleasing. We approached the *Fortunate* island (the Azores) if it be true, that Heaven has placed good fortune in any particular island.

The 11th, the wind fell calm, the sea was covered with bonnets de feu *(bonnets of fire)* a kind of mucilage, formed into the shape of a cap, with a progressive motion. In the morning we saw a ship.

The

THE 12th and 13th, some good regulations were made. It was agreed, that each passenger should have but one bottle of water a day. Breakfast was to be at ten every morning, and was to consist of salted meats and dry vegetables. Our afternoon meal, at four o'clock, was a rather better repast. All fires were to be put out at eight o'clock.

ON the 14th, we expected to see the island of Madeira, but we were too much westward; it was calm all day. We saw two birds, brown, and of the size of a pigeon, flying to the westward, as high as the masts. We took them for land birds, and judged, from their appearing, that some island was to our left hand.

THE 15th, the calm continued; but the wind rose a little towards night: an English brig passed us in the afternoon, and saluted us with his flag.

THE 16th, at sun rise, we saw the island of Palma before us; on the left is the island of Teneriffe with its Pike, which is in the shape of a dome, with a pyramid on the top. These islands were enveloped in a fog all day, and at night in storms of lightning: an appearance which terrified the mariners who first discovered them. It is known, that the Romans had heard of them; because Sertorius was desirous of retiring to them. The Carthaginians, who traded on the coast of Africa, knew them well. *Juba*, the historian, says, there are five of them; and describes them at large: he calls one of them the Isle of Snow, because it is covered with it all the year. The Pike is, in fact, covered with snow, although the air is so hot. These islands are the ruins of that large island of Atlantis, of which Plato speaks. By the depth of the cavities, out of which their mountains are raised,

one

one would think they were the ruins of this original world, when overturned by an event, the tradition of which remains among all nations. According to *Juba*, the ifland of Canary took it's name from the large dogs bred there. The Spaniards, to whom they belong, got excellent Malmfey * from thence.

The 17th, 18th, and 19th, we paffed through the midft of thefe iflands, having Teneriffe on our left, and Palma on our right; Gomera was to the eaftward. I took a draught of thefe iflands, which are cut in with very deep ravines (or furrows.)

We faw a flying fifh. A lapwing came and perched on our fhip, and took it's flight to the weft; it was of an orange-colour, it's wings and aigrette mottled with black and white, its beak is black as ebony, and a little bent.

The 20th, we left the ifland of Ferro to the weft, and loft fight of all the Canaries. The fight of thofe iflands, fituated in fo fine a climate, excited in us many fruitlefs wifhes. We compared the repofe, and abundance, the union and pleafures of thefe iflands, to our own unquiet life of agitation. Perhaps, at feeing us pafs by, fome unhappy Canarian was upon a burning rock, wifhing himfelf on board a fhip, that fteered under full fail for the Eaft-Indies.

The 21ft, we faw a land-fwallow, and afterwards a fhark. While we were in the latitude of thefe

---

* The wine at prefent brought from the Canaries, is chiefly *fack*, which name, it is generally fuppofed to have always been diftinguifhed by; yet I have heard fome firft-rate critics doubt very much, whether any human being could drink *fack and fugar* for pleafure; and they therefore fufpect, that Falftaff's fack was Rhenifh Wine. *T*.

iflands,

islands, we were becalmed all day, the wind rising in the evening only.

The 22d, the weather was so hot, as to occasion several bottles of Champagne to break, although they were cased in salt; this is a store, that most of the Officers going to India take with them; it is sold there at a pistole a bottle. This inundation, which penetrated every thing, destroyed some lettices and cresses, that I had sown in wet moss, where these plants grow surprizingly. This salted liquor was so very corrosive, as to entirely spoil all my papers that got wetted with it.

The 23d, we had a very fresh wind; the sea appeared to be grey and greenish, as upon banks, or in soundings; they pretend to find soundings above eighty leagues from the coast of Africa, which is but little raised in these latitudes. We saw a ship bearing away for Senegal.

The 24th, we found the trade wind, from the N. W. The ship rolled very much.

The 25th and 26th, fine weather and fair wind; we passed the latitude of the Cape de Verd islands, but did not see them; they belong to Portugal; fresh provisions are to be had there; but water, the chief article, is very scarce. We saw some flying fishes and a land swallow. The French wheat, in the Bread-room, heated to such a degree, that there was no bearing one's hand in it. It has happened sometimes, that ships have been set on fire by this means. In 1760, an English ship, loaden with hemp, was burnt in the Baltic. The hemp took fire of itself. I saw the wreck of her on the coast of the isle of Bornholm.

The 27th, an awning was spread from head to stern, to shelter the people from the heat. We saw some *galeres*, a species of living mucilage.

The 28th and 29th, we saw flying-fish, and a great number of tunny-fish.

The 30th, our men got ready for fishing, and took ten tunny-fish, the least of which weighed sixty pounds; we saw a shark. The heat increased, and the crew bore their thirst with great impatience.

The 31st, we took a bonnito; some thirty sailors in the night opened the water jars of several passengers, who by that means found themselves, as the crew were, reduced to a pint of water a day.

## Some OBSERVATIONS on the MANNERS of SEAFARING PEOPLE.

I will only speak of the influence the sea has upon these men, in order that those faults which are the consequences of their way of life, may meet with the indulgence due to them.

The haste which is absolutely necessary in operations on board a ship, renders them coarse in their expressions. Living at a distance from land, they think themselves independent; hence it is that they frequently speak of Princes, laws or religion, with a freedom equal to their ignorance. Not but they are in some circumstances, devout, and even superstitious. I have known more than one, who would not so much as touch a rope on a Sunday or Friday. But in general, their religion depends upon the weather.

The idleness in which they live, makes them fond of scandal and stories. The quarter-deck is the place where the officers deal out fables and wonders.

The habit of making new acquaintances continually, renders them inconstant in their society and taste: At sea they wish for land, on shore they murmur that they are not at sea.

In a long voyage, it is best to give way a little, and never to dispute. The sea naturally sours the temper; and the slightest contradiction will breed a quarrel. I have seen one arise on a question in philosophy. It is true these questions have sometimes caused no small mischief on shore.

In general, they are silent and thoughtful; who can be gay, when surrounded with dangers, and deprived of the principal necessaries of life?

Their good qualities however, must not be forgotten. They are open, generous, brave, and above all, good husbands. A seaman looks upon himself as a stranger when ashore, and mostly so in his own house. Unaccustomed to the manner of living, he leaves to his wife the management of a world, of which he is ignorant.

To these good and bad qualities of seamen, must be added the vices of their education. They are given to drunkenness. Every day a ration of wine or brandy is issued. There are seven men in a mess, and I have seen them agree among themselves to drink alternately the allowance of the whole seven. Some of them are given to thieving; and there are of these, men so dextrous as to strip their comrades while sleeping; others again, are of an extraordinary probity.

bity. The master and gunner, are commonly the men entrusted, upon whom devolves the government of the crew. One may add to these, the chief pilot, who, I don't know why, does not hold among us that rank which his merit deserves; he is but the first *officier marinier* \*. Upon these three men depends the good behaviour of the crew, and very often the success of the navigation.

The last man in the ship is the cook. The cabbin-boys are often used very barbarously. There is scarce an officer or sailor, that does not make them sensible when he is in an ill humour. They even amuse themselves on board some ships, with flogging them in calm weather, to procure a wind †. Thus, man, who is so often complaining of his weakness, seldom has power, but he abuses it.

You will gather from all this, that a ship is a place of dissention; that a convent and an island, which is a kind of ship, must be filled with discord; and that the intention of Nature, which is in other respects so plainly pointed out, is, that the earth should be peopled with families, and not with societies and fraternities.

---

\* In British men of war, the Captain and Lieutenants, are considered as Gentlemen by their office, and generally are so by their behaviour or birth. They all have commissions. The master, his mates, and the carpenter, gunner, &c. are only warrant officers, and in general are low born and educated, people, who by their good behaviour, and application in their respective branches in seamanship, have qualified themselves for their particular commands. These are what the Author probably means by *officiers mariniers*. T.

† This custom is not unknown to many of our cabbin-boys. T.

## APRIL, 1768.

The 1st, we saw some sharks and took one, as also a bonite. I intend to continue my observations on fishes at the end of my journal for this month.

The 2d, we had calm weather, and now and then squalls.—We are upon the borders of the southern trade winds. In the afternoon we had a squall that made us reef all our sails. We draw near to the line; and have now very little twilight.

The 3d, we took some bonnitos, and a shark. We were constantly surrounded by the same shole of tunny fish.

The 4th, we had a stormy sky, and a violent squall, with thunder at a distance. A sailor died of the scurvy. Many others are ill of it. This disorder shewing itself so early, spreads an alarm through the whole crew. We took several bonitos and sharks.

The 5th and 6th, yesterday morning at three o'clock, it blew a most terrible storm, and obliged us to reef all our sails except the mizen. I have always remarked, that the rising of the moon dispels the clouds very perceptibly. Two hours after it is above the horizon, the sky is perfectly clear. We had a calm these two days, and some drops of rain.

The 7th, we took some bonitos. I saw some glass cut with scissars under water; the cause of which I am ignorant of.

The 8th and 9th, we caught one shark, some sucking-fish, or remoras, and two tunny fishes.

Although near the line, the heat was not very troublesome to me; the air is cooled by the storms.

The 10th, the ducking at the line, was announced, we were within one degree. A sailor disguised in a mask, came to the Captain, and desired him to cause the old custom to be observed. This is a frolic designed to divert the melancholy of the crew. The sailors are very dispirited; the scurvy gets a-head among them, and we have not gone one third of the voyage.

The 11th, the ceremony of dipping was performed. The principal passengers were ranged along a cord, to which their thumbs were tied with a ribband. Some drops of water were poured on their heads, and they then gave some money to the pilots.

The wind was contrary; the sky and the sea very fine.

The 12th, we could not get past the line. The currents ran northward. We now see the polar-star no more. We saw a ship to the East.

The 13th, we crossed the line. The sea appeared at night, as if covered with phosphorus. The lower deck is cleaned every Sunday; the chests and hammocks of the crew are brought upon deck, and then pitch is burnt between decks; the third part of the water-casks were found to be empty, although we had not gone near a third of our voyage.

The 14th, 15th, and 16th, the winds varied. It was very hot. We were continually surrounded with bonitos, tunny-fish, porpoises, and flemish-caps.

caps. We saw a shark of an enormous size. The weather calm in general, but sometimes stormy.

The 17th, 18th, and 19th, the calms and the heats continued. The pitch melted from the rigging. Spleen and impatience increased aboard the ship. 'Tis not unusual to lay becalmed a whole month under the line. I saw a whale going to the westward.

The 20th, 21st, and 22d, the calm, and our uneasiness continued; the ship was surrounded with sharks. We saw one tied to a *paillaison*, in a large ridge of surf running from East to West. It was alive; some ship had certainly passed by just before us.

We catched some tunny-fishes, bonitoes, five or six sharks, and a porpoise, with a very sharp pointed head. The sailors say that the porpoise forbodes wind; in effect, at midnight it arose.

The 23d, we entered at last into the South-West trade-winds, which were to carry us beyond the other tropic. We took some bonitos and tunny-fish. As we were drawing one of these fishes out of the water, a shark catched it by the tail, and broke the line. We saw a frigate-bird; it is black and grey, and nearly of the same form as a stork. Its flight is very lofty.

The 24th and 25th, we had some squalls, which occasioned the wind to change. Towards evening the moon was encompassed with a large halo. We catched bonitos, and tunny fish.

The 26th, we saw frigate-birds, flying-fish, tunny-fish, bonitos, and a white bird, which the crew said was a booby. In the evening, all the sails being set, we were attacked by a violent squall, which laid us on one side for some minutes. Our ship is a bad sailor, and when the wind is quite fair, makes but about two leagues an hour.

The 27th, the sea ran high; the wind was fresh, and had some squalls of rain. We saw the same fishes, and a halcyon, which the English call the Bird of Storms\*. I shall reserve an article of my journal for sea-fowl.

THE 28th, we had fresh winds, and squalls, with rain. Six guns were carried forward, from the aft-part of the ship, —— that being deeper in the water forward, she might steer the better. We had very stormy weather, which is rare in these latitudes. Saw the same tunnies.

THE 29th, fine weather, but sometimes squally. We saw some frigate-birds, and a white bird, with wings marked with grey. At sun-set, we saw a ship to windward, steering the same course as we.

THE 30th, a fine fresh wind and beautiful sea. The air cooler. We saw the ship we had seen last night, a little to windward. She had crouded sail; we did the like; she hoisted English colours, we ours. We catched tunnies, and saw flying-fish.

\* Petrels, alluding it is said, to St. Peter, when our Saviour walked on the sea. They seem to walk in a ship's wake, particularly in storms. The common sailors call them *Mother Carey's Chickens*.

OBSER-

## OBSERVATIONS upon the SEA and FISHES.

There is scarcely so dismal a sight as the main sea. A man becomes presently impatient of being in the centre of a circle, the circumference of which he never attains to. It however presents some very interesting scenes. I do not speak of it when tempestuous only. During a calm, and especially at night in hot climates, it is surprizing to see the sparkling of it. I have taken in a glass some of those luminous points of which it is full; and have seen them move about with great vivacity. They are said to be the fry of fish; and are sometimes seen in a heap together appearing like moons. At night, when the ship is under way, and is surrounded by fish that accompany it, the sea appears like a vast firework, all sparkling with serpents and silver spangles.

I leave you to think what a prodigious quantity of living beings this element must be the country of. I confine myself to some observations upon different species of fishes found in the main sea.

The bonnet-flamand, which I believe the Ancients called *pulmo-marinus*, is a species of animal, formed of a very glaring substance. It is not unlike a champignon, or mushroom. Its upper part has a power of contraction and dilatation, by the which it moves very slowly. I know no other property of it; 'tis so common, that we found the sea covered with it for many days. It can change its shape and colour; but the shape naturally is always the same. They are found very large upon the coast of Normandy.

THE *ga'ere* is of the same substance, but seems endued with more intelligence and malignity. Its body is a kind of oval bladder, covered lengthways with a tuft or sail, which is always out of the water, in the same direction as the wind. When overturned by a wave, it rises again quickly, and always presents the convex side of its body to the wind. I have seen many of them together, ranged like a fleet of ships. There might perhaps, be some kind of sail contrived upon this principle, by means of which a bark might get on, although the wind were contrary. From the lower part of the *galere*, hang several long blue filaments, with which it seizes whatever attempts to take it. These filaments burn immediately, like the most violent caustic. I one day saw a young sailor who swam after, and attempted to catch one of them, burnt on the arm so terribly, that the fright nearly occasioned his being drowned. The *galere*, while alive, is the most beautiful colours; some of them are of a sky-blue, and some of a rose-colour. The *bonnet-flamand* \*, is found in our seas, and the *galere* in those near the tropics.

IN the latitude of the Azores, I saw a kind of shell-fish, floating and living on the surface of the sea, shaped like the beard of an arrow, or beak of a bird. It is small, transparent, and very easy to break. This is perhaps the same that is found in Ambergrease.

IN the same latitude, we found some snails, that were blue, and floated on the surface of the water, like bladders filled with air. Their shell was very thin and brittle, and filled with a liquor of a beau-

---

\* Or Flemish Bonnet.

tiful

# VOYAGE to the ISLE OF FRANCE.

tiful purplish blue colour. This is not however, the purple fish of the Ancients.

A SPECIES of shell-fish much more common, is that which sticks itself to the sides of the ship, by means of a ligament, which it shortens or contracts, in bad weather. It is white, shaped like an almond, and composed of four pieces. It puts out a number of filaments, that have a regular motion. They multiply so very fast, that the course of the ship is sensibly retarded by them.

THE flying-fish is very common between the tropics. It is of the size of a herring. It flies in a troop and at one single spring, the usual flight of a partridge. In the sea, 'tis hunted by the fishes, and in the air by the birds. It's destiny seems a very unfortunate one, that in the air the same danger should await it, which it fled from in the water. But it has a compensation for the misfortune, for as a fish, it often escapes from the birds, and as a bird from the fishes. 'Tis in storms chiefly, that it is seen flying from the *fregattes* and tunnies, which make prodigious leaps in pursuit of it.

THE *encornet*, makes nearly the same manœuvre as the flying-fish. It has the faculty of black'ning the water by throwing into it a very black ink, and it does not swim altogether so well; it is of a conoid form. These two kinds of fish frequently fall on board of ships, and are very fine eating.

THE tunny-fish of these seas differs in taste from that of the Mediterranean. It is very dry, and has no fat but in the eye. It has very little entrails. Its flesh appears pinched, or compressed together by the skin. Eight muscles, four large, and four
small,

small, form its body, the transverse section of which resembles that of a tree. They fish for it at sun-rise, and sun-set, because then the shade of the waves disguises the bate, which is made to represent a flying-fish. This shoal of tunnies followed us these six weeks past. They are easily known; among them there is one, which has a red wound on the back, from being struck with a harpoon a fortnight ago: but his course was not retarded by it.

Can a fish exist without sleep, and is sea-water of a healing quality to wounds? I have somewhere read that Monsieur de Chirac, cured the Duke of Orleans of a wound in the wrist, by ordering it to be steeped in the waters of Balaru.

The tunny when eaten fresh, is wholesome, though it occasions thirst,—it is dangerous in these latitudes to eat it salted—for one of our sailors having done so, his skin turned as red as scarlet, and he had a fever for twenty-four hours after.

Among the tunnies we took a number of bonitos. They are a sort of mackarel, some of which are as large as tunnies. In the flesh of many were found living worms, as big as a grain of barley, which did not seem at all troublesome to the fish.

Sharks are very numerous near the Line. As soon as it is calm the ship is surrounded with them. This fish swims along slowly, and without noise. It is preceded by many small fishes called pilot-fish, speckled with black and yellow. If any thing falls into the sea, they instantly reconnoitre, and return to the shark, who approaching his prey, turns himself, and devours it. If it is a bird, he does not touch

touch it; but when preſſed by hunger, he ſwallows every thing, even iron nails.

THE ſhark is the tyger of the ſea. I have ſeen ſome, more than ten feet long. By nature it is very ſhort-ſighted. It ſwims very ſlowly, from the round form of its head, which joined to the poſition of its mouth, that obliges it to turn upon its ſide, in order to ſwallow, preſerves a number of fiſhes from its voracity. It has no bones, but cartilages, like other fiſhes of prey, as the ſea-dog, the thornback, the polypus. Theſe like the ſhark, ſee but badly, are ſlow ſwimmers, and have their mouths placed quite beneath, and are alſo viviparous.

The jaws of the ſhark are armed with five or ſix rows of teeth above and below. They are flat, and ſharp at the ſides, which are ſerrated. They have but two rows perpendicular, the others are hidden, and diſpoſed in ſuch a manner, that they replace by an admirable mechaniſm, thoſe that frequently are liable to be broken.

THEY bait for it with a piece of fleſh, faſtened upon an iron crook. Before they draw it out of the water, they fix round the tail a ſliding knot, and as ſoon as it is upon the deck, and attempts to ſtrike, or wound the ſailors, they cut it off with a hatchet. This tail has but one fin, ſhaped like a ſickle. The Chineſe eſteem this as an aphrodiſiaque. In other reſpects, this fiſh is of no utility. Its fleſh has a taſte of the thornback, and a ſmell of urine, and is reckoned feveriſh. The ſailors fiſh for this creature, merely to deſtroy it. They put out the eyes, gut them, tie two or three together by the tails, and throw them into the ſea; a ſpectacle worthy of a ſailor. The ſhark is ſo vivacious, as to move, long after

after the head is cut off; yet, I have seen them drowned very fast, by being plunged several times in the sea, after being struck by a hook, which keeps their mouth open.

We almost constantly took upon the Shark, a fish called a Sucking-fish, or *Remora*, about as big as a Herring. It has upon the head an oval surface, a little concave, with which it fixes itself upon any body, by forming a vacuum, between the oval surface and the body, to which it adheres in the manner of a leathern sucker. I have put some of them alive upon an even smooth glass, from which I could not afterwards take them. This fish has this singularity, that it swims with the head and gills out of water, its skin is courfe and rough, and its mouth armed with several rows of small teeth. We often have eaten the Sucking-fish, and found the taste like fried artichokes.

Besides the Pilot and Sucking-fish, the Shark nourishes under it's skin an insect, shaped like the half of a pea, with a beak that projects a long way. It is a kind of louse.

The Porpoise is a fish well known. I have seen of one sort, that has the snout very pointed. The sailors, on account of its swiftness, call it the Sea-arrow. I have seen them go quite round about the ship, while she made two leagues an hour. They throw a dart at this animal, which pants when taken, and seems to complain; it is a bad fish; it's flesh is black, hard, grofs and oily.

I have also seen a *Dorado*, which they say, is the lightest of all fish. It is also said, that this is the Dolphin of the antients, so fully described by Pliny.

Be

Be as it may, we did not experience much of it's friendſhip to mankind; but ſaw, at a great depth, the ſhining of its golden fins, and it's back of a beautiful azure.

WE ſometimes ſaw, at half a league's diſtance, Whales, throwing up their jetdéau. They are ſmaller here than in the North; and appeared to me, a far off, like a boat, bottom upwards.

SUCH are the ſpecies of fiſh I have hitherto ſeen. Sharks are ſeen in a calm, and are commonly followed by the *Dorados*; the Porpoiſes appear when the wind freſhens. The Tunnies have followed us conſtantly for ſix weeks paſt.

IF this detail has been tireſome to you, conſider what my pleaſures muſt have been. There are none for a man, upon an element, with the inhabitants of which he cannot çonnect himſelf.

M A Y,

## MAY, 1768.

THE 1ft, at fun rife, the veffel we had feen fome days before, was in our wake, and gaining upon us infenfibly; at ten in the morning fhe was along fide of us. We remarked, that all her fails were very old, that the chefts and beds of the crew were upon deck. They afked us in Englifh, *What cheer? What's your fhip called? Where do you come from? Where are you bound?* We anfwered in Englifh, and afked them the fame queftions. She came from London, fixty-four days before; and was bound for China. She was pierced for twenty-four guns, and was of about five hundred tons burthen. She wifhed us a good voyage, and continued her way. Saw fome Frigate Birds, Tunnies, and Bonites.

THE 2d and 3d, again faw the Englifh fhip, which the Tunnies followed, after having borne us company fo long. We had violent fqualls from the Weft. Thefe variations, in my opinion, arife from the neighbourhood of *All Saints* Bay; and I believe the currents and leeway fhe made by not anfwering her helm, have carried her nearer to America * than we were aware of.

THE 4th and 5th, the wind was violent and changeable. We faw a Fouquet, a bird that is black and grey; fome Frigate Birds and Boobies, that were diving to catch fifh.

THE 6th and 7th, a good breeze and fine fea; laft night we had violent fqualls. We faw fome Frigate Birds taking their courfe to the N. E.

* The Abbè de la Caille fays, that in his Voyage to the Cape of Good Hope, the fhip was conftantly and confiderably to the weftward of the Reckonings. *T.*

# VOYAGE to the ISLE OF FRANCE.

THE 8th and 9th. Yesterday the wind was very violent, and the sea very high. The ship lay on her side, and the water came in at the ports. Towards the evening the wind fell calm, which it commonly does, when the sun gets in the quarter oppofite it. We saw a great number of land birds and some gulls; signs that we were near land, from whence these squalls arose.

THE 14th, Calm. At nine in the evening, as I stood talking in the gallery with the captain, I saw all the horizon enlightened by a very luminous fire, running from the East to the North, and shooting forth red sparks. In the day-time the clouds stopped and appeared like land to the Southward.

THE 14th, we had violent squalls with some thunder. Here the S. E. winds commonly end, but sometimes they reach to twenty-eight degrees of latitude. We now looked for the westerly winds, with which they double the Cape of Good Hope.

THE 17th, 18th, and 19th, the weather was fine although foggy; we perceived a surge coming from the West, which always precedes a wind from that quarter. Last night we saw a second luminous appearance, and in the afternoon a Whale to the S. W. a league and a half from us. They imagined in the morning, that they saw a sea fowl, called the Mouton de Cap, or Cape Sheep.† This bird is found in the latitudes of the Cape of Good Hope.

† Called by the English, Albatrosse. Their wings, when extended, will measure ten feet, sometimes more, and have one more joint than the wings of other birds; for this reason, if they are put on their feet upon deck, they cannot fly away, being unable to rise; but from the water. *T.*

## OBSERVATIONS on the SKY, WINDS, and BIRDS.

THE ſtars to the Eaſtward ſeem to be more luminous than thoſe to weſtward. One may diſtinguiſh beſides the croſs of the ſouth, the magellanick Conſtellation, which are two white clouds, formed by multitudes of little ſtars. One ſide of which are ſeen two ſpaces more dark than the other parts of the ſky.

In approaching the Line, the twilight decreaſes ſo much, that the day is almoſt entirely diſtinct from the night. It is eaſily explained, why the twilight increaſes with the refraction of the rays toward the poles. In theſe regions, ſcarcely inhabited, light is mingled with the darkneſs, eſpecially in the Aurora Borealis, which in all places, is the greater, the leſs the ſun is elevated above the horizon. How very inconvenient would it have been, had the night between the tropics partaken of day light. The night ſeems made for the Blacks of Africa, who wait the cloſe of day, that they may dance and revel: 'Tis at this time, that the wild beaſts of theſe parts come to refreſh themſelves in the rivers, and that the turtles go on ſhore to lay their eggs. Is there not then a a ſenſible heat in the rays of the ſun, although refracted? The torrid zone would have been uninhabitable, had there been long twilights. In other reſpects, the night in theſe climates is finer than the day. The riſing moon diſpels the vapours with which the air is impregnated. I have ſo often made this remark, that I am of the ſailors opinion, who ſay that the moon ſwallows up the clouds. On the other hand, can the

influence

influence of the moon upon our atmosphere be denied, when we allow it to have so great a one upon the ocean *.

On this side the Line, the winds in general are N. E. and on the other side, S. E. These winds appear to arise from the air being dilated by the sun, and reflected by the poles. The S. E. winds extend farther than the N. E. as may be seen by the journal of winds. They are commonly met with in three or four degrees of N. latitude. The S. pole is moreover colder than the N. perhaps because the sun is longer on the northern side. Navigators who have attempted to discover the southern continent, have found ice in forty-five degrees †.

These winds continually waft to America, the vapours raised by the sun from the Atlantic. Those of the South-Sea, serve to fertilize a part of Asia and Africa. The wind in general blows harder by day than by night.

Without clouds there would be no rivers; and they do not contribute less to the beauty of the Heavens, than to the fruitfulness of the Earth.

I have frequently admired the rising and setting of the sun: 'tis a spectacle not less difficult to describe than to paint. Figure to yourself the horizon of a beautiful orange colour, tinged with green, which as it approaches to the zenith, loses itself in a lilach

* This is a part of natural philosophy which has been very little attended to by the learned; it is commonly said, that the principal changes of the weather, occur at the time of new and full moon; and more particularly when she is nearest the earth. *T.*

† And some have sailed as far as 56 deg. before they met with ice. *T.*

D hue

hue, while the reft of the fky is of a moft glorious blue. The clouds floating to and fro of a clear pearl coloured grey, fometimes difpofed in long ftreaks of crimfon or fcarlet; all the tints lively, diftinct, and bordered with a fringe of gold.

One evening the clouds to the weftward, appeared in the fhape of a vaft net, like black filk. As foon as the fun began to pafs behind it, each mafh of the net looked as if it raifed in a thread of gold. The gold then changed into flame colour and fcarlet, and the deeper part of the fky was coloured with light teints of purple, green, and fky blue.

A strange variety of landfcapes are frequently formed in the fky, in which the moft uncouth figures prefent themfelves to the imagination. We fee in them, promontories, fteep and rugged rocks, towers, and villages, over which the light diffufes all the colours of the prifm. 'Tis to the brilliancy of their colours we muft attribute the beauty of the birds of India, and the fhell-fifh of thefe feas; but why are not the birds of the fea of thefe countries fo handfome as ours? I will referve the examination of this problem to another article; and now defcribe to you thofe I faw flying about our fhip, with the names given them by feafaring people. You may imagine that this defcription cannot be a very accurate one.

The bird moft commonly met with in all latitudes, is a fpecies of fwallow\*, or halcyon, called by the

---

\* Taken for the king's fifher, or a fpecies of it. Meige's defcription of the Alcyon, in his dictionary, differs totally from the author's, and is as follows. "A fea-bird, that lays her eggs on the fands—She is a little bigger than a fparrow; her feathers purple, mixed with white; her neck long and fmall; her bill green, long, and flender." It is faid when fhe lays, be the fea never fo ftormy, it becomes prefently calm, until the young be hatched and brought up, which is the fpace of forty days. *T.*

Englifh

English, the *foul-weather bird*, or *petrel*. It is of a blackish brown, skims on the surface of the water, and in bad weather follows the wake of the ship. It is probable that why it follows ships at that time, is to find a shelter from the wind; for the same reason it flies between the two surges in skimming the water's edge.

As high up as Cape Finisterre, we saw some sea-mews, the wings of which are bordered with black. They are about the size of a duck, and fly, fluttering their wings, on the surface of the sea. They do not fly far from land, whither they retire every evening.

We saw the frigate-birds first in 2 and half deg. of N. latitude. They were thought to come from the Island of Ascension, which is in 8 deg. S. latitude. In form and size, they are like a stork, are black and white, have wings that extend a great way, and they have a long neck. The males have under their bills, a puff of skin, round as a ball, and red as scarlet. This is the lightest of all sea-birds. It never rests upon the water, yet is seen three hundred leagues from land, whither, 'tis affirmed, that it returns every evening to roost.

The booby is something larger, but more compact. It is white, mingled with grey, and dives when pursuing its prey, which is fish. The point of its beak hooks downwards, and the sides of it are full of little sharp points, which assist it in seizing its prey. The frigate-bird is at war with the booby, which is better furnished with arms, although the former has more swiftness and cunning. When the booby has filled its craw with fish, the frigate attacks it, and makes it give up its spoils, which it receives in the air.

The *goelettes*, are found in great flocks, denote shallow water, and that the land is near. They are white, and by their flight and shape may be taken for pigeons.

The *envergure* * is a bird something bigger, of the height of a large duck. It is white under the belly, and of a greyish brown on the wings and back. It takes its name from the great extent of its wings.

The *damiers*, are found only near the Cape of Good Hope. They are as big as pigeons, have a black head and tail, a white belly, the back and wings marked regularly with black and white, like the checks of a draught-board.

After the *damiers* we saw the *mouton-de-cap*; 'tis a bird something larger than a goose, has a flesh-coloured beak, very extensive wings, mixed with grey and white. They are seldom found but in the latitude of the Cape of Good Hope. I have seen all these birds at rest upon the water except the *frigate-bird* and the *envergure*. The sight of them is an indication of the latitude, when we have been many days without taking an observation, or when the currents have made us lose way in our longitude. It is to be wished that able seamen would give the world their observations hereon. Some species do not go far from the land, and roost there every night. *Goelettes* seen out at sea, are signs of some land, or broken rocks being near; but the *manches-de-velours*, or *sea-mews*, are a certain token of its neighbourhood.

There are also some species of bladed grass, or floating *algæ*, which should be attended to. These

* Not mentioned in the Encyclopedie  *T.*

several notices may be of use, instead of a method which is not yet discovered, of determining the longitude. They make an observation of the variation morning and evening; but this is not to be depended on. One cannot every day see the sun rise and set; moreover the variation, which is the declination of the needle, varies from one year to another under the same meridian.

## JUNE, 1768.

The 1st, the westerly winds having announced themselves, we now hoped we should soon double the Cape.

The 2d, the necessary precautions for this purpose were taken. New cordage was put to the wheel of the rudder, and some additional ones to the shrouds, for securing the masts. We bent four new sails. The boats, and all things that were moveable on board, were strongly lashed. The wind was very fresh. We saw some birds, but the *frigates* no longer appeared.

The 3d, 4th, and 5th,—each day the wind was very fresh, except yesterday when it subsided a little. We saw every day a prodigious number of *grelettes*, *moutons*, and *damiers*, and the Cape reed\*, which resembles the long trumpet used by shepherds. The sailors make a kind of trumpets of these hollow stalks. The sea was covered with surf, another sign of our being near the Cape. Fifteen men are rendered unfit for service by the scurvy.

The 7th at noon, a bird of the size of a goose, with short wings, tawny coloured and brown, a head like a hen, a short tail, shaped like a leaf of trefoil, has fixed upon our masts for some time. By all the bearings, we ought to find the Cape hereabouts. Saw the same birds.

The 9th, disorders and dejection increase in the ship. One of the mates died of the scurvy.

\* English sailors call it trunk-weed. *T.*

THE 12th, as the sea appeared greenish, we sounded, but found no bottom. The wind very fresh, and a great sea.

THE 13th, we at length came into soundings of ninety-five fathoms, a muddy and greenish bottom. This rejoiced us exceedingly. The great depth convinced us that we had lost way to the westward. We saw two ships, one a-stern, the other over our starboard cat-head. The soundings ascertain where we are, but inform us, that we have misreckoned above two hundred leagues in our journal.

THE 15th, blew fresh. The vessel a-stern hoisted English colours, and soon passed by us at about a league and a half to leeward. The other hoisted French colours, and as she was before the wind, she lowered her sails in order to join us, bearing up as near as she could. Our captain did not think proper to come to, she proved to be the Digue man of war, that sailed a month before us. Towards evening she hoisted all her sails, and steered in our course.

The 17th, it proved calm. We saw some whales and *dorados*.

THE 18th in the morning we had a gale of wind, that obliged us to remain till eleven at night under our mizen. There rose at the extremity of each wave a white powder like the dust blown by the wind along a road. At seven o'clock we shipped a sea at the great cabbin windows. At eight o'clock it hailed, and at midnight the weather grew fine.

THE 22d, the wind very fresh and a rolling sea. The opinion of the Ancients that the weather was calm during the solstice, was erroneous. I have this

afternoon

afternoon read an obfervation in Dampier's voyages, that the fun's difappearing at about three in the afternoon behind a range of high and thick clouds, is a fign of a violent ftorm. When I went upon deck, the fky difcovered all thefe figns defcribed by Dampier.

THE 23d, at half paft twelve in the night, a great fea beat in four of the five great cabbin-windows, though the dead-lights were barred like a St. Andrew's crofs. The veffel pitched, as if fhe would have ftood an end in the water. Hearing the noife, I opened the door of my chamber, which was inftantly filled with water and the furniture that floated about. The water ran out at the door of the great cabbin like the fluice of mill; above, thirty hogfheads of water came in by this accident. The carpenters were called, lights were brought, and new boards nailed againft the windows as quickly as poffible. We now ran under a mizen, and the wind and fea were truly frightful.

THIS diforder was fcarcely put to rights, before a large cheft that ferved for a table, full of falt and bottles of champagne, broke its lafhings. The rolling of the fhip threw it to and fro like a die. This enormous box weighed many tons, and threatened us with being crufhed to pieces in our rooms. At laft it burft open, and the bottles rolling about and breaking, caufed a confufion that is inexpreffible. The carpenters returned, and with the greateft difficulty replaced and faftened it.

THE rolling of the fhip not fuffering me to fleep, I lay down upon the bed in my boots and morning-gown: my dog feemed in the greateft fright, and while I amufed myfelf with foothing him, I faw a flafh of light'ning through the crevis of the porthole, and

and heard it thunder. 'Twas about half paſt three in the morning. In a moment, a ſecond clap of thunder broke, and the dog began to fly about and howl. The light'ning flaſhed again in an inſtant. Thunder immediately following, I heard 'em cry out upon deck, that ſome ſhip was in danger; in fact the noiſe was like the report of a cannon fired near us, as it did not roll at all. Perceiving a ſtrong ſmell of ſulphur, I went upon deck, and immediately felt it exceſſively cold. Every thing was ſilent, and the night ſo dark, I could diſtinguiſh nothing. I preſently perceived ſomebody near me, and aſked, what was the matter? The man anſwered, " They are " carrying the Quarter-maſter to his birth; he has " fainted away, and ſo has the Pilot. The thunder " has fallen upon the ſhip, and ſhivered the main- " maſt." Indeed, I found the main-top-ſail yard was fallen upon the main-top. Neither maſt nor rigging appeared, the crew were all retired to the Council-Chamber *.

They made a ring upon the fore-caſtle. The thunder had deſcended ſo far along the maſt. A woman who had juſt lain in, had ſeen a globe of fire at the foot of her bed; yet nobody could diſcover any trace of the fire. — Day light was looked for with impatience.

At day break I again went upon deck. Some very black clouds, appeared, and others of a copper colour. The wind was weſterly, where the horizon appeared of a flaming red, as if the ſun was going to riſe in that quarter. The Eaſt was totally black. The ſea formed monſtrous waves, that roſe like pointed mountains, compoſed of a number of ſmaller hills; on their ſummits were raiſed ſpouts of foam,

* There is no Council-Chamber in our Engliſh ſhips, nor do I know what part is ſo called by the French in theirs. *T.*

coloured

coloured like so many rainbows. They were thrown so high, as to appear from the quarter-deck, to be higher than the tops. The wind made so much noise in the rigging, that we could scarcely hear each other speak. We ran before the wind under a mizen only. A piece of the top-mast hung from the end of the main-mast, which was split in eight places to a level with the deck. Five of the iron rings with which it was bound, were melted. The gangways were covered with the broken pieces of the top, and main top-mast. At the rising of the sun, the wind also rose with a redoubled and inexpressible fury. The ship no longer to be guided by the helm, went which way soever the wind or the waves drove her. The mizen-sail having gibed its braces, broke soon after; the force with which it was continually striking against the mast, we feared would have broken the latter by the board. In an instant, the forecastle was under water. The waves broke over the larboard cat-head, in so much, that the bowsprit was not to be seen. Clouds of surf inundated even as high as the poop. The ship, by not steering, presented her side to the waves, and at every roll took in water even to the foot of the main-mast, and rose again with the utmost difficulty.

THE Captain in this moment of danger, called out to the Pilots to put before the wind; but the vessel could not be in the least affected by the helm. He ordered the sailors to reef the mizen, which the wind was carrying away piece-meal; the poor fellows were sheltering themselves under the quarter-deck, some crying, others fallen on their knees, and praying. I crept along the larboard gangway, griping fast by the tackling, and was followed by a Dominican who was chaplain of the ship, a passenger, and by several of the seamen, and we at length did reef the sail, though
 above

above half of it was carried away. They wanted to have bent a stay-sail, in order to put before the wind, but it was torn like a sheet of paper.

We remained then like a log, rolling about in a most frightful manner; having one time let go the tackle I held by, I slid as far as the foot of the main-mast, where the water was up to my knees. In short, next to God, we were indebted for our safety, to the strength of the ship, and to her having three decks, without which she must have filled. Thus we were tossed about till the evening, when the storm abated. The moveable furniture was almost entirely topsy-turvy, or broken to pieces: and I more than once found myself upright on my feet upon the wainscot of my cabbin.

Such was the tribute that we paid in the streights of Mozambique\*. The passage through which is more dreaded by seamen, than doubling the Cape of Good Hope. The Officers declared, they never saw so great a sea. All the upper works of the ship were so shaken by it, that into the joints of the pilasters of the great cabbin, I put mutton bones, which were crushed to pieces by the play of the timbers.

The 24th, at four in the morning it fell calm, the sea was still very high. The people worked hard all day, in bringing the main-yard to its right place, and in fitting two fishes to strengthen the main-mast. The effects of the light'ning are not to be described. The

---

\* In this strait the Aurora Frigate, with the East-India Supervisors on board, is supposed to have been lost. The Portugueze have a large settlement at Mozambique, which is situated on an island in 15 deg. S. The town is populous and well fortified; and the harbour safe and commodious. *T.*

mainmaſt is ſplit in a zig-zag, five feet of the maſt immediately under the top, is ſplintered, forward, or towards the head of the ſhip; then five feet on the afterſide, or towards the ſtern, is ſplintered; and ſo five feet alternately, the whole length of the maſt to the deck; ſo that the ſound on the one ſide, anſwers to the ſhattered on the other. In theſe cracks I could not perceive any ſmell or blackneſs, the wood being of it's uſual colour.

We ſaw ſome Moutons de Cap. The weather killed the remains of our live ſtock, and doubled the number of men ſick of the ſcurvy.

The 25th, was ſpent in belaying and faſtening the two fiſhes round the maſt; they were two pieces of timber, forty-five feet long, hollowed out in grooves, to fit the circumference of the maſt. Every man put his hand to this work, on account of the ſickly ſtate of the crew. A Whale paſſed us, within piſtol ſhot, it was ſcarcely the length of the long boat.

The 26th, middling weather; *Te deum* was ſung according to cuſtom, to thank God for having paſſed the Cape, and the Straits of Mozambique.

The 27th, we completed the maſt ſo far, that it would carry the main ſail. One man died of the ſcurvy; and twenty-one men were rendered unfit for ſervice by ſickneſs.

The 29th, a child of only eight days old died of the ſcurvy. There are now twenty-eight ſailors in the Lazarette. To make out the watch, we have been forced to take the domeſtick ſervants that are on board, and alſo the paſſengers, that are not of the Great Cabbin.

The

# VOYAGE to the ISLE OF FRANCE.

The 30th, our uneasiness was encreased, by the melancholy condition of the crew. Here the westerly winds are at an end. We keep in a high latitude, that we may have the S. W. winds which blow constantly hereabouts, and endeavour to keep to windward of the island of Rodorigue, to make the Isle of France with the greater certainty.

## OBSERVATIONS that might be of use for the better Government of Seamen.

THERE did not seem to me to be a proper subordination among the officers; the superiors are afraid of the interest of their inferiors. The chief part of these appointments being obtained by favour, I do not think that an authority can be established among them as it ought to be; and the evil being dependent upon the manners of the persons concerned, is, in my opinion, without remedy.

No ship should stay more than three months at sea, without going into port. The sailors have not water enough for a longer trip; in these hot climates; being frequently reduced to half-a-pint a day. Could not that part of the ship, where the ballast is put, be divided into leaden cisterns and filled with fresh water; or could not some kind of wax or mastic be found out, with which the casks might be done over to prevent the water from corrupting. It is sometimes so much tainted, and so full of worms, as to be really intolerable.

As for the salt water, that is rendered fresh by a machine, it is not thought wholesome: besides, a great deal of sea-coal must be taken on board, which
occupies

occupies too much room, and is subject to take fire; and the additional dangerous inconvenience of keeping a Furnace burning night and day.*

The seamen are very ill victualled; their biscuit is full of worms; the salt beef, in a short time, becomes both a disagreeable and unwholesome food. Could not provisions be dressed and preserved in fat. The Great Cabbin was served with meat so prepared, which kept as well as the salted beef.

When on shore, the sailors will spend as much money in a week, as they have been a year in earning. I should think each man might be provided with proper cloathing, which they should be obliged to take care of, by the frequent reviews of its condition by proper officers. Such a precaution would certainly, in some degree, prevent their extravagance. Several other regulations might be thought of, which properly attended to by the officers, would tend much to their cleanliness and decent appearance. The major part of these poor fellows need always be under a tutor.

* Experience has shewn, that Dr. Irvin's method is of great utility. T.

JULY,

## JULY, 1768.

THE 3d. This evening one of the carpenters died of the scurvy; forty people are now ill of it, and it makes a sensible progress, owing to the exhalations from the hold filled with masts, that have, for a long time been layng in mud.

THE 9th, one of the sailors upon the watch died suddenly. We have all been very faint and weak to-day; some have had vertigoes and sickness at their stomachs. We are, notwithstanding, more than one hundred leagues to windward of any known land.

THE 11th, fair wind; sixty-six of the men are now sick in their beds; if we should remain eight days longer at sea, we must infallibly perish.

THE 12th, fine weather and sea; there are no more than three foremast men to each watch; the officers and passengers help to work the ship.

THE 13th, at half past eight this morning, land appeared. We are so cast down, that the news rejoices no body. Eighty men are now ill with the distemper.

THE 14th, on approaching the land, many of the people found themselves sick: I felt uneasiness all over me, and sweated abundantly. We hoisted the colours and fired guns for assistance; but a pilot alone came on board. He told us of the differences among the chief people of the island, about which, I suppose, he thought us very anxious: on the other hand, many of the people on board were of opinion, that the

the complaints and miseries we had laboured under, would be a matter of great concern to the inhabitants on shore.

WE presently left to our right, two small inhabited islands, called Round Island, and the Isle of Serpents: we next passed within gun-shot of *Coin de Mire*, another island on the left. We kept at a good distance from the shore, on account of the shoal, at *Point aux Cannoniers*.

At half past one, in the afternoon, we entered the harbour; two hours after, I landed, thanking God for having delivered me from the dangers and fatigues of so dreadful a voyage.

We were at sea four months and twelve days, without touching at any port. According to my journal, we have sailed about three thousand eight hundred marine, or four thousand seven hundred common leagues: and have lost eleven persons, including the three men carried away by the sea, and one who died as he was going ashore.

## OBSERVATIONS on the SCURVY.

THE scurvy is occasioned by the bad quality of the air and of the provisions. The officers, who are better fed and better lodged than the sailors, are the last attacked by this disorder, which affects even the animals on board: my dog was very much troubled with it. There is no absolute cure for it, but the air of the land and the use of fresh vegetables, although there are some palliatives which may moderate it's effects; as the use of rice, acid liquors, coffee,

coffee, and abstinence from all salted provisions. Great virtues are attributed to the use of turtle, but like other prejudices, this is adopted by seamen upon slight grounds only. At the Cape of Good Hope, where there are no turtles, the scurvy is cured as quickly as in the hospital at the Isle of France, where the patient is fed with broths of this animal. On our arrival, almost every body used this remedy; but not being fond of turtle, I did not eat of it, but of fresh vegetables; I was well before any of them.

The scurvy's first symptoms is a general lassitude; the sick person wishes for rest, is uneasy in his mind, and disgusted with every thing; all day long he is in disquiet, and is only relieved from it by the night: it's next, are red spots on his breast and legs, and bleeding ulcers in the gums. There are frequently no external symptoms; but, if a man gets the slightest wound imaginable, it is incurable, while at sea; and makes the most rapid progress. I myself had a very slight wound at the end of my finger; in three weeks the sore had taken off the skin entirely; and notwithstanding all the remedies that were applied, extended itself to my hand. A few days after my landing, it healed of itself. Before the sick were landed, they took care to expose them for a whole day to the air from the shore. Notwithstanding these precautions, it cost one man his life, who was not able to bear the change.

I cannot describe to you the miserable situation we were in at our arrival. Figure to yourself a ship, with it's main mast shattered to pieces by light'ning, with a waft upon it's ensign, and firing minute-guns as signals of distress; sailors more like spectres than men, sitting upon deck; the scuttles all open and emitting a vapour that infected the air; the forecastle and poop covered with sick men, exposed there for the benefit of the sun, and who died even while speaking to us. I shall never forget a lad of eighteen years old, to whom I had promised some lemonade the evening before. I was seeking for him among the rest, when they shewed him to me, lying dead in the cook-room.

# LETTER V.

## NAUTICAL OBSERVATIONS.

BEFORE I give you an account of the Isle of France, I shall add to my journal the observations of the most able seamen upon the voyage we have made.

REGULAR as the trade winds are in general, they are, notwithstanding, variable along the coast, and in the neighbourhood of islands.

A BREEZE blows off the land almost every night, along the shores of the great continents. This wind blowing in a different direction from the sea breeze, brings the clouds together into one long motionless range, which vessels rarely fail seeing as they approach the land.

NEAR the coasts, it is in general, stormy, especially in the neighbourhod of islands. The winds in thefe parts vary much. At the Canaries, the S. and S. E. winds blow fometimes for eight days fuccefsively.

The trade winds are firft met with, about twenty-eight degrees North latitude; but they feldom continue fo far as the Line. An experienced feaman has given me the following account of the ceafing of the trade winds, which he has with much labour collected from more than two hundred and fifty journals of this voyage:

In January, between the 6th and 4th degrees of North latitude.
In February, between the 5th and 3d degrees.
In March and April, between the 5th and 2d degrees.
In May, between the 6th and 4th degrees.
In June, in the 10th degree.
In July, in the 12th degree.
In Auguft and September, between the 14th and 13th degrees.
And during the months of October, November, and December, they blow as far as the Line.*

† Between the trade and the general winds, by which is meant the trade winds fouthward of the Line, the wind is variable and ftormy. The general winds extend much farther than the trade; they reach as far as twenty-eight degrees fouth. Beyond which

---

* The fouthern trade wind has been known to blow farther north than the Line; and the northern, at other times, to be extended to the fouthward of the Line: but this rarely happens. *T.*

† B Varenius, in his *Geographia Generalis*, gives a particular account of the winds, (*cap.* 20. and 21.) and of the variation of the needle, (*cap.* 38.)—and in the appendix prefixed by Sir *Ifaac Newton*, and Dr. *Jurin*, to the edition they publifhed in 1712, (*page* 31 and 49) are collected Dr. *Halley*'s obfervations upon the fame fubjects. *T.*

latitude the winds vary more than in the seas of Europe; and the higher the latitude the more violent they are; blowing generally from the N. to N. W.; and from the N. W. to the S. S. W.—when they get round to the S. a calm succeeds.

Near the Cape of Good Hope, S. E. and E. S. E. winds are frequently met with. It is a general maxim to keep to the windward of the place intended to be made; yet not too much so, as the ship would make too much leeway. It is best to cross the Line as much to the Eastward as possible.

If a ship is in want of provisions, she may be better supplied at the Cape de Verd Islands than at Brasil, where they are very dear; besides that, the air of the place is very unwholsome. Turtle is catched in great plenty at the island of Tristan d'Aconia, but water is hard to be got, on account of the trees, which grow in the sea.

It is dangerous to put in at the *Cape of Good Hope* from April to September; but the anchorage is perfectly safe at *False-bay*, which is very little distant. If a vessel misses the Isle of France, it may put in at Madagascar, at Port Dauphin, or Bay of Antongil; but there are dangerous epidemical distempers, and hurricanes on that coast, which last from October till May.

Returning to Europe, there is St. Helena, an English settlement; and the island of Ascenfion; where, however, nothing can be got but turtle. In time of war, the two islands are commonly cruizing stations, all ships from the other side of the Cape endeavour to make them, in order to ascertain their route.

The

# VOYAGE to the ISLE OF FRANCE.

The charts moſt in repute are Monſieur Dapre's; ſailors are alſo much indebted to the learned and modeſt Abbé de Caille. But the geography of theſe parts is yet very imperfect. The longitude of the Canaries, and of the Cape de Verd iſlands, is not well laid down. Between Cape Blanco and Cape Verd, the chart ſays, there are thirty-nine leagues difference, although there really are not twenty.

A SHOAL is ſuſpected to be at about twenty minutes South of the Line, and about twenty-three degrees ten minutes longitude: in 1764, two French ſhips touched the bottom.

SEAMEN are liable to be led into great errors by the currents. I am of opinion, that nothing certain relative to them can be determined upon, 'till a method is diſcovered, of aſcertaining the quantity of a ſhip's leeway: even the angle ſhe forms with her Wake, will not lead to a deciſion of this matter; becauſe the ſhip and her trace have one cauſe, the ſhip's motion.

THE hardineſs of the navigators, who firſt made theſe voyages, without experience and without charts, cannot be ſufficiently admired. Thoſe of the preſent day have much more information, and leſs reſolution. Navigation is become a mere routine. Ships ſail at a particular ſeaſon, make the ſame places, and ſteer the ſame courſes. It were to be wiſhed, that ſome veſſels might be riſked in making diſcoveries, that might aſſure the ſafety of others.

## LETTER VI.

THE Isle of France was discovered by a Portugueze, of the family of Mascarenhas, who called it *Isle de Cerné*. It was afterwards possessed by the Dutch, who gave it the name of *Mauritius*. They abandoned it in 1712, and soon after the French, inhabitants of the Isle of Bourbon, which is only forty leagues distant, came and settled themselves there.

THERE are two ports in this island; that on the S. E. where the Dutch settlement was, and where remains of their buildings are still seen, is the principal port. It may be entered before the wind; but it is difficult to get out of it: the winds being almost ever at S. E.

THE smaller port, or Port Louis, is to the N. W. a ship may go in or out of it, large, before the wind. It's latitude is twenty degrees ten minutes S, and it's longitude, from the meridian of Paris, fifty-five degrees E. This is the capital of the island, though situated in the most disagreeable part of it. The town, called also the Camp, and which has scarcely the appearance of a market town, is built at the bottom of the port, and at the opening of a valley, which is about three quarters of a league long, and eight hundred or a thousand yards wide. This valley is formed by a chain of high mountains, covered with rocks; but without trees or bushes. The sides of these mountains are covered six months in the year, with a burning herb, which makes the

country

country appear black, like a colliery. The edge of the rocks, which form this dismal vale, is broken and craggy. The highest part is at the extremity, and terminates in a rock, standing by itself, which they call the *Pouce*. This part, however, has a few trees; and there issues from it a rivulet, which runs through the town; but the water is not good to drink.

As for the town or camp, it consists of wooden houses of one story high; each house stands by itself, and is inclosed in pallisades. The streets are regular enough, but are neither paved nor planted with trees. The ground is every where so covered, and as it were staked with rocks, that there is no stirring without danger of breaking one's neck. The town is neither walled nor fortified in the least; except that on the left, when looking to the sea, there is a sort of intrenchment of stone, reaching from the mountain to the harbour; on this same side is Fort-Blanc, that defends its entrance; on the other side is a battery upon the Isle of *Tonnelliers*.

According to the measurement of the Abbé de Caille, the Isle of France is ninety thousand, six hundred and sixty-eight fathoms in circumference; it's greatest diameter is thirty-one thousand, eight hundred and ninety fathoms from N. to S.; and twenty-two thousand, one hundred and twenty-four from E. to W.; its superficial content is four hundred thirty-two thousand, six hundred and eighty acres, of one hundred perches the acre; and twenty feet the perch.

THE N. W. part of the island is apparently level, and the S. W. covered with ridges of mountains, from three hundred to three hundred and fifty fathom high.

high. The higheft of all is four hundred and twenty-four fathom, and ftands at the mouth of the river *Noire*. The moft remarkable, called *Pieterboth*, is four hundred and twenty toifes high; it is terminated by an obelifk, which is again covered with a cubical rock, upon which no perfon has ever yet been. At a diftance, this pyramid and it's capital, refemble the ftatue of a woman.

THE ifland is watered by above fixty rivulets, fome of which have no water in the dry feafon, efpecially fince fo much timber has been cut down. The interior part of the ifland is full of ponds, and in this part it rains nearly all the year round, the clouds being ftopped by the mountains, and the woods at the top of them.

I CANNOT give you a more perfect account of a place in which I am but juft arrived. I expect to pafs a few days in the country, and will endeavour to defcribe to you what relates to the foil of this ifland, before I fpeak of it's inhabitants.

PORT LOUIS,
Aug. 6, 1768.

## LETTER VII.

*Of the Soil and natural Productions of the* ISLE *of* FRANCE.

EVERY thing here differs from what is seen in Europe, even the herbage of the country. To begin with the soil: It is almost every where of a reddish colour, and mixed with veins of iron, which are frequently found near the surface, in the form of grains, the size of a pea. In the drier parts, especially near the town, the ground is very hard. It resembles pipe-clay, and to make trenches in it, I have seen them cut it with axes, as they do lead. As soon as it rains, it becomes soft and tenacious; notwithstanding they have not yet been able to make it into bricks.

THERE is no real sand in the soil. That which is found on the shore, is composed of fragments of madrepores and shells, which will calcine in the fire.

THE ground is almost every where covered with rocks, from the size of one's fist to a ton weight. They are full of holes, the bottom of which is in the form of a lentil.

MANY of these rocks are formed of concentrical laminæ, like an onion. Some of them are in large masses, that adhere together. Others seem as if they had been broken, and were again joined together. The island is in a manner paved with these rocks, and the mountains are formed entirely of these strata, which are oblique to the horizon, although parallel to each other. They are of an iron grey colour, vitrify in the fire, and contain a great deal of iron ore. I saw at the foundry, some grains of beautiful copper and lead, that were taken from some of the fissures in the rocks, but in a very small quantity. Experiments of this nature afford no encouragement here. The mineral appears to be too much dispersed. In the broken pieces of these stones, there are little cavities cristalized, some of which contain a down *, that is white and very fine.

I know only of three species of herbs or gramen, that are natural to the soil.

Along the sea-shore is found a sort of turf, that grows in beds, very thick and elastic. Its leaf is very small, and so sharp pointed, as to prick through one's clothes. The cattle will not touch it.

In the hottest part of the island, the pastures are of a kind of dog's grafs, which spreads much upon the ground, and puts out little branches from the joints. This herb is very hard. The oxen like it very well, if not too dry.

The best herb grows in the airy and windward side of the island. 'Tis a gramen, with large leaves, and is green and tender all the year.

The other species of herbs and shrubs that are known, are, a plant that yields for fruit, a husk filled with a kind of silk, of which an advantageous use might be made.

A kind of asparagus, prickly, and that grows above twelve feet high, round the trees, as the bram-

* Probably a species of the Asbestos. *T.*

ble

ble or briar. It is not yet known whether this is good to eat.

A kind of mallow shrub with small leaves, that grows in the paths, and sides of the roads. There is also a kind of thistle with yellow flowers, the seeds of which kill the birds that eat them; and a plant that is like the lilly, bearing long leaves. It grows in marshy ground, and has a flower of a grateful smell.

Upon walls, and by the sides of the roads I found some tufts of a plant, whose flower resembles the plain red July-flower; It has a bad smell, and this singular property, that only one flower flourishes upon each branch at one time.

At the foot of the neighbouring mountains, there grows a sweet basil, the smell of it is like that of a July-flower. Its stalk is ligneous. It is of a healing quality.

The *Raquettes*, of which they here make very dangerous hedges, bear a yellow flower, marbled with red. This plant is stuck full of very sharp prickles, that grow upon the leaves; and also upon the fruit. The leaves are very thick. The fruit is never used, and is of a sour taste.

The *Veloutier* grows upon the sand on the sea-shore. Its branches have a down upon them, like that of velvet. The leaves are entirely covered with glittering filaments. It bears flowers in clusters. This shrub exhales an odour, that at a distance is agreeable, less so when you draw near, and when quite close is perfectly loathsome.

There

There is a kind of plant, half bramble, half shrub, that produces in pods, bristled with prickles, a sort of nut, very smooth and hard, of a pearl colour grey, and the size of a musquet-ball. Its kernel is very bitter. These nuts are good for the venereal disease.

In the parts of the island that are cleared, there grows a great number of a kind of shrub, that has large leaves, in the shape of a heart. Its smell is sweet enough, and like that of balm, whose name it bears. I know of no use made of it, except in baths.

Another plant equally useless, is the false potatoe, which grows twining along the sea-side. It spreads on the ground like the *liseron*. Its flowers are red, and like a bell. It thrives in the sand.

Upon the borders of the woods is found a ligneous herb called, *Pannier-grass* *. They have attemptnd to make thread and cloth of it, which is not bad. Its leaves are small. Taken in barley-water, they are good for complaints in the breast.

There is a great variety of shrubs all comprized under the general name of †*liannes*, some of which are as thick as a man's leg, and grow round the trees, making the trunks look like a mast furnished with rigging. They, however, support the trees against the hurricanes, of whose violence I have seen frequent proofs. When they fell timber in the woods, they cut about two hundred trees near the root, which remain upright till the *liannes*, which hold them, are cut down also. When this is done, one whole part of the forest seems to fall at once, making a most

---

* Herbe à pannier. *T.* * A Rattan, or Supple Jack. *T.*

horrid

horrid crash. Cords are made of their bark, stronger than of hemp.

There are many shrubs which bear a flower like that of the box-tree.

A PRICKLY and spungy shrub, with a red flower, in a hoop, and scolloped. Its leaf is large and round. The fishermen use the stalk of it (which is very light) instead of cork.

ANOTHER shrub, which is a very pretty one, called, † *bois-de-demoiselle*. Its leaf is scolloped at the edge, like that of the ash, and its branches ornamented with small red seeds.

BEFORE I proceed, you will observe, that I know nothing of botany. I describe things as I see them; but if you will rely upon my opinion, I declare to you, that I think every thing inferior to the productions of Europe.

THE meadows do not produce a single flower, but are entirely covered with small stones, and overgrown with an herb as hard, and as tough as hemp. No plant bears flowers of a pleasant smell, nor is any shrub in the Island to be compared to our white thorn. The liannes have not the fragrancy of the honeysuckle or ivy. Not one violet in all the woods. As to the trees, they have large whitish trunks, that are bare, except a little kind of nosegay of leaves of a dull green. I will describe them in my next letter.

PORT-LOUIS, ISLE-OF-FRANCE, *Sept.* 15*th*, 1768.

† Lady's Wood.

## LETTER VIII.

SOME days ago I perceived a large tree in the middle of some rocks, and being desirous of cutting a piece with my knife, was surprized at the whole blade entering without my using the least force. It was of a substance like a turnip, and of a very disagreeable taste; for some hours after, (although I did not swallow any part of it) my throat was much enflamed, and felt as if pricked by pins. This tree is called *mapou*, and is looked upon as poisonous.

The trees of this country take their names in general, from the fancy or caprice of the inhabitants.

The *bois-de-canelle*, which is not like the real cinnamon-tree, is one of the largest in the island. It is the best I have seen for joiner's work, and resembles walnut-tree, both in colour and veins. When it is worked green, it smells like human excrement, and like the blossoms of the real cinnamon. This is the only resemblance I could perceive between them. The seed of it is inveloped in a red skin, which has an acid, yet not a disagreeable taste.

The stinking-wood, deservedly so called from its horrid smell, is very good for carpenter's use.

The iron-wood, its trunk seems blended with the roots, and shoots up in a kind of ribs or spars, like so many boards. It turns the edge of the axe that fells it.

The

The ebony-wood; its leaves are large, the lower side white, the upper of a dingy green. The center only of this tree is black, the fap and the bark being white. In a trunk, from which may be cut a timber fix inches fquare, there is frequently no more of real ebony, than two inches fquare. This wood, if worked while green, fmells like human excrement, and its flowers like the July-flower; the very reverfe of the cinnamon, whofe flowers are ftinking, and the wood and bark of a pleafant fmell. The ebony bears a fruit like a medlar, full of vifcous juice, that is fweet and pleafant tafted.

There is another fort of ebony here, veined with black.

The citron-tree bears fruit in cool and damp places only; the citrons are fmall, but full of juice.

The orange-tree alfo thrives in a foil of this kind, its fruit is bitter and fharp-tafted. Many of them grow in the neighbourhood of the Great-Port; yet I doubt if thefe two fpecies are natural to the ifland. The fweet orange is very rare, even in gardens.

There is found here, but rarely, a fpecies of the *fandal-wood*. Somebody gave me a piece of it, which was of a greyifh white. It had a faint fmell.

The *vacoa*, is a kind of fmall palm-tree, whofe leaves grow fpirally round the trunk; they make mats and bags of them.

The *latanier*, is a large kind of palm-tree, it bears at the top, one leaf only, in the fhape of a fan, with which they cover their houfes.

The

THE *palm-tree* rises in the forest above all the other trees. It bears at the head a cluster of palms, whence there issues a shoot, which is all this tree affords fit to be eaten; and to get at this, the tree must be cut down. This shoot, which they call the cabbage, is formed of young leaves, rolled one over the other, very tender, and of a very pleasant taste.

The *manglier*, or *mangrove**, grows entirely in the sea. Its roots and branches creep along, and interweave themselves in the sand, so that it is impossible to pull them up. Its wood is red, and stains of an ugly colour.

I TOOK notice that the greater part of these trees have but a very thin bark, some of them even have nothing but a sort of skin over them, differing widely from the trees in the North, which nature has furnished with a variety of coats, to protect them from the cold. Most of them have their roots upon the surface of the earth, and twist round the rocks as they shoot up. They are but short; their heads little, furnished with leaves, and are very heavy; which with the *liannes* that grow round them, is their only support against the hurricanes, which would else presently tear up the firs and chesnuts.

As to the uses they are fit for, none can compare for durability and solidity to the oak, to the elm for pliancy, to the fir for the lightness and length of its timber, or to the chesnut for its usefulness in general. Their foliage has the same disagreeable quality as is

---

* The mangrove is also called *paletuvier*; its wood is very proper for building, and of its bark, the people in some part of the East-Indies make clothes. The elephants are extremely fond of the young leaves of this tree, and eat them with avidity. *T.*

common to every tree, whose leaves laſt the year round, being hard, and of an ugly dark green. Their wood is heavy, brittle, and eaſily rots. Thoſe that in other reſpects are fit for cabinet-work, ſoon turn black, when expoſed to the air, which gives their furniture a very diſagreeable look.

ALONG the margins of the rivulets which flow through the woods, are the moſt pleaſing retreats imaginable. The waters run through the midſt of the rocks; in one part gliding along in ſilence,—in another, falling precipitately from a height, with a confuſed and murmuring noiſe. The borders of theſe ravines are covered with trees, from which hang large bunches of *Scolopendria*, and *Liannes*, which falling down, are ſuſpended by their own twigs. The ground about them is rugged, with great pieces of black rock, overgrown with moſs and maidenhair. Large trunks over thrown by the hand of time, lay, covered with fungus, waved with various colours.

FERN grows here in infinite variety. Some, like leaves ſeparated from the ſtem, meander among the ſtones, and draw their ſubſtance from the rock itſelf. Others ſpring up like a tree of moſs, and reſemble a plume of ſilken feathers. The common ſort is of twice the ſize here, that it is in Europe. In lieu of the groves, and reeds, which ſo beautifully variegate the borders of our rivers, along the ſides of theſe torrents, grow a kind of water-lillies,

---

* *Spleenwort*, or *hartſtongue*, a medicinal herb, Pliny ſays, it was called in his time *Scolopendria*, *lingua cervina*, or *Aſplenus*. There is a fiſh, and alſo an inſect, called *Scolopendria*, both of which were called by the Ancients *millipeda*, and the Italians now call them *Centogambo*. T.

in great abundance, with very large leaves, in the form of a heart. They are called *Songes*. It will float upon the water without being wet, and the drops of rain amafs together upon it, like globules of fhining filver. Its root is an onion, of a malignant quality. 'Tis diftinguifhed into the black, and the white.

NEVER were thefe favage defarts enlivened by the fongs of birds, nor have they ever feen reluctant maid with downcaft eye, and lift'ning ear attend to the fond lover's tale. The ear is fometimes grated by the croaking of the perroquets, or pierced by the fhrill cry of fome malicious monkey.

YET, notwithftanding the barrennefs of the foil, even thefe rocks might be habitable, if the Europeans had not brought hither more and greater evils, than Nature herfelf, has heaped upon it.

The PORT, *October* 8, 1768.

## LETTER IX.

### Of the ANIMALS natural to the ISLE OF FRANCE.

THE Monkey of *Madagascar*, called *Maki*, does not in the least resemble those of this Island; nor the Baboons of the Cape of *Good-Hope*.

THE Monkey of the Isle of France, is of a middling size. It is of a reddish grey cast, and has a long tail. This animal is fond of society. I have seen them in troops of sixty at a time. They frequently come in droves, and pillage the houses. Scouts are placed on the tops of trees, and the points of the rocks, who as soon as they see any dogs or hunters approach, cry out, to alarm the others, who immediately decamp. They will climb up the steepest mountain, and rest upon the slightest edge of a precipice, where no other quadruped of its size dare venture. Thus Nature, which has covered even the holes of the rocks with herbage, has also created Beings to enjoy the benefit of it.

THE *Rat* seems a native of this island. There are prodigious numbers of them; and it is said, that the place was abandoned by the Dutch, because of this creature. In some houses they are so numerous, that
30,000

30000 \* are killed in a year. They make large hoards under ground, both of corn and of fruits, and climb up to the tops of the trees to eat the young birds. They will pierce the very thickest rafters. One may see them at sun-set, running about in all parts, and in one night they will destroy an entire crop. I have seen a field of maize, in which they have not left one single ear. They are exactly like the rats of Europe, and have, very possibly, come from thence in ships.

Mice are very common here; the havock they make is incredible.

It is said, that there were formerly a great many *Flamingos*; this is a large and beautiful sea-fowl, of a rose-colour; they say also, that three of them yet remain, but I never saw them.

Many *Corbigeaux* fly about, and are reckoned the best game the island produces; but are difficult to shoot.

There are *Paillencus* of two sorts, the one of white, like silver, the other having the beak, claws, and the tail red. Although this is a sea-bird, it builds its nest in the woods. Its name is not at all suited to its extraordinary beauty. The English more

---

\* This number may appear improbable, and I should have been inclined to think the Author misinformed, had I not been told by a Gentleman, upon whose veracity I can depend, that upon his return from the Havanna in the year 1766, in the Valiant man of war, the rats increased to such a degree, as to destroy a hundred weight of biscuit a day. The ship was at length smoked between decks, in order to suffocate them. This had the desired effect, and six hampers were filled daily for some time with the rats killed by this means. *T*.

*properly*

properly call it the *Tropic Bird*. It keeps near the sea, and is not intimidated at the sight of man.

TURTLES used frequently to be found on the shore, but now rarely. Their flesh is like beef; the fat green, and well tasted.

I HAVE seen many sorts of *Parrots*, but none very handsome. There is a species of green *Perroquets*, with a grey head. They are as large as sparrows. It is impossible to tame them. These also are enemies to the harvest, but they are very good to eat.

IN the woods are found black-birds, which when called to by a sportsman, will come to the end of his gun. This is a kind of game much in request.

THERE is a pigeon called the *Dutch-Pigeon*, of a most magnificent plumage; and another sort, which although, of a very pleasant taste, are so dangerous, that those who eat them are thrown into convulsions.

Two sorts of *Bats* are found here; one like ours, the other as big as a small cat, very fat; and is eaten by the inhabitants as a rarity.

THERE is a specious of sparrow-hawk, called the *Chicken-eater*; it is also said to eat *grasshoppers*.

THE sea-side is full of holes, in which lodge a great number of *Toulouroux*, they are a kind of amphibious crab, and make burroughs under ground like moles. They run very fast; and if you attempt to catch them, they snap their claws, and present their points, by way of menace.

ANOTHER amphibious and very extraordinary creature, is the *Bernard L'Hermite*, a kind of lobster, whose hinder part is not provided with a shell; but it instinctivly lodges itself in empty shells, which it finds upon the shore. One may see them run along in great numbers, each with its house after it, which it abandons for a larger when its growth makes it necessary.

THE most destructive insects on this island, are the *grasshoppers*. I have seen them light upon a field, like a fall of snow, and lay upon the ground several inches deep. They will eat up the verdure in the course of one night. This is the most dreaded enemy of agriculture.

THERE are many sorts of snails, and a large butterfly, which has upon its body the figure of a Death's Head. It is called *Hai* ‡, and flies about chiefly in rooms. It is said that the down of its wings will blind those whose eyes it touches.

The houses are full of ants, which destroy provisions of every kind. The pantries are not safe from their ravages, except they stand in water. Numbers of them are killed by an insect called a *Formicaleo*.

THE § *Centpieds*, or *Centipedes*, are frequently found in damp places. This insect seems destined to drive mankind from the unwholesome air they breed in. Its sting is very painful. My dog was bit by one of them, which was more than six inches long; the

‡ *Odious or Hateful*; so called, the Author says, from the fear it excites. *T.*

§ This, I suppose to be the insect *Scolopendria*, beforementioned. *T.*

wound

wound turned to a kind of ulcer, and was three weeks in healing. I was highly pleased with seeing one of them carried off by a vast unmber of ants; they had seized it by all its legs, and bore it along as workmen do a large piece of timber.

The yellow wasp with black rings upon the body, is not less formidable for its sting, than the scorpion, which is very common here. It builds in trees, and even in houses, its hive is of a substance like paper. There was one of them in my chamber; but I soon grew weary of so dangerous a guest.

The wasp called *Maçonnel*, or the *Mason*, builds itself a nest of earth, which one would think, was the work of a swallow, were any in the island. It lodges in rooms that are not frequented, and chiefly in the locks, which are filled with its labours.

One frequently finds in the gardens, leaves of the size of a sixpence; this is the work of the wasps, who shape with their teeth these circular pieces, with a nicety and readiness truly admirable. They carry them into their nests, and having rolled them into the shape of a horn, deposit their eggs in them.

There is a species of insect like an ant, which is not less industrious with regard to their habitations. They make great havock among the trees and timber, the wood of which they reduce to a powder; with this dust they construct little caverns of about an inch broad, under which they live; these caverns or pipes, are black, and will sometimes run over the timber of a whole house. They will penetrate through trunks, or furniture in one night. I found no remedy so effectual as to rub the places they frequented very often.

ten with garlick. They call thefe infects *Carias*. Many houfes are quite ruined by them.

THERE are three fpecies of *Cancre'as*, the dirtieft of all the *Scaraboea*. One of them is flat and grey; the moft common one is of the fize of a cockchafer, of a reddifh brown. It attacks furniture, efpecially books and papers, and harbours conftantly in the offices and kitchens. The houfes are very much peftered with them; efpecially in wet weather.

IT has for an antagonift, a fpecies of *Scarabæa*, or green fly, very gawdy and very nimble. When the *Can.relas* is met with, and touched by this fly, it becomes motionlefs. The fly then feeks for fome crack or chink, to which it draws the *cancrelas* and thrufts it in, depofits an egg in its body, and then leaves it. This touch, which fome look upon as a charm, is the ftroke of the fting, the effect of which is inftantaneous, this infect being elfe hard to kill.

IN the trunks of trees there is found a large worm with paws, that picks the trees, they call it *Montac*. The blacks, and even the white people eat them greedily. Pliny obferves, that they were ferved up at the moft capital tables in Rome, and were fattened with meal for that purpofe. That found in the oak-tree was in the higheft eftimation; and was called *cofſus*. Thus have abundance and fcarcity combined in the fame tafte; and like all other extremes, approached very near to each other.

THERE are lady-birds on the fides of the rivulets, of a fine violet colour, with a head like a ruby. This infect is carnivorous. I have feen it carrying a beautiful butterfly through the air.

THE

The apartments are, at certain seasons, filled with moths, or small butterflies, that come and singe themselves in the candle. They are so numerous, that the candles are frequently obliged to be put into cylinders of glass. They draw into the houses a very handsome small lizard, about a finger's length. Its eyes are lively; it climbs along the walls, and even along the glass, lives upon flies and other insects, and watches with great patience for an opportunity of catching them. It lays eggs that are small and round like peas, having a white and yellow shell, as the eggs of pullets. I have seen some of these lizards so tame, that they would come and take sugar out of a person's hand. Far from being mischievous, they are on the contrary, very useful. Some very beautiful ones are to be seen in the woods, of an azure, and changeable green, marked with crimson on the back, like Arabic characters.

An enemy that is still more terrible to the insects, is the *Spider*. Some of them have bellies as big as a nut, with large paws, covered with hair. Their webs are so strong, that even small birds are catched in them. They are of use, in destroying the wasps, scorpions, and centipedes. There is a little white louse, that harbours in fruit-trees, and destroys them; and a bug, whose bite is more dangerous than that of the scorpion, and is succeeded by a tumour as big as a pigeon's egg, which continues for four or five days.

You will observe, that the temperature of this climate, so tempting to the inhabitants of Europe, is so favourable to the propagation of insects, that in a short time, the fruits would be eaten up by them, and the island itself become uninhabitable; but

but the fruits of thefe meridional countries, are clothed with a thick rind, and afterwards with a fkin, a very hard fhell, or an aromatic bark, like the orange or citron, infomuch that the flies can introduce their worms into very few of them only. Many of thefe noxious animals are at perpetual war with each other, as the fcorpion and the centipied. The *Formicaleos* lays fnares for the Ant; the green fly pierces the *Cancrelas*; the *Lizard* hunts the *Butterfly*; the *Spiders* fpread nets for every infect that flies; and the hurricane which rages once a year, annihilates at once a great part, both of the prey, and of the devourers.

Port-Louis, *Dec.* 7, 1768.

## LETTER X.

I am now to write to you concerning the sea, and its productions, you will then know at least as much as the first Portugueze that landed in this island. If I can add to this a metereological journal, you will by degrees be acquainted with the whole natural history of this country; from hence we shall go on and treat of the inhabitants, and of the course they have taken for the improvement of their country, where, as in every other part of the world, good and evil are mingled together. Plutarch would have us deduce harmony from these contrarieties; but though good instruments, are very common, good Musicians, are found but rarely.

Whales are often seen to windward of this island, especially about September, the time of their coupling. I have seen many this season, that kept themselves upright in the water, and came very near the coast. They are smaller than the northern ones. There is no whale fishery, but the Negroes are not unacquainted with the method of harpooning them. * Sea Cows are sometimes catched here; I have eaten of them, their flesh is like beef; I never saw any of this fish.

The Vieille, is a blackish fish, and in form and taste a good deal like the cod fish. One extraordinary

* Whales are in such plenty upon the equally southern coast of Brazil, that they constitute the greatest part of the food of the Negroes, belonging to the Planters near the sea; as I have been informed by a person who lived several years in that country. *T.*
  Herodotus in Lib. 4 says that in the Borysthenes, in his time there were Whales. *T.*

circumſtance, is, that the fiſh on the windward-ſide of the iſland is never unwholſome. Thoſe then that attribute this poiſonous quality to the Madrepores are miſtaken ; the iſland being on all ſides ſurrounded by banks of coral. I ſhould rather think it occaſioned by ſome venomous tree falling into the water, which conjecture is the more probable ; becauſe at one ſeaſon, only, ſome particular ſpecies of gluttonous fiſh are ſubject to this inconveniency. Moreover that ſpecies of Pigeon whoſe fleſh occaſions convulſions in the eaters of it, proves that the poiſon is in the iſland itſelf.

Among the fiſh to be ſuſpected are a number of white ones, with a large belly, and a great head, ſuch as the Captain and the Carangue. Theſe two ſorts are of an indifferent taſte. Thoſe that have their mouths paved, that is to ſay, a rugged bone in their palates are thought to be never dangerous.

In general, the ſmaller the fiſh, the greater the danger.

The Water-pullet, a ſort of Turbot, is the beſt of all the fiſh catched here,—the fat is green.

Perroquets, that are not only green, but have yellow heads, white and crooked beaks, and go in a body like the birds of that name.

The Hog-Fish, is ſmall and oddly ſhaped ; its head is like a pike, upon its back are ſeven points as long as its body, the prick of them is very venomous ; they are united by a membrane like the wing of a bat ; it is ſtreaked with brown ſtripes, which begin at the muzzle, exactly as thoſe of the Zebra at the Cape. The fiſh is ſquare like a trunk, and

which

which name it bears, is armed with two horns like a bull; there are many species of them: they never grow large.

The EEL is tough, they are of the conger fort, some of them are seven or eight feet long, and as thick as a mans leg. They harbour in the creeks of the rivers, and sometimes devour those who are imprudent enough to bathe there.

There are LOBSTERS or CRAY-FISH of a prodigious size, their paws are not large, they are blue, marbled with black. I have seen here a species of lobster that is smaller and of a beautiful form.; it was of a sky-blue; it had two little claws, divided into two articulations, like a knife with the blade shutting into the handle.

There is a great variety of CRABS. The following seemed to be most worthy of notice.

A sort that is rugged with tubercules and points like a madrepore; another that has upon its back the impression of five seals; another with something in the shape of a horse-shoe at the end of its claws; a sort covered with hair, that has no claws, and that adheres to the sides of ships; a crab marbled with grey, the shell of which though smooth and polished is very uneven. Many irregular and strange figures are observable among these, which are notwithstanding perfectly alike upon each crab; that with its eyes at the end of two long tubes like telescopes, which when it is not using them, it deposits in grooves along the side of its shell.

A Crab with red claws, one much larger than the other; a small crab with a shell thrice as big as itself, in which it is covered over as by a buckler, so that its claws cannot be seen when it walks.

In many places along shore and some feet under water are found a multitude of large *Boudins de Mer*, red and black. In taking them out of the water they emit a white and thick slime, that immediately changes into a number of small and glutinous threads. I believe this animal to be an enemy of the crab species, amongst which it is to be always met with. Its vicious glear is very fit to entangle their claws, which otherwise could have no hold upon its elastic hide, and cylindrical form. The seamen give it a very gross appellation which I will render in latin *mentula monachi*. The Chinese hold it in high esteem, looking upon it as a powerful aphrodisiac.

I think I may rank among the shell-fish a shapeless Mass, soft and membranous, in the middle of which is one single flat bone that is a little arched. In these species the usual order seems to be reversed, the animal is on the outside of the shell.

It is thought a great singularity, that all univalves of which there are many, are turned from left to right, in looking at the shell when lying on its mouth, and the point towards ones-self: there are very few exceptions to this rule. What law can have determined them to begin their volute on the same side? Is it the same that has caused the sun to turn from West to East? In this case the sun may in some degree be the cause, as it is of their colours, which are the more beautiful the nearer to the line. There is much ingenuity and variety in the hinges of shell-fish, and our artists might improve by attending to the construction of them.

The Oyster called the *Tulier* is common here, and is of the same sort as those that are used as holy water

# VOYAGE to the ISLE OF FRANCE.

water pots in the church of St. Sulpice, at Paris; and is perhaps the largeſt ſhell which the ſea produces: ſome of them are found at the Maldivia Iſlands, which are not to be drawn by two oxen without difficulty. It is rather extraordinary that this oyſter is found in Normandy as a foſſil, upon which coaſt I have ſeen it.

Apparently, ſhell-fiſh do not live peacebly together, any more than other animals do. Many of them are found broken to pieces on the ſhore; thoſe that are taken whole are always pierced. I too have ſeen a ſnail armed with a pointed tooth, with which it pierced the ſhells of muſcles: twas brought from the Streights of Magellan.

The ISLE of FRANCE is ſurrounded with Madrepores, a kind of vegetation of ſtone formed like a plant or ſhrub. They are ſo very numerous that the rocks ſeem formed of them only.

Among thoſe that adorn and diverſify the bed of the ſea and adhere to it by their roots, are, the collyflower; the cabbage, whoſe appearance is very like that plant; it is of the large ſort, as well as another madrepore, the ſtages of which grow ſpirally; it is very brittle; another that by the high ſhooting of its head and the robuſtneſs of its branches, reſembles a tree; a very beautiful ſpecies, which I called the ſheaf; it ſeems formed of ſeveral bunches of ears of corn; the pencil or pink,—at the center of each opening, there is a little piece that is green.

A BEAUTIFUL MADREPORE, growing in the form of an iſland with its ſhores and Mountains; another, like an icicle; another, the leaves of which are digitated like a hand: the ſtag-wood, with horns very detached

detached and brittle: the beehive, a large fhapelefs mafs, the whole furface of which is full of regular holes; the pale blue coral, which is rare,—within, it is of a deeper blue; the jointed coral, black and white, containing a fmall piece of red coral which has not yet been feen here; vegetations of coral, blue, white, yellow and red, fo brittle, and fo much pierced that one cannot fend any of it to Europe.

AMONG the *Litophites*; a plant like a long ftraw without leaves, buds or buttons; a vegetation like a foreft of trees; their roots are very much interwoven, and have each a fmall nofegay of flowers; the fubftance of this *Litophite* is of the nature of wood, and burns like it in the fire; it is notwithftanding claffed among the Madrepores.

I HAVE feen three forts of fea ftar-wort, but nothing remarkable in either. Formerly ambergreafe was found upon the coaft; (there is even a little ifland to windward called by that name): It is fometimes brought from Madagafcar.

IT is not now doubted but that the Madrepores are the work of an infinity of fmall animals, altho' they have a perfect refemblance of plants; I was pleafed to be experimentally convinced of this, it being delightful to me to look upon the Univerfe as peopled. Befides I conceive fo regular a work can only be carried on by fome agent endewed with intelligence and a love of order. Thefe vegetations refemble ours fo much, the component matter apart, that I am even much induced to believe our vegetables alfo to be * productions of the labour of a multitude of living animals combined together for that purpofe. I had much rather look upon a tree as a republick, than as a machine without life. and actuated by I know not

* See letter 29 where this fubject is difcuffed.

what

what laws of Hydraulics. I could support this opinion by many curious observations, for which I may perhaps some time hence have leisure. These researches may be useful, but when not employed to a good purpose, do but divert our attention from the more laudable pursuits on which it should be employed, and habituate it to fix upon any thing trifling that presents itself. Our histories are frequently made up of calumnies, our moral treatises, of Satires, and our societies and academies of slander and epigrams. And after all this, men lament that friendship and confidence no longer exist; not considering the impossibility that they should do so; among persons, each of whom carries a shield upon his heart, and a poignard under his cloak.

Let us talk little, or let us form systems, *Tradid·tmundum disputationibus*. Let us dispute then, but without being angry.

PORT LOUIS, 12*th of January* 1769.

## METEREOLOGICAL JOURNAL.

### QUALITIES OF THE AIR.

### JULY, 1768.

DURING this month the winds blew from the south-west as it usually does all the year. There is a strong breeze all day, and at night it is calm. Altho' tis now the dry season, yet it frequently rains, with violent squalls, that last but a short time. The air is very sharp; in so much that cloth clothes are indispensably necessary.

G　　　　　　　　　　AUGUST.

## AUGUST.

IT rained almost every day. The tops of the mountains are covered with vapours like smoke, which descend upon the plains with gusts of wind. These rains frequently form rainbows upon the sides of the mountains, which however are not the less black on that account.

## SEPTEMBER.

THE wind and weather as before. 'Tis the season for harvest. If heat and moisture are the sole causes of vegetation, why does nothing shoot at this time? It is no less hot than in May in France. Can there be any spirit of life attending the return of the sun? The Romans paid honours to the western wind, and fixed the period of its arrival at the 8th of February. They called it *Favonius*, or the Fosterer. 'Tis the same as the Zephyr of the Greeks. Pliny says it serves as a husband to all things that draw their existence from the earth.

## OCTOBER.

THE same temperature; the air is a little hotter, it is always coldest in the interior part of the island. At the end of this month they sow their wheat, and in four months after is their harvest; they then sow maize, which is ripe in September. Thus have they two crops on the same land; but these are scarcely a compensation for the other plagues with which this island is pestered.

## NOVEMBER.

THE heats begin to be felt, the winds change, and sometimes get round to the N. W. Storms of rain fall.

No ship from France. No letter. It is grievous at this distance to be in constant expectation of our chief happiness from Europe.

## DECEMBER.

THE heats are excessive. The sun is in the zenith, but the air is tempered by plentiful rains. I think I have felt it hotter in the summer at Petersbourg. At the beginning of the month I heard thunder for the first time since my arrival.

THE 23d in the morning the wind blew from the S. W. and seemed to presage a storm. The clouds gathered at the top of the mountains. They were of an olive or copper colour, and one long range of them was higher than the rest and motionless. The smaller ones that were below blew about with a surprising rapidity. The sea broke upon the rocks with a great noise. Many of the sea birds flew for shelter to the land. The domestic animals were very uneasy. The air was gloomy and hot although the wind was still high.

ALL these signs presaging a hurricane, every body hastened to strengthen their houses with supporters and props, and to block up their doors and windows.

ABOUT 10 o'clock in the evening the hurricane announced itself by horrible gusts of wind, which were followed by not less horrible intervals of calm, in which the wind seemed to collect new powers. It kept augmenting the whole night; my apartment being very much shaken, I went into another. The good woman I lodged with, wept, and was in despair at the thoughts of her house being destroyed. Nobody went to bed. Towards morning the wind redoubled its efforts. I perceived that one side of our pallisade fence was falling, and that part of the roof of the house was raised at one corner; I got some planks and cords, by means of which I prevented the damage that would else have happened. In crossing the yard to give directions about this work, I frequently thought I should have been blown down. Some walls at a distance were falling, and some roofs were torn to pieces, the timbers of which were blown away as if they had been cards.

About 8 in the morning some rain fell, and the wind not at all abated, blew it horizontally along with such violence, that it entered like so many Jets-dëau at every the smallest opening. It spoiled several of my papers.

At 11 o'clock the rain fell in torrents. The wind subsided a little, the ravines in the mountains formed prodigious cascades on every side. Large pieces of the rocks broke off with a noise like that of Cannon, and as they rolled down, cleared to themselves a path among the woods. The rivulets overflowed into the plain which by this time was like another sea, neither banks nor bridges being any more to be seen.

At one o'clock the wind whirled about to the N. W. and drove the surf of the sea in large clouds along the land. The ships in the harbour were run ashore, and kept firing guns as signals of distress, but in vain, for no succour could be sent to them. By these repeated gusts, the buildings were acted upon the contrary way, and with nearly equal violence. About noon the wind shifted to the E. and then to the W. Thus it went quite the circle of the horizon in the four-and-twenty hours, as usual,— after which a perfect calm succeeded.

Many

Many trees were blown down, and bridges carried away. Not one single leaf remained in our gardens. Even the herb dogs-tooth so remarkably hardy, seemed in some places to be cut to the very edge of the ground.

During the tempest a good man of this place whose name is *Le Roux*, a joiner, sent his blacks and workmen to help those that might want their assistance, and this without any gratuity. Good actions should never be passed over without notice,—especially in this place.

There was an eclipse at 4 min. past 5 on the 23d, but the bad weather prevented its being seen.

The hurricane comes regularly every year in December, and sometimes in March. As the winds make the tour of the horizon, there is not a cavern in the island unfilled with the rain, which destroys a great number of rats, grasshoppers and ants,—they are not seeen again for some time.

It holds the place of a winter, but the ravages made by it are more to be dreaded. That of 1760 will be a long time thought of. A shutter was seen lifted into the air and then darted like an arrow, upon a roof at some distance. The lower masts of a 64 gun ship were twisted round and broken off. No tree in Europe could withstand the force of these whirlwinds. How the trees of the country are protected we have seen above.

## JANUARY, 1769.

Rainy weather, hot and gloomy; great storms, but little thunder. The gales of wind blowing very hard in this season all navigation is at a stand from December till April.

The Meadows recover their verdure, the earth presents a pleasanter prospect, but the sky a dismal one.

## FEBRUARY.

STORMY weather, and violent gusts of wind. The Happy, a passage boat sent to Madagascar, and the Favorite, a ship, are both lost.

THE 25th of this month the clouds gathered together by a N. W. wind, formed themselves into a long range from the Flag Mountain to the Isle of *Tonneliers*. It is motionless: claps of thunder innumerable proceeded from it. The storm lasted from 6 in the morning till noon, during which time a number of thunderbolts fell; one of them killed a Grenadier, and another, a Negro woman; an ox upon the Island of *Tonneliers* had the same fate: a gun in an officer's house was melted. The people here say, that the thunder never falls within the town; for my part I never heard any so loud, and could not help thinking it very like a bombardment. I am of opinion that if they had fired one cannon, the explosion would have dispelled the motionless clouds from whence the thunder issued.

## MARCH.

THE rains are not so frequent, and the winds always from the S. W. The heat is now tolerable.

## APRIL.

THE season is fine, and the herbage begins to be dry, and should it now be set on fire, the landscape would be totally black for seven months to come.

## MAY.

TOWARDS the end of this month the winds according to cuftom turned to N. W. We have now the dry feafon. I was in the plains, called *Williams* plains, and found the air of a temperature perfectly pleafant and refrefhing.

## JUNE.

THE winds blow almoft conftantly from the S. E. and the fhowers of fmall rain again begin to fall.

No malady feems peculiar to this country, but the people have all thofe we have in Europe, as the apoplexy, fmall-pox, pleurifies and obftructions in the liver, which laft I fhould imagine proceeded rather from vexation, than from the bad quality of the water as is the general opinion. I have feen a ftone taken from a Negroe of the place which was bigger than an egg. Violent gouts and paralytic diforders are common.

THE Blacks and children are very fubject to worms: the former have in the venereal difeafe dreadful chops or clefts in the foles of their feet. The air is as good as in Europe, but has no medicinal virtues, and I would by all means diffuade gouty perfons from coming here, having feen fome people keep their beds for fix months together.

THE change of the feafons, makes a very fenfible alteration in the conftitution of the inhabitants. They are liable to bilious fevers, and the heat occafions ruptures. but temperance and bathing will keep a man in health. I cannot however but obferve that in cold countries, the people are more healthy and their spirits more vigorous, and it is worthy of remark, that history mentions no celebrated man that was born between the tropics, except *Mahomet*.

## LETTER XI.

### MANNERS OF THE WHITE INHABITANTS.

THE Isle of France was uninhabited till discovered by Mascarenhas. The first French people that established themselves here were some Husbandmen from Bourbon. They brought with them simplicity of manners, goodfaith and confidence, a love of hospitality and even an indifference with respect to riches. Monsieur de Bourdonnais who was in some measure the founder of the colony, brought workmen into it that were good sort of men, and some others whom their parents sent from home for misconduct, and whom by his discipline he made good and useful members to society.

WHEN he had rendered the island respectable by the labour he exerted for its encouragement, and it was thought a proper place to touch at in the way to India, people of all ranks poured in upon it. Among whom were the persons sent out by the India Company. The principal employments on the island being vested in their hands, they lived in a state equal to that of the nobles in Venice, and to their aristocratical manners joined something also of a spirit of financing, which

which is always prejudicial to the spirit of agriculture. Every appointment was at their disposal, and their power was alike absolute in judicial matters, as in matters of trade. Some of them cleared the lands, and erected buildings, which they sold again at an exorbitant rate to those who came thither to settle. An outcry was raised against the oppressors, but so great was their power, that no redress could be obtained.

Several seafaring people established here, who for a long time could not understand that the dangers and fatigue of the trade to India was to them, in proportion as the honours and profits of it were to those for whom they laboured. This settlement so near to the Indies raised great expectations on their first coming. But before their establishment was effected, they became discontented, and much more so afterwards.

The company sent out a military force, among whom were some officers of high birth. These had no idea of degrading themselves so far as to rank or connect with men who had formerly been Merchants Clerks; except to receive their pay of them: they liked the seamen as little as the merchants,—their manners were too blunt and unpolished. Thus their pride standing in the way of their fortune, they continued as poor as when they left France.

Some of the King's troops touched here, and staid some time. A few of the officers tempted by the serenity of the climate and a love of ease, fixed their abode here. Every thing and every body being subject to the company only, the subaltern did not meet here with the distinction and respect paid to him in garrisons, and which were so flattering to his vanity,— being without employment he was looked upon as an alien

alien among the mercantile people, each of whom had his particular interest to attend to.

OTHER settlers here, were the Missionaries of St. Lazarus, who availing themselves of the simplicity of the first inhabitants, had exercised a dominion over them uncontrouled: but when the body of the people increasing very fast, divided and dispersed itself, they were content to attend to their pastoral functions, and to some of the better sort of families who countenanced their visits.

NEXT landed some merchants who brought money with them, though to no great amount. In an island without trade they added to the abuses of brokerage already practised, and introduced besides monopolies of every kind.

THEY quickly became odious to the other inhabitants, who wanting the means of imposition, were themselves imposed upon, and gave their oppressors the epithet of *Banians*, a name there held in as much abhorrence as that of Jew in France. They also affected to despise the distinctions of rank, looking upon every man after his having crossed the line, to be the equal of his neighbour.

AT length the late war in India, inundated upon the Isle of France, the scum of Europe and of Asia, Bankrupts,—ruined Libertines,—Thieves, and wretches of every kind, who driven from the former by their crimes, and from the latter by the bad success of our arms, attempted to reestablish their fortunes upon the ruins of the public. On the arrival of this set of men, the complaints both general and particular of the inhabitants were augmented; every character was traduced with an Asiatic ingenuity, hitherto unknown to
the

the caluminators of our climate; no woman was now looked upon as chaste, nor any man as honest: all confidence and esteem, were at an end. Thus by vilifying all mankind, they thought to reduce all mankind to their own level.

ALL their hopes being founded upon a change of the administration, they at last effected their design. The company in 1765 yielding up to the King, a colony which had cost them so much trouble and expence;—Order and peace were now expected to resume their seat, but it was found that this change had added new leaven to the fermentation: for a number of persons were sent by authority from Paris to make their fortunes in an island, uncultivated and without any settled trade, and where paper is the only currency. These then were malecontents of another sort.

A party of the inhabitants who were grateful enough to continue their attachment to the company, saw with grief, the introduction of the royal jurisdiction. The other party that had reckoned upon the new government, seeing that none but oeconomical plans were adopted, felt their disappointment the more severely, on account of the expectations they had formed.

To these new differences were added the dissentions of bodies of men, who were at continual variance even in France,—the departments of the marine, the pen,—and the sword;—In short, the mind of every individual, being neither occupied by business, nor amused by public entertainments, retired within itself, to brood over its own inquietudes.

Discord reigns all over the island, and has entirely extirpated that love of society which might be expected

pected to prevail among Frenchmen banished to a desart, surrounded by the seas, and at the end of the world. Each man is discontented;—each man wants to get a fortune—and to leave the place. To hear, them talk one would think the island would be again uninhabited, every man declaring he will go away next year, and some of them have held this intention for thirty years past, yet remain to make the same declaration the year ensuing.

An officer from Europe soon loses here his military ardour. In general he has but little money and is in want of every thing; his house is without furniture: provisions when bought retail are excessively dear, and he finds himself the sole consumer between the inhabitants and the merchant, who seem to strive who shall impose upon him most. This forces him to act upon the defensive,—he buys by wholesale, and makes the most of all opportunities of getting good bargains, every commodity being of double value after the departure of the ships. The anxiety of providing for his family being at an end, another ensues, he torments himself with the thoughts of being an exile from his native country, and being destined to remain he knows not how long in one destitute of every comfort and convenience, want of employment and company, aided by the hopes of gain, allure him to engage farther in that commerce, which mere necessity at first drove him to.

There are without doubt some exceptions to this general character of the military, and were they not even numerous, I should recite them with pleasure. M. de Steenhovre, the commanding officer is a pattern of every virtue,

The regiments furnish a number of workmen;
for

for the heat is not so excessive as to prevent the white people from working in the open air. That advantage however for the benefit of the colony has not been made in this respect, that might have been. Among the recruits sent from Europe, there are frequently wretches capable of the most atrocious villainies. I cannot for my part conceive but that the sending of culprits whose crimes have rendered them unworthy to remain in their native country, must be of bad consequence to any colony in an incipient state. These unhappy creatures frequently become so desperate, as to murder each other with their bayonets upon the most trifling occasion.

ALTHOUGH the seamen do but come and go, they yet have a great influence upon the manners of the the inhabitants. Their policy consists in complaining of the places whence they come, as well as of those they arrive at. They would have you believe that their lucky hour has passed them without their making a proper advantage of it,—they speak of themselves constantly as ruined men; they tell you how dear they have bought, and to what loss they have sold. The truth of this matter is, that they think no bargain a good one, unless they get a 150 per cent by it. A cask of claret costs 150 livres, and every thing else in proportion. One would scarcely imagine that European goods were dearer here than in India, and Indian goods dearer than in Europe. This however is the case. The seamen are much regarded by the inhabitants who indeed could hardly exist without them. Their murmurings, and perpetual going to and again give the island the appearance, and in a degree the manners of an inn.

From so many of such different conditions, results as it were a people of different nations who hate each other

other moſt cordially. Probity and honour are in no
eſteem. The *cunning* man is here the man of wit. It
is however in my opininion a character worthy only
of foxes; it is certainly not a property natural to the
human ſpecies, and a wretched ſociety muſt that be,
where it is looked upon as an eſtimable quality. On
the other hand, miſtruſtful or wary people are much
diſliked; this may appear a contradiction, but the
reaſon is, that there is leſs to be got, from perſons uſed
to be on their guard, who may detect and expoſe thoſe
who would impoſe upon them. They will flock a-
bout a man whom they know to be artful, and will
aſſiſt him to the utmoſt in duping the ignorant.

THEIR inſenſibility with reſpect to the feeling
which conſtitute the happineſs of a generous mind,
is extreme. They have no taſte for arts or literature,
but deeply regret their abſence from the Opera and the
Women of Paris. Every ſentiment of humanity is
here depraved, nay, I may ſay extinct. I was once
at the funeral of a conſiderable merchant, but ſaw no
ſigns of affliction; his brother-in-law remarked indeed that they had not dug the grave ſo deep as it
ſhould have been.

THIS indifference extends to all things about them.
The ſtreets and courts are neither paved, nor planted
with trees; the houſes are meer cabbins of wood,
which may be eaſily removed from one place to another upon rollers. The windows have neither glaſs
nor curtains; and the houſes have but little furniture, and that little very ſhabby.

THERE is a ſort of exchange, where people meet at
noon and in the evening; here they make their bargains, and rail at, and talk ſcandal of their neighbours. The married people in the town are very
few

few. Those who are not rich, plead their circumstances as an excuse for continuing single: others say they will not settle till their return to France; but the true reason is, their seldom or ever meeting with a repulse in their attempts upon the negro girls. Besides, there are very few good matches for the men, ten thousand franks * being a fortune but seldom heard of.

The greater part of the married people live upon their plantations. The women scarcely ever come to town but to a ball, or to confess at Easter. They are most passionately fond of dancing. No sooner is a ball announced, than they come in crouds, brought in palanquins, which are a sort of litter, and carried upon the shoulders of four negroes, four others following as a relay. As many children as there are in the family, so many of these vehicles are there, and each attended as above by eight blacks. The husbands who are prudent and saving, are very averse to these excursions, as hindrances of the business of the plantations; but the roads are so bad, that a wheel carriage here is of no use.

The women are rather pale, but well made, and in general handsome,—they have naturally a great flow of wit and spirits, and if better educated would be most agreeable companions, but I have known some so ignorant as to be unable to read.

At their meetings they are reserved and silent; each woman brings with her some secret pretensions, either from the fortune, the employ, or the birth of the husband: others reckon upon their youth or their beauty; an Europian looks with disdain upon a Creole, who as often looks upon the European as an adventurer.

* L 437,10 or thereabouts, according to the rate of Exchange.

Not-

Notwithstanding that the tongue of scandal is ever speaking to their prejudice, they are in my opinion far more deserving than the men, by whom they are neglected for the black slaves. Such of the women as are really virtuous, are the more to be commended, that it is by no means owing to their education that they are so. They have at once to combat with the heat of the climate, the indifference of their husbands, and the prodigality and ardour of young officers, skilled in seduction and regardless of repulse: if then Hymen complains and with justice of the infidelities of the fair sex, whom can we thank but ourselves, who have introduced the manners of France upon the shores of Africa.

In other respects they have very many good qualities,—are domestic, sober, (drinking water only, except rarely), and neat in their apprrel to an extreme. The dress most common here is of muslin trimmed with rose coloured taffaty. They are extravagantly fond of their children, who run about the house naked, very soon after they are born; are never put in swaddling clothes, but are frequenely bathed, eat fruit as they think proper, live without care, and without study, and soon grow strong and robust. The puberty of both sexes makes a very early appearance. I have known girls married here at eleven years old.

This manner of bringing up children which approaches so near to a state of nature leaves them in an almost utter ignorance; but the vices of the negro women, which they imbibe with their milk, and their caprices, which they are suffered to exercise upon the poor slaves to a degree of tyranny beyond all bounds, adds to this ignorance all the depravity incient to society. To remedy this evil, the principal
people

people send their children while very young into France, from whence they return with vices perhaps more amiable, but certainly more dangerous.

The number of Planters on this island, is scarcely four hundred. There are about a hundred women of condition, about ten only of whom live in the town. The evening is their visiting time—and for want of conversation, they game, or soon grow tired of each other. At eight o'clock the evening gun fires, and every body goes home.

Farewell, my dear friend; I am really grieved to think that in speaking of mankind as they are, the truth carries with it the air of a satire.

Port Louis, Isle of France, 10th of February, 1769.

## LETTER XII.

### Of the BLACKS.

In the Population of this Island, I must include the INDIANS and NEGROES.

THE the first are the Malabars, or Malayans, a mild and gentle people, who come from Pondicherry, where they let themselves as servants for a term of years. They are almost all of handicraft trades, and occupy a suburb, called the Camp of the Blacks. This people is of a deeper hue than the islanders of Madagascar, who are perfect Negroes; but have features as regular as a European, and not the frizled hair. They are sober, thrifty, and much given to women. They wear on their heads, a turbant, are clothed in long muslin gowns, and carry large rings of gold in their ears, and silver bracelets on their wrists. Some of them let themselves to the rich people, and are called *Pions*, a kind of domestic like our running footmen, who executes every commission, with the most profound gravity; and by way of distinction, carries a cane in his hand, and a poignard in his girdle. It were to be wished, that a great number of Malabars were established here, especially as labourers; but I never saw one of them fond of farming work.

THE Blacks who till the ground, are brought from Madagascar, where a slave may be bought for a barrel fel of powder, for a few mufquets, linen, or efpecially for piaftres; the greateft price paid is * fifty crowns, and that rarely.

This nation have neither fo flat a nofe, nor fo black a fkin as the Negroes of Guinea. Some of them are only to be called brown, and fome, as the *Balambous*, have long hair, of a brown, or carrotty colour. They are active, ingenious, have a quick fenfe of honour and of gratitude, far lefs mindful of injuries done to themfelves perfonally, than of thofe offered to their family,—which laft, they deem an infult of the higheft degree. When in their own country, they make a variety of things with much art and induftry. Their *zagaye*, or half-pike, is very well forged, although they have nothing but ftones for both anvil and hammer. Their linens, or *pagnes*, which are weaved by women, are very fine, and beautifully coloured. Their manner of throwing this garment round them, is extremely graceful. Their head-drefs is very regular, in rows of curls and braids, nicely ranged one above the other.; this is alfo the work of women. They are paffionately fond of dancing and mufic, and play upon an inftrument called a *Tamtam*, which is a kind of bow, with a gourd bottle fitted to it. The found of it is very foft, and is a pleafing accompanyment to their fongs, of which, love is always the fubject. The girls dance to the fongs their lovers compofe, while the fpectators beat time, and applaud the peformance.

They are very hofpitable. A Black who is travelling, enters, though unknown, into the firft cottage he comes to; fits down with the inhabitants of it, and partakes of their repaft, without being quef-

* 7 l. 10 s.

tioned, whence he comes? or whither he is going? This custom is general.

These arts, and these manners, they bring with them to the Isle of France, where they are landed with a rag round their loins. The men are ranged on one side,—and on the other, the women, with their infants, who cling for fear to their mothers. The inhabitant having examined them, as he would a horse, buys what are for his purpose. Brothers— sisters—friends – lovers—are torn asunder, and bidding each other a long farewell, are driven weeping to the plantations they are bought for. Sometimes they turn desperate *, fancying that the white people intend eating their flesh, making red wine of their blood, and gunpowder of their bones.

They are treated in the following manner: At break of day, a signal of three smacks of a whip calls them to work, each of them betakes himself with his spade to the plantations, where they work almost naked in the heat of the sun. Their food is maize, bruised, and boiled, or bread made of Manioc †, and their clothing, a single piece of linen. Upon the commission of the most trivial offence, they are tied hand and foot to a ladder; the overseer then comes with a whip like a postilion's, and gives them fifty, a hundred, or perhaps two hundred lashes upon the back. Each stroke carries off its portion of skin. The poor wretch is then untied, an iron collar with three spikes put round his neck, and he is then sent

---

* Ludicrously extravagant, as this fancy may seem, reflection upon the barbarities exercised upon them, must allow the possibility of its suggesting itself, especially in minds so ignorant as the slaves are described to be. *T.*

† A root, for which the English have no name.—'Tis poison, if eaten raw, but wholesome and good, if boiled. *T.*

back

back to his tafk. Some of them are unable to fit down for a month after this beating, which punifhment is inflicted with equal feverity on women as on men.

In the evening, when they return home, they are obliged to pray for the profperity of their mafters; and before they go to reft, they wifh him a good night.

There is a law in force in their favour, called the *Code Noire*, which ordains, that they fhall receive no more than thirty lafhes for any one offence,---that they fhall not work on Sundays,---that they fhall eat meat once a week,---and have a new fhirt every year; but this law is not obferved. Sometimes when grown too old to labour, they are turned out to get their bread where they can. One day I faw a poor creature who was nothing but fkin and bone, cutting off the flefh of a dead horfe to eat;—It was one fkeleton devouring another.

When a European feems affected at thefe fights, the inhabitants tell him, he does not know the Blacks ---That they are fuch gluttons as to go and fteal victuals from the neighbouring houfes;---fo idle, that they take no manner of care of their mafter's bufinefs, nor do what they are fet about;—that the women are totally inattentive to family affairs, and fo little concerned about children, that they had rather procure an abortion, than bring them into the world.

The Negroes are naturally lively, but after having been fome time in flavery, become melancholy. Love feems the only paffion their forrows will permit them to be fenfible of.. They do all in their power to get married; and if their own choice is fuffered to take place,

place, they generally prefer thofe who have paffed the prime of their youth ; who, they tell you, *make better foup than the very young ones.* They give the wife all they poffefs. If their miftrefs is the flave of another planter, they will go three or four leagues in the night to fee her, through ways one would think impaffable. When under the influence of this paffion, they are alike fearlefs of fatigue or of punifhment. Sometimes they appoint a rendezvous in the middle of the night, and perhaps, under the fhelter of a rock, they dance to the difmal found, of a bladder filled with peas : but the fight of a white perfon, or the barking of a dog, immediately breaks up the affembly.

They have alfo dogs with them, and it is an undoubted truth, that thefe animals know perfectly, even in the dark, not only a white man, but a dog that belongs to a white man,—both of whom, they fear and hate; howling as foon as they approach.

The dogs of the white people feem on their parts, to have adopted the fentiments of their mafters ; and at the leaft encouragement, will fly with the utmoft fury upon a flave, or upon his dog.

In fhort, the Blacks are fometimes unable to endure their hard lot, and give themfelves up to defpair. Some,—hang or poifon themfelves ; others will get into a little boat, and without fails, provifions, or compafs, hazard a voyage of two hundred leagues, to return to Madagafcar, where they have been fometimes feen to land ; and have been taken, and fent back to their mafters.

In general, they fecrete themfelves in the woods, where they are hunted by parties of foldiers, and by other

other negroes with dogs. Some of the inhabitants form parties of pleasure for this purpose---put up a Negro as they would a wild beast, and if they cannot hunt him down---will shoot him---cut off his head---and bring it in triumph to town upon the end of a stick. Of this I am an eye-witness every week.

WHEN a *Maron-Negro* is catched, he is whipped, and one of his ears cut off: The second time, he is again whipped, the sinews of his hams cut across, and he is put in chains: for the third offence he is hanged; but is kept in ignorance of his sentence, 'till put in execution.

I HAVE seen some of them hanged and broken alive. They went to execution with joy, and suffered without a cry. I once saw even a woman, throw herself from the top of the ladder. They believe that they shall find more happiness in another world, and that the Father of Mankind is not unjust, as men are.

SOMETIMES they are baptized, and are told they thereby become the brethren of the white people, and will go to Heaven. But they are hardly to be made believe that the Europeans can ever be instrumental to their going to Paradise; saying, that on earth, they are the cause of all the sufferings they endure. They say, that before Europeans landed in their country, they fought with sticks headed with iron; that they now, taught by us, kill each other at a great distance with fire and balls; that in order to procure slaves at a cheap rate, we foment continual divisions and wars among them; that formerly they followed the impulse of Nature, without fear of those grievous distempers, with which we have poisoned the constitutions of their women: that we suffer them to languish, without clothes, and without nourishment, and

beat

beat them inhumanly without reason. Of all this, I have seen frequent instances. A female slave came one day, and throwing herself prostrate at my feet, told me;---that her mistress made her rise so very early every morning, and sit up every night so late, that she was almost totally without sleep; and that when overcome with fatigue, she did chance to drop asleep, her mistress caused her lips to be rubbed with ordure, which if she did not lick off, she underwent a whipping. A relief from this intolerable grievance, was what she begged I would intercede for.---I did so; and obtained my request. Intercessions of this kind, are sometimes complied with, and the punishment is redoubled a few days after. I was a witness to this conduct, in a Counsellor, whose Blacks complained of him to the Governor; and who assured me, that on the morrow he would have them flead from head to foot. Not a day passes, but both men and women are whipped for having broken earthen ware---for not shutting the door after them, or some such trifling reason; and when almost covered with blood, are rubbed with vinegar and salt to heal their wounds. On the key, I have sometimes seen them so overwhelmed with grief, that they have been unable even to utter a cry,---others biting the cannon to which they are tied.—My pen is weary of writing this recital of horrors; my eyes of seeing, and my ears of hearing their doleful moanings. Happy you, who when tired of continuing in town, can retire to a country where fertile plains are seen, with rising hills, villages, harvests and vintages, the plenty of which chears the hearts of a people who accompany their labours with dancing and singing.—Signs these, at least, of happiness. The sights I see, are poor Negro women bent over a spade, the companion of their labour,—their children flung at their backs---Negroes, who pass trembling and shrinking before,

before me,---sometimes I hear the sound of their \*_Tambour_ afar off; but far more frequently, the smack of the whips, that eccho in the hills like the report of a pistol, and cries of, " Mercy ! Master, Mercy !", which at once strike my ears and pierce my heart.

If I seek a retirement, I find a country, barren, rugged, and rocky; mountains whose summits, inacceffible, retard the course of the clouds, and breaking them, form torrents that rush into abyffes equally horrible and and tremendous. The winds that roar in the deferts, the hollow, difmal found of the waves dashing upon the breakers, the sea before me, vast, and extending to regions unknown to the human race, all combine to deprefs and dejeét my fpirits, and to furnish me with ideas fit only for an exile and an outcast.

Port-Louis, *April* 15, 1769.

P. S. Whether coffee and fugar are really neceffary to the happinefs of Europe, is more than I can fay, but I affirm---that thefe two vegetables have brought wretchednefs and mifery upon America and Africa. The former is depopulated, that Europeans may have a land to plant them in ; and the latter, is ftripped of its inhabitants, for hands to cultivate them.

It is thought more for our intereft to have plantations for cultivating ourfelves the commodities we want, than to purchafe them of our neighbours. But

---

\* I fuppofe this to be the inftrument they dance to, as before-mentioned. *T.*

But

But since carpenters, bricklayers, masons, and other workmen from Europe, can work in the open air, and exposed to the sun, why should not white men be employed in all sorts of labour! But what then is to become of the proprietors of these lands? I answer, they would become the richer by this means. An inhabitant would live at his ease, were he to employ twenty farmers,---possessed of twenty slaves, he struggles in vain with an insurmountable poverty. The number of slaves here are computed at 2000. A yearly recruit of an eighteenth part of that number, is found absolutely necessary. Hence we see that the colony left to itself, would in eighteen years be extirpated.----So true is it, that without liberty and property, population must decrease,---and that injustice and good husbandry are incompatible.

The *Code Noir*, is said to be made for relief of the slaves. Be it so---Yet does the cruelty of the masters exceed the punishment it permits, and their avarice with-hold the food, the rest, and the rewards it decrees. If the poor wretches complain of this infringement, to whom do they seek for redress? to judges, who are perhaps the tyrants, under whose oppression they languish.

But say they, these people are not to be restrained, but by severities. Punishments must be inflicted, iron collars with three points, whips, fetters for their legs\*; and chains of iron for their necks must be made

---

\* I cannot help attempting to describe in this place, a sort of Iron Mask, or as it is more properly called a Muzzle, great numbers of which, I am told, are kept by several wholesale ironmongers in this city, to supply the orders of merchants and planters in the West-India islands.—I have seen one of them at the house of a Gentleman, as well known for his universal benevolence,

as

made use of---they must be treated like savage beasts, or the white people could not live like men. From this principle, so grosly unjust, no consequences can be deduced, but what are equally unjust and inhuman; nor does it suffice, that these poor Negroes are victims to the avarice and cruelty of the most depraved of men, but they must also be the sport of their sophistical arguments.

Our priests tell them, that the slavery of their present life, will ensure to them a spiritual liberty in Heaven. But the greater part are bought at an age too late to learn French, and our Missionaries do not understand the language of the country. Moreover,

as for his particular perseverance in behalf of the African Negroes, and who uses it as an IRON argument against the toleration of Slave holding.——It is fastened round the neck of the wretched Culprit, by a collar, from which rise some Bars of iron, forming the Mask and Head-piece;——before the mouth is a round plate of iron, wherein are bored holes, to allow a small portion of breath to the wearer.——There is also a place for his nose.——A flat piece of iron goes into the mouth, and acts upon the tongue and glands, as a slavering-bit does upon those of a horse.——Worn by a man working beneath the scorching rays of the sun in the torrid zone, it soon attains a violent degree of heat, which with the constant flowing of the saliva, in a little time, excoriates the nose, mouth, and chin, and must occasion a TORMENT, the very idea of which it would give me pain to convey to the Reader.——In England, we put upon a vicious *horse*, or a mischievous *dog*, a muzzle of LEATHER,——this,——self-preservation dictates,——but what cogent motive can urge the slave-holder, to put upon his fellow-creature—upon a MAN——A MUZZLE OF IRON.——I will tell the Reader.——'Tis to prevent him, when at work, from sucking, or eating of the sugar-canes, herein denying him that indulgence which the ALMIGHTY GOD charged the Israelite, by the remembrance of his own slavery in Egypt, to shew to HIS BEAST, when treading out the corn,—or from putting an-end to his wretched existence, by cramming himself with the dirt of the ground.——A practice to which the despairing wretches are frequently driven by the merciless treatment of their worse than Egyptian Taskmasters. T.

those

those who have been baptized, are not a jot better treated than the rest.

The Planters add, that the Negroes merit the vengeance of Heaven, for the traffic they carry on. Are we then to take upon us to be their executioners? Let us leave the destruction of kites to the vultures.

I am concerned to see, that Philosophers, who enter the lists with so much alacrity to combat other abuses, scarcely speak of this slavery of the Negroes, beyond a degree of pleasantry. Indeed, 'tis a subject they seem desirous of avoiding. They speak of the massacre of Paris, and of the Mexicans by the Spaniards, as if the crimes of our days, and in which the half of Europe are concerned either as principals or accessaries, were not equal to them. Can they believe the iniquity of murdering a number of people of a different persuasion than ourselves, to be greater, than that of bringing misery and torment of the severest nature upon a whole nation, to whom we are indebted for those delicacies which our luxury has rendered necessary to us? Those beautiful rose and flame-colours, in which our Ladies are dressed, cotton, of so general use, coffee and chocolate, now the only breakfast admitted to polite tables; the rouge with which the pallid beauty gives new bloom to her complexion;---all these are prepared by the industrious hand of the enslaved and oppressed Negro. Ye women of sensibility and sentiment, who weep at the affecting story of a novel, or the representation of a tragedy, know, that what constitutes your chiefest delight, is moistened with the tears, and died with the blood of men.

## LETTER XIII.

AGRICULTURE. Herbs, Vegetables, and Flowers imported.

THE greater part of the plants, trees and animals, I am about to describe, have been brought here by order of government. Some of the inhabitants have contributed their endeavours for this purpose; among others, Messrs. de Cossini, Poivre, Hermans, and le Juge. I wished to have learnt the names of the others, that I might have mentioned them with the respect which is their due. The gift, or introducing of a useful plant, being, in my opinion, of more consequence, than the discovery of a gold mine, and a monument more durable than a pyramid.

I SPEAK of them in the following order; first, the plants, which being once sown, ever after sow themselves, and are, as it were, naturalized in the country; secondly, those that are articles of cultivation in the country; thirdly, the produce of the kitchen-garden; fourthly, of the flower-garden. I shall pursue the same method with the trees and shrubs. Of those I know, I shall omit none.----Whatever Nature has not disdained to form, we certainly ought not to think too insignificant to describe.

AMONG the plants that grow wild, is found in some of the plains round the town, a kind of indigo, which

I apprehend to be foreign to this ifland. It is of no ufe.

The Purflain grows in fandy places; I take this to be natural here, being reckoned among that clafs of Plants, which when rotten, manures the ground, and which Nature feems to have made the growth of dry and fandy foils, to facilitate vegetations of other kinds.

Water-Cresses, are found in every rivulet. They have been brought here thefe ten years. The Dandelion and wormwood grow fpontaneoufly in rubbifh, or ground newly opened; but above all, the mullen expands its large downy leaves, and fhoots up its girandole of yellow flowers to a furprizing height.

The Bulrufh (not the Chinefe plant fo called) is a grafs about the height of well-grown rye. It extends itfelf daily, and choaks the plants that grow near it. It is apt to be tough when dry, and fhould therefore be cut before ripe. It is green for five months only in a year, and it is afterwards fet on fire, notwithftanding the burning of it is prohibited. The flames of it burn and parch up the out-fkirts of the woods.

The White-grafs, (fo called from the colour of its flower) was brought here, as being proper for forage, but no animal will eat of it; the feed refembles that of cherville. It multiplies fo faft, that it is become one of the plagues of hufbandry.

The Brette, which fignifies in the Indian language, a leaf good to eat, is a fpecies of the morell. There are two forts of it; one called the *Brette* of Madagafcar. Its leaf is rather prickly, but of a pleafant tafte, and is purgative. The other is commonly

monly ferved up to table as fpinnage, and is the only food of which the Blacks may eat at difcretion, and grows all over the ifland. The water in which it is boiled becomes very bitter. In this liquor, mingled and ftill more imbittered by their tears, the Negroes fteep their Caffave.

Among the plants cultivated in the country, is, the Caffave-Root. It grows in dry foils; its juice has loft the poifonous quality it formerly had: 'tis a fhrub, whofe leaf is like that of hemp, with a root as thick and as long as a man's arm; when rafped, and unpreffed, they make cakes of it, that are heavy like dough. Three pounds of this are allowed for the food of a Negro for one day. This vegetable grows and fpreads very faft.---M. de la Bourdonnois brought it from America. 'Tis a ufeful plant, being eafily fheltered from the hurricanes, and enfures a certain fubfiftence to the Negroes, for the dogs will not eat it.

The Maize or Turkifh corn grows very beautifully here. 'Tis a precious grain; turns to good account, but will not keep more than a year, as the mites get into it: this, I think, a good reafon why the cultivation of it fhould be encouraged in Europe, as it cannot be with-held long from market. It ferves as food for the flaves, the fowls, and the cattle. 'Tis worthy remark, that the inhabitants fpeak highly of the excellence of Maize and the Manioc, but never eat of either. I have feen little cakes of them in a defert, and when they are made with a great deal of fugar, of wheat-flower, and yolks of eggs, they are very eatable.

WHEAT grows well here, but not to any great heighth. They put the feed into the ground by single grains, becaufe of the rocks; they cut it with knives, and threfh it out with fmall fticks. It will not keep fo long as two years. Pliny tells us, that in Barbary and Spain, it was put in full ear into holes in the earth, taking care to introduce a proper quantity of air. Varro fays, that it would keep by this means for fifty years, and millet, for a whole century. Pompey found at Ambratia fome beans preferved in this manner, fince the time of Pyrrhus, which was near 120 years. But Pliny will not admit of the cultivation of the earth by flaves of any kind, whofe work, he fays, is never done effectually. Although the meal of the wheat that grows here is not fo white as that from Europe, yet I prefer the bread of it, to that of european meal, which either grows vapid, or ferments during the voyage.

RICE, the beft, and perhaps the moft wholefome of all aliments, thrives very much. It keeps longer than the wheat, and yields more plentifully. A wet foil agrees with it beft. There are above feven different fpecies of it in Afia, one of which grows beft in a dry foil; it were to be wifhed, that this grain were cultivated in Europe, on account of its extraordinary fertility.

THE fmaller kind of millet yields abundantly. It is feldom given but to the blacks and the beafts. Oats thrive exceedingly, but the cultivation of them, or of any thing elfe, which the blacks or the beafts only derive benefit from, is very little attended to.

THE Tobacco is not good. None is planted but by the Negroes for their own ufe.

VOYAGE to the ISLE OF FRANCE. 113

THE *Fatague*, is a grafs, bearing large leaves, of the nature of a fmall rofe-tree. They import it from Madagafcar, and make of it the moft delightful artificial meadows.

EXPERIMENTS have been made, but without fuccefs, to make Saint-foin, Trefoil, Hemp, Flax, and Hops grow here.

You will obferve, that our vegetables in general degenerate here, and that thofe who wifh to have them good, are fupplied every year with feed from Europe, or the Cape of Good-Hope. The fmall peas are tough, and taftelefs; the French beans are hard; there is a fort larger, and more tender; called Cape-peas; it is worth tranfplanting to France. Another fort of beans which they barrel, they chop the hufks to pieces, and drefs them as peas. There is another kind of bean (with a pod a foot long) which they plant and form arbours of. The grain is very large; but of no fort of ufe.

ARTICHOAKS grow here, their leaves are very large, and the fruit but fmall. The *Cardoon* * is always tough here; but being alfo very prickly, and growing to a great height, it makes very good hedges.

THE *Giromon*, is a pumpkin, not fo large as ours; and if poffible, of a more infipid tafte. The cucumber is fmaller, and not fo plentiful as in Europe. The melons here are good for nothing, altho' much boafted of on account of their fcarcity. The *Pafleque*, or Water-melon, is fomething better than the other.

* A kind of thiftle,—there is one fort of this plant that is ufed in fallad. *T.*

I  The

The climate suits these fruits very well; but the loominess of the soil, is against them. Gourds grow here to an enormous size, and are of particular utility; they serve the Blacks for plates and dishes.

The *Briugella* or *Aubergine*, is of two sorts; the one bears a small, round and yellow fruit, and has a very prickly stem; it comes from Madagascar. The other, which is known in Paris, is a violet-coloured fruit, of the size and form of a large fig. When this fruit is well seasoned and boiled, it is not bad eating.

There are two sorts of pepper; that known in Europe, and another natural to this place; it is a shrub bearing very small fruit, that shine like so many grains of coral upon the most beautiful green foliage imaginable. The Creoles use it in all their ragouts. It is stronger than any other kind of pepper, and will burn like a caustick. They call it mad pepper.

The *Pine-Apple*, the most beautiful of all fruits, for the variegated colouring of its scaly rind, for its purple crest, and for its fragrant smell, which is like that of a violet, never ripens here perfectly. Its juice is very cold, and prejudicial to the stomach. Its bark is on the contrary very hot, and tastes like pepper; perhaps as corrective of the juice. Nature frequently contrasts the qualities of the same subject;—the bark of the citron is of a hot nature, the juice of a cooling;—the rind of the pomegranate is astringent, the seeds are laxative. &c.

Strawberries begin to thrive in the cool parts. They have neither the fragrancy nor the sweetness of ours; they yield but sparingly, any more than the rasberries, which are much degenerated. There is a
species

species of them from China, very beautiful, and in great plenty, which grow to the size of cherries, but have neither taste nor smell.

SPINAGE is scarce here. Garden cresses, sorrel, cherville, parsly, fennel, and cellery, have stringy stems, and are raised with great difficulty. Leeks, lettuce, endif, and colliflowers, are smaller, but not so tender as ours. Cabbage, the most useful of all vegetables, and which is found in all parts, thrives very well here. Burnet, purslain, and sage, grow in abundance; but especially the *Capucine* which grows upon large espaliers, and is very long lived.

ASPARAGUS is not much larger than a packthread, and has degenerated in taste as well as in bulk, and so have carrots, parsnips, turneps, sasafras, and radishes, which are of a biting taste. There is, however, a radish from China, that grows very well here. The beet-root grows beautifully, but is very sticky. Potatoes, *selanum Americanum*, are not bigger here than nuts. The Indian ones, called *Cambar*, frequently weigh above a pound a-piece; their skin is of a beautiful violet-colour, but within they are very white and tasteless; they however, serve for food for the blacks. They increase very fast, as well as the Jerusalem artichoak, some sorts of which are preferable to our chesnuts. Saffron is an herb that tinges the ragouts with yellow, as do the stamina of the European kind. The ginger here, is not so hot as that of India. What is called here, the Pistachia-nut, which is not the fruit of the pistachia-tree, is a small almond, that grows in the ground in a wrinkled shell. It is pleasant eating when roasted, but is hard of digestion. They cultivate it here, in order to extract oil for burning. This plant is a sort of phenomenon in botany, it being uncommon for vegetables that yield

yield fruit of an unctuous nature, to bear them below the surface of the ground.

CHIVES, leeks, and onions are smaller than in France, and even than in the Isle of Bourbon, which is so near.

AMONG the plants of the flower garden, I shall speak first of our own, and then of those of Asia and Africa.

THE tuberose, larksfoot, the large daisy of China, pinks of a small species, flourish here as in Europe; large pinks, and lillies bear a number of leaves, but seldom flowers. The anemony, ranunculus, Indian-pink, and rose, do not thrive here, any more than the July-flower, or poppy. I saw no other flowers that we know of in Europe among the curious, except the above-mentioned. Many people have attempted, but in vain, to transplant hither, thyme, lavender, the field-daisy, violets, and wild-poppy, the red of which, with the azure of the blue-bell, so beautifully decorate our golden harvests. Oh! happy France! a corner of whose fields, is, in my eyes, more desirable, than the most beautiful garden this island affords.

AMONG the flowering-plants of Africa, I know but one, the *belleimmortelle* of the Cape, the seeds of which are as large and red as strawberries, and grow in a cluster at the top of a stem, the leaves of which are like pieces of grey cloth;—another *immortelle*, with purple flowers, grows all over the island: a reed, the size of a horse-hair, which bears a group of leaves, white in the inside, and violet-coloured without: at a distance, that bouquet appears in the air; it comes from the Cape, as does also a sort of tulip, bearing

but

but two leaves, which lie upon the ground, and seem to adhere to it: a Chinese plant that sows itself, and bears little flowers like roses; upon its stem there are five or six, variegated alike, from a deep blood-red to the brightest scarlet. None of these flowers have any smell, and those which are known to have it in Europe, lose it on their being transplanted hither.

ALOES flourish here. Their leaves turn to good account,—the sap of them afford a medicinal gum, and the threads are very fit for a manufacture of cloth. They grow upon the rocks, and in the parts scorched by the sun. The one grows out in leaves, strong, thick, and as large as a man, and is armed with a long shaft: from the center grows a stem as high as a tree, furnished with flowers, from which drops gum-aloes in a perfect state. The others are upright, like tapers, several spans high, and have a number of very sharp prickles about them: these last are marbled, and resemble serpents that crawl upon the ground.

NATURE seems to have treated the Africans and Asiatics as barbarians; in having given them these at once magnificent, yet monstrous vegetables, and to have dealt with us as beings capable of sensibility and society. Oh! when shall I breath the perfumes of the honeysuckle? again repose myself upon a carpet of milk-weed, saffron, and blue-bells, the food of our lowing herds?—and once more hear Aurora welcomed by the songs of the Labourer, blessed with freedom and content.

PORT-LOUIS, Isle of France, *May* 29, 1769.

LET-

## LETTER XIV.

SHRUBS and TREES brought to the Isle of France.

THE rose-tree thrives so well here, that hedges are made of it; but the flowers are not so tufted, nor is the smell so fine as ours; there is of different sorts, among which, a small one from China, is in bloom all the year round. The jessamines of Spain and France are perfectly naturalized in this soil; those of Asia, I shall speak of in their place. There are pomegranate-trees with a double flower, and with fruit upon them, but they are good for little. The myrtle does not grow so beautiful here as in Provence. These are all the shrubs from Europe.

Those from Asia, Africa, and America, are, the *Cassis* * with a scalloped leaf; it is not at all like ours, is a large shrub, overgrown with yellow flowers of a strong smell, that look like small tufts: it yields a bean, with the grain of which they dye black. Being prickly, it makes good hedges.

The *Fou'sapatte*†, an Indian word, signifying the *Shoemaker's flower*; its flower rubbed upon leather,

---
\* Black currant bush.
† I should rather suppose it a corruption of the Portuguese name, in which language, *Frol de Zapate*, or *de Zopatero*, signifies the shoe-flower, or the shoemaker's flower. *T.*

stains

stains it black. The foliage of this shrub is of a beautiful green, and larger than that of the yoke-elm; in the middle of which glitter the flowers like pinks, but of a deep red. They have nurseries of this shrub, of which there are various sorts.

The *Poinciillade*, originally from America, is a species of bramble, bearing girandoles of yellow and red flowers, from which shoot tufts of a flame-colour. This flower is very beautiful, but soon fades; it yields a bean. Its leaves are divided like that of all leguminous shrubs.

Jalop bears flowers shaped like a funnel, of a crimson red; they blow only in the night, and have a smell like the tuberose. I have seen two sorts of them.

The Vine of Madagascar, is a rattan of which they make cradles; it gives a yellow flower. Its downy leaves seem as if covered with meal.

The *Mougris* is a jessamine, with a flower like the orange-tree. Some have double, and some single flowers, of a very agreeable smell.

The *Franchipanier* is still another jessamine, that grows in the form of stagwood; from the extremity of these hornes sprout bunches of long leaves, in the center of which are large white flowers, shaped like a funnel, and of a charming smell.

The Indian *Lilach*, grows here, and dies soon; its leaf is scolloped, and of a beautiful green. It is loaded with clusters of flowers, which have a pleasant smell enough, and turn to seed. This shrub rises to the height of a tree, and in a handsome form; its

green

green is finer, but the flowers not so beautiful as those of our lilach, which does not grow here.

The *Pepper-tree* is a rattan, or *lianne*, which creeps along the ground like ivy; it shoots well, but yields no fruit. It is not yet known whether the soil will agree with the tea-tree, which has been brought hither from China, as well as the rattan,—this last is used as commonly in India, as the osier is in Europe.

The *Cotton-tree* grows in the driest parts of the island; like a shrub, it bears a pretty yellow flower, to which succeeds a pod, containing the flocks. Cotton is not cultivated here, for want of mills to grind it: and till ground it is not an article of commerce.

The *Sugar-cane* ripens here in perfection; the inhabitants make an indifferent sort of liquor of it, which they call *flangourin*. There is but one sugar-house in the whole island.

The *Coffee-tree* is the most useful plant of any that grows here. It is a species of jessamine, its flower is white, leaves of fine green, shaped like laurel-leaves, and are opposed to each other. It's fruit is a red olive, like a cherry, which separates into two beans. They plant them at seven feet and a half a-sunder, and when they grow as high as six feet, they crop them. It lives seven years only, and when three years old is in its prime. The annual produce of each tree is valued at one pound of berries. A black can attend to one thousand feet of these in a year, exclusive of what else he cultivates for his own subsistence. The island does not yet produce coffee enough for it's own consumption. The inhabitants reckon it to be next to the Mocha coffee in quality.

Among

AMONG the trees of Europe, the pine, the fir, and the oak grow to a middling stature, and then decay. I have also seen here cherry, apricot, medlar, apple, pear, olive, and mulberry-trees; but without fruit, though some of them had flowers. The fig-tree produces a tolerable fruit. The vine does not succeed upon props; but when in arbours, bears grapes, which, like those in the gardens of Alcinous, ripen one part after another:* a good vintage cannot therefore be expected. The peach-tree gives fruit enough, and well tasted, but they are never luscious. There is a white louse that destroys them.

THESE trees are constantly full of sap; burying them in the ground might perhaps be of use to retard their vegetation. It is as necessary here to protect them from heat, as from the cold in the North of Germany. These trees lose their leaves in what is called the cold season, that is, when it is summer with you; notwithstanding, the heat and moisture are equal to what you have in the spring: there must therefore be some latent cause of vegetation of which we are ignorant.

FOREIGN trees, brought here for curiosity only, are the laurel, which thrives very well; as does also the *Agathis* of various sorts, the leaves of which are scolloped; it bears bunches of flowers, white and streaked, to which succeed long leguminous pods. The Chinese frequently represent this shrub in their landscapes.

* In Europe the fruits of the same tree are ripe nearly at the same time; here 'tis quite the contrary, they grow ripe in a regular succession; which causes a remarkable difference in the taste of fruits gathered from one and the same tree.

The *Polché* comes from India; it's foliage is tufted, the leaf is in the shape of an heart. It affords a pleasant shade, and answers no other purpose, it's fruit being sticky and good for nothing.—It is in the form of a medlar.

The *Bamboo* at a distance, looks like our willow. 'Tis a reed which grows as high as the tallest trees, and shoots out branches, furnished with leaves like those of the olive: They make the most delightful avenues, in which the wind murmurs incessantly. It grows fast, and its canes may be applied to the same uses as the branches of osier. There are many India pictures in which this reed is badly enough represented.

The fruit-trees are the *Attier*, whose triangular flower, of a solid substance, tastes like the pistachia; its fruit is like a pine-apple : when it is ripe it is full of a white and sweetish cream, which smells like the orange-flower. It is full of black kernels: the *Atte* * is very pleasant, but being very heating, soon cloys, and gives a pain in the stomach to those who eat it.

The *Mango* is a very beautiful tree : The Indians often represent it upon their painted silks. It is covered with superb girandoles of flowers like the Indian chesnut. To these succeed a great number of fruits, shaped like a large flat plumb, covered with a rind which smells like turpentine. This fruit has a vinous and agreeable taste; and, but for its smell, might vie with the best fruits of Europe. It is never prejudicial to those who eat it, and I should think, a wholesome and pleasant drink might

---

* The *Atte*, or *Ata*, is the name given by French naturalists to the fruit of the cinnamon-tree. *T.*

be

VOYAGE *to the* ISLE OF FRANCE. 123

be made from it. This tree has one inconvenience attending it---being covered with fruit at the time of the hurricanes, which ftrip it of the greater part.

THE *Banana-tree* grows every where. It has no wood, or ftock; being only a tuft of flowers, which fpring up in columns, and blow at the top in large and long leaves, of a beautiful fattiny green. At the end of a year, there iffues from the fummit a long ftem, all hung with fruit in the form of a cucumber; two of thefe ftems are a load for a black; this fruit, which is mealy, is alfo pleafant and very nutritive. The blacks are very fond of it; and it is given to them on the firft of January, as a new year's gift; they count their years of forrow by the number of Banana feafts they have regaled at. Linen cloth might be made of the thread of the banana-tree. The fhape of the leaves like belts of filk, the length of its item, the upper part of which hangs down from the height of a man, and whofe violet-colour at the end, gives it the look of a ferpent's head; may have occafioned its being called by the name of Adam's fig-tree. This fruit lafts all the year; there are many forts of it; from the fize of a plumb, to the length of a man's arm.

THE *Gouyava-tree* is fomething like a medlar. Its flower is white, and its fruit fmells like a bug. It is aftringent, and is the only fruit of this country, in which I have found worms.

THE *Jam-rofe* is a tree which affords a very fine fhade, though it does not grow high. It bears a fruit of a fmell like a rofe-bud, and of a fweetifh, but infipid tafte.

THE

The *Papa*, is a kind of fig-tree without branches. It grows fast, and rises like a pillar, with a capital of large leaves. From its trunk shoots out a fruit like a small melon, of an indifferent taste: the seeds taste like cresses. The body of this tree is of a substance like a turnep. The female *Papa* bears flowers, only; in form and smell as agreeable as the honeysuckle.

The *Badamier* is of a form that seems calculated purposely for a shade. It rises like a very fine pyramid, in different stories, distinct and separate from each other. Its foliage is very fine, and it yields almonds which are well tasted.

The *Avocat* is a handsome tree enough. It bears a pear (which encloses a large stone,) of a substance like butter. When it is seasoned with sugar and citron juice, it is not bad to eat; though it is heating.

The *Jaca* is a tree of a beautiful foliage, but the fruit it bears is a monstrous one. 'Tis as big as a large pumpkin, and has a rind that is green and shagreened all over. It is full of seeds; the outside, which is a white skin, sweet and clammy, is good to eat, but has an ugly smell, like that of rotten cheese. This fruit is aphrodisiac, and the women here are passionately fond of it,

The *Tamarind-tree* has a beautiful head; its leaves are opposed to each other on one side, and close at night, like most other leguminous plants. It's pod contains a mucilage which makes excellent lemonade.

Orange-trees are of many sorts, among them is one yielding an orange called a *mandarine*. A large

large kind of *Pamplemouſſe*, of a red colour, and but middling taſte. A citron * that bears very large fruit, but with little juice in it.

The *Cocoa-tree* is planted here, 'tis a kind of palm, which thrives in the ſand: this is one of the moſt uſeful trees in the Indian trade, though it affords nothing elſe than a bad ſort of oil, and cables as bad in their kind. It is reckoned at Pondicherry that each cocoa-tree is worth a piſtole a year. Travellers ſpeak much in praiſe of its fruit; but our flax will ever be preferred to cotton, for making cloth, our wines to its liquor, and our filberds to its nut.

The *Cocoa-tree* flouriſhes ſo much the beſt near ſalt-works, that ſalt is always put in the hole, wherein the fruit is ſown, to facilitate the blowing of the bud ‡. The cocoa ſeems deſigned to float in the ſea, by the wad which ſurrounds it, and helps to bear it up, and by the hardneſs of its ſhell, impenetrable to the water. It does not open by a joint, as our nuts do, but the juice comes out at one of the three orifices which nature has contrived at its extremity, and has afterwards covered with a cuticle. Cocoa-trees have been found upon the borders of the ſea in deſart iſlands, and even upon ſhoals of ſand. This, is the kind of palm which fringes the banks of

---

* Called by the Engliſh in the Eaſt-Indies, *Pomplemoſe*, and in the Weſt-Indies, *Shaddock*. T.

‡ In thoſe parts of the Eaſt-Indies, where fiſh are in plenty, a quantity of the refuſe of them is laid about the bottom of every cocoa-tree. But this practice is very prejudicial to the health of the inhabitants;—the iſland of Bombay was the moſt unwholſome of all our ſettlements, till a ſtop was put to the corruption of the air by this animal putrefaction, and the natives now have recourſe to ſome leſs peſtiferous manure for their cocoa trees. T.

the rivers between the tropics, as the fir does thofe of the north, and the date, thofe of the burning mountains of Paleftine.

I THINK I am not deceived, in faying that the cocoa is calculated to float upon the fea, and to fow itfelf afterwards in the fands. Every feed has its own peculiar method of propagating itfelf; but an inveftigation of this matter, would make me digrefs too much from the fubject. I may, perhaps fome day or other undertake it, and when ever I do, it will be with del'ght. The ftudy of Nature compenfates for our difappointments in the ftudy of mankind, as we cannot but trace throughout the whole, the harmony with which Intelligence and Beneficence unite to render the fyftem compleat. But if it were poffible, that we fhould be deceived even in this;—if all things by which mankind is furrounded, were combined to diftract him; at leaft, let our errors, be errors of our own choofing, and let us give the preference to thofe which afford confolation, rather than excite difguft.

THOSE who imagine that Nature in raifing fo high the heavy fruit of the cocoa-tree, has loft fight of that law which decrees the pumpkin to creep upon the ground, do not confider that the head of the cocoa-tree is but fmall, and can therefore afford but little fhade. 'Tis under the leaves of the oak, men feek a fhelter from the fun's fcorching rays. Why not rather obferve, that in India, as in Europe, thofe trees which bear a mellow fruit are but of a middling height, that in falling it may not be deftroyed; on the contrary, thofe producing fruit of a hard nature, as the cocoa, chefnut, acorn, and nut, are lofty, their fruit being not liable to be damaged by falling to the ground? Moreover, the trees that are furnifhed with a number of leaves yield as well in

India

India as in Europe, a defirable fhelter without danger. There are fome, as for inftance, the *Jaca*, which bear fruits of a very great fize; but then they bear them near to the trunk, and within reach of the hand: thus, Nature, which man is ever accufing of imprudence, has contrived with equal bounty for his fhelter, and his nourifhment.

A KIND of crab has been lately difcovered to burrow at the foot of the cocoa-tree. Nature has provided this animal with a long claw, at the end of which is a nail, ferving to extract the fubftance of the fruit by the holes I have defcribed. It has not the large pincers of other crabs;—they would be ufelefs to it. This animal is found upon the Ifle of Palms, to the northward of Madagafcar, difcovered in 1769, by the fhipwreck of the *Heureux*, which was loft there in going to *Bengal*.

AT the ifle of *Sechelle*, there is juft difcovered a tree bearing double cocoa-nuts, fome of which weigh upwards of forty pounds. The Indians attribute great virtues to it. They believe it to be a production of the fea, becaufe the currents formerly threw fome of them upon the coaft of Malabar. They call it the *fea-cocoa*. This fruit, *mulieris corporis bifurcationem cum natura & pilis repræfentat*. Its leaf, fhaped like a fan, will cover half a houfe. Order is obfervable in every work of nature,—the tree which bears this enormous fruit, bears three or four only at the moft: the common cocoa-tree bears bunches of more that thirty; I have tafted both, and think their flavour very much alike. They have planted the fea-cocoa in the ifle of France, and it begins to bud.

THERE are ftill fome other trees, which though curious, are of little or no ufe, as the *Date*, which feldom

dom bears fruit; the Palm, which is called here the *Araque*; and that which produces *sago*. The *Caneficier*, and the *Cusbor*, bear flowers, but no fruit. The *Canellier*, (of which I have seen avenues) like a pear-tree in growth and leaves. Its little bunches of flowers smell like excrement. Its cinnamon has very little of the aromatic. There is only one *cacao-tree*\* in the island; and the fruits of this never ripen. They should bring thither the *muscadine* and the *clove*†. Time will decide as to the success of these trees, transplanted from under the Line to 20 deg. of latitude.

Some time ago, were planted here, layers of the *Ravinesara*, a species of the *muscadine* of Madagascar; of the *Mangoustan* and the *Litchi*, which are said to produce the finest fruit in the world; the *Vernis*, whence is extracted an oil to preserve furniture; the tallow-wood, its seeds are impregnated with a kind of wax; a tree from China, which bears citrons in bunches, like raisins; the silver tree of the Cape; and lastly, the *Teeque*-wood, nearly equal to the oak for buiding of ships. The greater part of these trees vegetate here with difficulty.

The climate of this island seems too cold for the trees of Asia, and too hot for those of Europe. Pliny observes, that the temperament of the air is more necessary for the culture of plants, than the qualities of the soil; and says, that in his time, pepper and citron-trees were seen in Italy; and incense-trees in Lydia; but that they merely vegitated. I am however of opinion, that the coffee-tree might be naturalised in the south of France, for it delights in a

---

\* The tree of whose fruit chocolate is made. *T*.
† They were brought in 1770.

cool

cool and temperate air. These expensive experiments can scarcely be carried on by any but Princes; and yet, the acquisition of one plant unknown before, is a circumstance, by which a whole nation may be benefited. To what purpose have been all the wars upon our Continent? Of what consequence is it now-a-days, that Mithridates was once conquered by the Romans, and Montezuma by the Spaniards? Unless some benefit accrue, Europe might with reason, weep over her unprofitable trophies; but whole provinces in Germany subsist upon potatoes brought from America, and our fair ladies are indebted for the cherries they eat, to Lucullus. The desert was indeed costly; but for this, our fore-fathers paid. Let us be wiser,—let us collect together the good things which nature has scattered abroad.

If labour should ever become necessary for my health, I will make a garden after the Chinese fashion;—the situation they delight in, is on the banks of a river;—they chuse an irregular piece of ground, on which are old trees, large rocks, and rising hills. They form round it a boundary of rugged rocks, placed upon one another, so that their junctures cannot be perceived. Hereon grow clumps of *scolopendria*, tendrils with blue and purple flowers, and borders of moss of different colours. A stream of water meanders among these vegetables, whence it escapes in cascades. Health and enjoyment are diffused over such a spot as this, while the European's garden presents him with no other view but that of a dreary brick-wall.

Of the hollow grounds they make pieces of water, which they stock with fish, surround with banks

banks of turf, and plant with trees. They are particularly careful that no level spot or strait line shall appear ; nor any masonry ; How often does the fancied skill of the artist, mar the simplicity of Nature's handy work ?

The plain is diversified with tufts of flowers, and walks of green sod, in which fruit-trees are planted. The sides of the hills are variegated with clumps of shrubs, some bearing fruit, others flowers ; the summit is crowned with trees whose spreading branches afford a pleasing retreat from the parching rays of the sun.

There are no strait walks, discovering to you every object at once ; but winding paths, which open them to your view in an agreeable succession. Nor are their objects, statues, or vases, useless, as they are large ;—but a vine bending under a load of ripening grapes, and adorned with rose-bushes, and other flowers :—the mind is at the same time delighted with a sonnet or epigram upon the bark of an orange-tree,—or a philosophical maxim upon a piece of broken rock.

This garden is not an orchard,— a park,— a lawn,—but an agreeable assemblage of them all;— 'tis itself a country, with hills, woods, and plains, where each object contributes to the perfection of the whole. A Chinese has no more idea, of a regular garden, than he has of cutting a flowering shrub into the squared form of a chest of tea.

Travellers say, that there is no leaving these delightful retreats, but with a kind of regret ; for my part, I would enhance the pleasures of them

by

by the society of an amiable woman, and by having in my neighbourhood such a friend as yourself.

Port-Louis, *July* 10, 1769.

---

LETTER XXV.

ANIMALS brought to the Isle of France.

SUCH pains have been taken for the improvement of this colony, that even foreign fishes have been imported to it; the *Gourami* comes from Batavia, 'tis a fresh-water fish, like a salmon, but of a finer flavor, being reckoned the best fish that is eaten in India. The Chinese *Goldfish* is brought here, but loses its beauty as it increases in bulk. These two species breed very fast in the ponds and lakes.

It has been attempted, but without success, to bring frogs here, that they might eat the eggs which the musquito lays upon the surface of the standing waters.

But a bird has been brought from the Cape, that is of infinite service, they call it the *Gardener's Friend*. It is brown, the size of a large sparrow, and lives upon worms, snails, and small serpents, which it not only eats when pressed by hunger, but makes an ample

ample store of, by sticking them upon the prickles of the hedges. I have seen but one of them, which, though deprived of its liberty, retained the manners of its kind, and suspended the meat which was given it, upon the wires of its cage.

A BIRD that has multiplied very fast in the island, is the *martin*, a species of the Indian *sanjonnet* *, with a yellow beak and claws. It differs but little from ours, except in plumage, which is less spotted. In chirping, however, as well as in an aptitude to talk, and to mimic other birds, it perfectly resembles the European. It will perch upon, and peck at beasts without fear, but the prey it pursues with an unwearied perseverance, is the grasshopper, numbers of which species are destroyed by it. The martins always fly in pairs, and assemble constantly at sun-set in flocks of some thousands. After a general chirping, the whole republic fall asleep, and at day break, again disperse by pairs to the different quarters of the island. This bird is not fit to eat; yet they are sometimes shot, though shooting them is prohibited. Plutarch relates, that the lark was adored at Lemnos, because it eat and destroyed the grasshoppers-eggs: but we are not Grecians.

SEVERAL pairs of ravens were let loose in the woods to destroy the rats and mice. Three cocks are all that are left of them. The people accused them of killing their fowls, and herein were at once accusers, judges and executioners.

THE ravages of the Cape bird cannot be denied, 'tis a species of small *tarin*†, and is the only inhabitant

---

* Called by some the *Starling*, by others the *Fiskin*. T.

† A kind of lark,—'tis a bird well known in France, and admired for its song—and aptitude to talk. T.

of thefe forefts that is heard to fing. They were brought here firft as curiofities, but fome of them efcaped to the woods, where they breed very faft, and live upon the fpoils of the harveft. Government gives a reward to any body that kills one.

There is a beautiful *titmoufe* here, with a number of white fpecks on the wings; and the *cardinal*, whofe head, neck, and belly, at a particular feafon, are of a lively red; the reft of its plumage is of a pearl-coloured grey.—This bird comes from Bengal.

There are three forts of partridges, all fmaller than ours. The cry of the male refembles that of a cock when hoarfe; they rooft at night upon the trees, for fear of the rats.

They have put in the woods fome *pintadoes*\*, and Chinefe pheafants, and into the lakes fome geefe and wild ducks: They have alfo tame ducks here, efpecially the Manilla ones, which are very beautiful; and European barn-door fowls; a fpecies of fowl from Africa, whofe flefh and bone are black; a fmall fpecies of fowl from China, the cocks of which are very fierce and bold, and for ever a fighting with the Indian cocks. I faw one of them attack a large Manilla duck, which feized the little champion with its beak, and fmothered it with its belly and claws: and although the cock is fometimes drawn half dead from this perilous fituation, it will return to the charge with redoubled fury.

Many people make a great deal of money of their poultry, on account of the fcarcity of other provifi-

---

\* So called by the Spaniards, from the beauty of its plumage, which feems as if painted. It is believed by fome to be the *Storm Bird*, or *Procellaria Capenfis*. *T.*

ons. Pigeons succeed well, and are the best birds of flight in the island. They have also brought two species of turtles, and of hares.

There are in the woods wild goats, wild hogs, and especially stags, which had multiplied to such a degree, that whole squadrons were supplied with venison for provisions. Their flesh is very good, especially during the months of April, May, June, July and August. Some of them have been taken when young, and brought up tame; but they will not breed in that state.

Among those that we may call the domestic quadrupeds, are sheep that fatten and lose their wool, goats that thrive prodigiously, and oxen of the Madagascar breed, that have a great wen upon their neck; the cows of this breed give but very little milk; those from Europe give much more, but their calves degenerate. I saw once, two cows and two bulls from Bengal, which were no bigger than an ass. This breed did not succeed.

Butchers meat is sometimes not to be got. Pork is the substitute on these occasions, and is better than our's in Europe; notwithstanding which, it will not salt to keep, on account of the salt's being too sharp or acid. The female of this animal, is subject in this island to bring forth monsters. I was once shewn a little pig, preserved in spirits, the snout of which was produced in the manner of an elephant's trunk.

Horses are very dear, and by no means fine ones. A common horse cannot be bought for less than a hundred pistoles. They fall to decay very
soon

soon at the Port, from the exceffive heat. They never are fhod, though the ifland is fo rocky. Mules are rarely feen. The affes are fmall, and but few in number. The afs would be a truly ufeful animal in this country, as it would lighten the fevere labours of the poor negroes. Every load, how heavy foever, is carried on the heads of the flaves.

A SHORT time fince, two beautiful wild affes were brought from the Cape, a male and female,---they were of the fize of a mule, and ftriped on the fhoulders like the zebra, from which, however, they differed in other refpects. Thefe animals, though young, were not to be tamed.

THE breed of cats degenerates greatly on this ifland, they grow lean and thin flanked. The rats fcarcely fear them,—the dogs are therefore the rat-catchers, and my *Favorite* has often diftinguifhed himfelf in this fervice. I have feen him ftrangle the largeft rat of the fouthern hemifphere. The dogs at the long run, lofe their hair and their fenfe of fmelling ; but it is faid that they never go mad here.

PORT-LOUIS, *July* 15, 1769.

## LETTER XVI.

### TOUR THROUGH THE ISLAND.

MONSIEUR de Chazal, Councillor, and M le Marquis d'Albergaty, both of them fond of Natural Hiftory, propofed to me fome time fince, to go and fee a famous cavern about a league and a half from hence. We embarked upon the Great River, which, like the other rivers of this ifland, is not navigable for floops, above a mufquet fhot from its mouth. A fmall fettlement is eftablifhed there confifting of an hofpital and a few ftorehoufes; and here alfo begins the aquæduct that fupplies the town with water. Upon a little height, in the form of a fugar-loaf, there is a kind of fort to defend the bay.

AFTER croffing the Great-River, we took a guide, and walked through the woods weftward, for near three quarters of an hour. It was not long before we came to the entrance of the cavern, which feemed like the hole of a cave, the vault of which had fallen in. Many roots of the *mapou* grow perpendicularly down it, and barr up a part of the entrance. The head of an ox was nailed in the center.

WE breakfafted before we defcended this abyfs. After which, we lit flambeaux and candles, and furnifhed ourfelves with tinder-boxes to ftrike fire, if neceffary.

WE

WE went about a dozen paces down the rocks at the mouth of it, and then found ourselves in a vaft, and far more fpacious cave than I had ever feen before.

ITS vault is formed of a black rock.

ITS width was about thirty-feet, and its heighth, twenty.

THE foil is very compact and adhefive, and is covered with a fine earth.

ALONG each fide of the cavern, about breaft-high, extends a large fillet with mouldings, which I fuppofe to be the work of the waters, which flow down in the rainy feafon, of different heights;— the land, as well as river fhells that we faw here, confirm this conjecture. Yet the country people fancy it to be the ancient crater of the volcano. It rather appeared to me as having been the bed of fome fubterranean river.

THE vaulted roof is covered with a fort of dry fhining varnifh, or ftony concretion, which extends itfelf to the fides, and in fome places, even to the floor of the cave, and forms thereon ferruginous ftalactites, which broke and crackled under our feet, as if we had been walking upon frozen fnow.

WE walked on for fome time, and found the foil perfectly dry, except at about three hundred paces from the entrance, where a part of the roof is mouldered away. The water had oozed through in this place, and had fettled in different parts of the ground beneath.

FROM

From thence the roof gradually lowered, 'till we were at length obliged to go upon our hands and knees; being almost stifled with heat, I would go no further. My companions being more curious, more active, and in a proper deshabille, continued their route.

As I returned, I discovered a plant about the size of my finger, which hung to the roof by very small filaments. It was more than ten feet long, had neither branches nor leaves, nor did it appear to have ever had either. It was unbroken at both ends, and was filled with a kind of milky juice.

I returned to the entrance of the grotto, and sat down to breathe the fresh air, and in a little time heard an inarticulate noise, and then, by the light of the flambeaux the Negroes carried, saw my fellow-travellers returning in their caps, shirts, and drawers, so dirty and so red, that they looked like so many actors in an English tragedy. They were bathed in sweat, and all besmeared with this red earth, over which they had crawled upon their bellies, without being able to go much farther than I had done.

This cavern chokes and fills up daily. Methinks, magnificent store-houses might be constructed, by making partition-walls to keep out the water.

We returned home that evening.—This excursion made me desirous of another. I had been invited on my first arrival by Monsieur de Messin, who lives about seven leagues from Port-Louis, upon the Black-River, to spend some days at his house. As his pirogue came every week to Port-Louis, I took the opportunity of going in her on her return.—The

perogue

pirogue is a kind of boat cut out of a single piece of wood, and goes either with oars or sails.

We embarked at midnight, and in about half an hour rowed out of the harbour. The sea ran high, and dashed with great violence upon the breakers, over which we were several times driven by the surf, without knowing it. The night being very dark, the master told me he would land, as he thought it dangerous to proceed till day-light.

We had gone, I suppose, about a league and a half; the blacks carried me to shore on their shoulders; after which they took two pieces of wood, one of *veloutier*, the other of *bambou*, and kindled a light by rubbing them together. This practice is very ancient; Pliny tells us, it was in use among the Romans, and that nothing is so fit for the purpose of striking fire, as a piece of ivy-wood rubbed against the laurel.

Our people seated themselves round the fire, smoaking their pipes, which are a kind of crucible at the end of a long reed, and which they hand round as they sit. I gave them some Eau-de-Vie, then wrapping myself in my cloak, went to sleep on the sand.

At five o'clock they called me to go on board again. The day breaking, I saw the tops of the mountains covered with thick clouds, which blew along at a great rate; the weather was hazy, and the wind drove the fog along the vallies; the main sea grew white with foam, and the pirogue, carrying both her sails, made a great way.

When

WHEN we were at that part of the coast called *ficq-en-flacq*, about a league and a half from land, we found a prodigious short and broken sea, with squalls of wind, so violent as to oblige us to down both our sails. The master said to me in his Patois jargon, "*Ça n'est pas bon, Monsié*." I asked him, if there was any danger, he answered me twice, "*Si vous n'a pas gagné malheur, ça bon.*"—In short, he told me, that a fortnight before, the pirogue had overset, and drowned one of his comrades.

It was a lee-shore, and so covered with rocks, that there was no possibility of landing; and had we passed the island, we could not have made it again without the utmost difficulty. As we could not carry sail, the men took to their oars. The sky grew more and more louring, which made it necessary to hasten as much as possible. The men having drank some eau-de-vie, pulled stoutly, and by dint of arms, and at the risk of being twenty times overset, we once more got into tolerable smooth water, and coasted along between the shore and the breakers.

During the storm, the blacks were as easy and unconcerned as if they had been safe on shore. Their belief in Predestination, and their indifference for life, gives them a tranquillity, which all our boasted philosophy can never attain to.

I landed about nine in the morning at the mouth of the Great-River: M. de Mesfin was agreeably surprized at the arrival of his pirogue, which he did not expect that day, and received me with the utmost cordiality. His estate includes all the valley through which the river flows.—It is imperfectly described in the chart drawn by the Abbé de le Caille; he has omitted a branch of the mountain, on the
right-

right-hand shore, which extends towards the promontory *du Tamur*. Moreover, the course of the river is not so strait as he represents it, for at a short league's distance from the mouth, it turns to the left hand. This learned astronomer having given us a description of the out-line only of the island, I propose to make additions to his plan*, according as the information I procure in these excursions may furnish me with opportunity.

There is great plenty of every thing at Black-River; of game, venison, and both fresh-water and sea-fish. While we were at dinner one day, a servant came to tell us that some *lamentins* † were seen in the bay, we ran down immediately; they cast nets a-cross the entrance, and when drawn a-shore, we found a great quantity of the sword-fish, of skait, two sea-turtles, and other kinds of fish; but the lamentins were escaped.

The utmost regularity and good order is observed in this, as in every other plantation I have been at. The negroes cabbins are ranged in lines, like tents in a camp. Each man has a small piece of ground allotted him for growing tobacco and gourds;—flocks, and poultry, are bred in great numbers upon these plantations. The harvests are plentiful, but receive great damage from the swarms of grasshoppers.

The convenience of commodities from thence to the town, is inconvenient and hazardous, it being impossible for a carriage of any burden to get along by land, the roads are so bad; and the wind being in general contrary on the voyage from thence to the Port.

† A kind of sea-cow.
* I wish the author had furnished us with this plan. T.

AFTER

AFTER a stay of a few days, I determined to return to town by a tour over the plains *de Villiams*; for this purpose my host furnished me with a guide, and a pair of pistols, lest I should meet with any of the * Maron Negroes.

I set out at two in the afternoon for Palma, the plantation of M. de Cossigni, about three leagues off; where I proposed to lay that night: there being none but foot-paths over the rocks, I was obliged to walk. When I had gone over the mountains of Black-River, I found myself in a vast forest, through which a narrow path only is grubbed up, and which passes close by a lonely house, the solitary retreat of a man, who in France had squandered a considerable fortune, and who now drags on a wretched and miserable life in this gloomy desart, without property; the land round his house not being his own, and without society; except that of a few negroes, his slaves. As I passed, he was sitting at his door, in his shirt and drawers only, with his legs naked and his sleeves tucked up, diverting himself with rubbing a monkey with the juice of red mulberries, himself being all over smeared therewith.

* The Dutch who came here in the year 1638, upon forming a settlement, found themselves in want of slaves, for the cultivation of their lands, and applied to the French, who were settled on the island of Madagascar, to supply them with some of the natives from thence for this purpose. The French complied, and sold them fifty, whom they had taken by force from among the inhabitants. These, exasperated at the outrage, attacked, and massacred the invaders.——The poor people who had been sent to the Mauritius, fled from their servitude to the woods, from whence they made such continual incursions upon their former masters, that at length they determined to quit the place, rather than be subject to the dangers which constantly attended them. The slaves were now the sole resiants; such of their progeny as escaped the vigilance of Monsieur de la Bourdonnais, are the Maron negroes, mentioned by the author. *T.*

FROM

From thence, about half an hour's walk brought me to the side of tamarind-river, whose waters flowed with a loud noise over a bed of rocks. My black found a ford, and carried me over upon his shoulders. I saw before me the mountain of three-paps, which rose to a very great height, and on the other side was the plantation of Palma. My guide persuaded me to go along the side of this mountain, assuring me that we could not fail of finding the path that led to the top. We got quite round it, after having walked above an hour: but seeing the man was at a lofs, I returned immediately, and again reached the foot of the mountain, before the sun was set. I was much fatigued, and very thirsty, and could I have got water, would have passed the night there. But I determined otherwise; and although there was no sign of a path, began to ascend the mountain thro' the woods, being sometimes forced to clamber over huge rocks, or to drag myself along by the trees, and at others, being supported by my black servant, who came after me. I had not walked half an hour, before night came on, and was then without guide, except the steepness of the mountain. Not a breath of wind was stirring, the air was intensely hot,—and ready to faint with heat, fatigue, and thirst, I lay down several times, determining to stay all night where I was. At length, after an infinite deal of trouble, I perceived that I ascended no longer. Soon after, a breeze from the south-east refreshed me exceedingly, and the appearance of some lights at a distance, afforded me an additional comfort. The side I had quitted was inveloped in total darkness.

I now began to descend, and frequently slid down upon my back, without being able to prevent it. The noise of a rivulet was my only guide, and I at length reached it, very much bruised. Although in a
violent

violent perspiration, I drank heartily, and having felt herbage under my hand; had the additional good fortune to find some water-cresses, of which I ate several handfuls. I continued to approach the fire I saw before me, carrying my pistols ready cocked in my hand, fearing I might find an assembly of Maron negroes; but it proved to be a part of the wood that was lately cleared, in which there were several trunks of trees still burning. No body was near. I halloo'd, and listened, in hopes at last to hear the barking of a dog,—but in vain, no other sounds were to be heard, than the distant murmurs of the brook; and the whistling of the wind among the trees.

My black and my guide kindled some brands, by the light of which we walked over the ashes of this burning wood, towards another fire a little farther. Here we found three negroes watching some flocks, that belonged to a neighbour of M. de Cossigni. One of them conducted me to Palma. It was now midnight, and every body was fast asleep. A negroe, whom our noise had awakened, informed me that his master was abroad;—he, however offered me all the accommodation the house afforded. I rose early in the morning, intending to go to Mr. Jacob's, who lived about two leagues off upon the high grounds of *Williams-plains*; a fine broad road being cleared all the way to his house, I soon arrived there, and was received with his usual hospitality.

The air is so much colder here than at the Port, and the place I had just left, that I found the fire-side the best situation towards evening. This part is the best cultivated of any in the whole island, and is watered by several rivulets, some of which, especially one they call the deep-river, runs in beds

of

### VOYAGE *to the* ISLE OF FRANCE.

of a depth frightful to look down. The road from hence to town running close by the side of this river, on my return I observed it particularly, and suppose I could not be less than three hundred feet above its channel. The sides are covered by five or six stories of very large trees, rising one above another; a sight which gave me a violent swimming in my head.

As I came nearer to the town, I perceived the heat of the air increase, and the herbage insensibly lose its verdure, till I reached the Port, where every thing is dry and barren.

PORT LOUIS, *August* 15, 1769.

## LETTER XVII.

### JOURNEY ON FOOT OVER THE ISLAND.

AN Officer had proposed to me a tour round the island on foot, but just before we were to have set out, excused himself from going,—I therefore determined to go alone.

I knew I might depend upon *Côte*, one of the King's blacks, who had accompanied me before; he was little, but he was very strong, of approved fidelity, sober, of few words, and fearless of danger.

I had bought a slave a little time before, and called him by your name, hoping it would be an omen in his favour. He could not speak French, nor was his constitution healthy; but he was well made, and of a very decent appearance.

I took my dog with me by way of guard in the night, and to look out for game in the day time.

Knowing that I should be very often alone, and that these woods were without inns, I provided every thing which I thought might be necessary for myself or my people. My baggage weighed two hundred pounds, and consisted of a kettle, some plates, a quantity of rice, biscuit, maize, a dozen
of

of wine, six bottles of eau-de-vie, some butter, sugar, citrons, salt, tobacco, a small hammock, linen, a plan of the island, some books, a sabre, and a cloak.

I DIVIDED the whole into four packs, two of sixty pounds, and two of forty; and got them tied to the ends of two very strong reeds. *Côte* took the heaviest, and *Duval* the other. I, for my part, was in my waistcoat, and carried a double-barrelled gun, a pair of pistols in my pocket, and my couteau de chasse.

I DETERMINED to begin my course on the leeward-side of the island, proposing to keep constantly close to the shore, that I might form a judgment of its defence, and to make observations upon any objects of natural history which might present themselves.

M. de Chazal offered to accompany me as far as his estate, situated five leagues from the town, in the plains of *Saint Peter*, and M. le Marquis d'Albergati, agreed to do the like.

WE set out early in the morning of the 26th of August, and went all the way along shore. From *Fort-Blanc*, to the left of the Port, the sea washes a sandy strand, that is not at all steep, 'till it gets to the point of a plain, on which *Paulm* battery is raised; though this shore is level, a descent would be impracticable, on account of a long bank of rocks, which run along shore at two musquet-shots distance, and forms a natural defence. From this place the shore becomes steep, and the sea runs so high, that it would be impossible to land hereabouts; and it would be equally impossible for cavalry or artillery to make good their landing upon the plain, because of the rocks with which it is covered all over. There are no trees, except a few *mapous* and *veloutiers*. The shore is no longer steep at *little-river* bay, where there is a small battery.

HERE we dined with M. de Seligny, a man of singular merit. He shewed us the plan of a machine, by which he cut a canal to the Neptune, a ship that was run a-ground here in the hurricane in 1760. They were two iron rakes, put in motion by two large wheels that were supported upon barges; and whose effect was increased by levers, again supported by rafts.

WE saw also a cotton-mill of his invention, which was worked by water. It was formed of a number of small metal cylinders, in a parallel position to each other. Children are taught to hold the cotton to two of these cylinders, the cotton passes and the seed remains. This same mill answered the purpose of a pair of bellows to a forge,—to grind meal,—and to make oil. He informed us, that he had discovered a vein of coal, some iron ore of an earth very proper for making crucibles, and that the cinders, which are called *nymphea*, burnt with coal, produced glasses of a variety of colours. In the afternoon we took leave of this useful and unrequited member of society.

WE took a path which was about a musquet-shot from the shore, and having forded the river *Belleisle*, whose mouth is very narrow, after walking about a quarter of a league we entered a wood, which leads to M. de Chazal's house. This estate, which is called *St. Peter's-Plains*, is still more rocky, than the rest of the way. In many places, the negroes were obliged to lay down their burdens, and to assist us to clamber. When we were within half an hour's walk of our journey's journey's end, *Duval*, being no longer able to stand under his load, was obliged to lay it down. We were much perplexed by this accident; for night was coming on, and the other negroes were gone before. How was he to be found again if we left him in these woods? I struck a light with the lock of my gun, and kindled a fire with some straw and dry sticks; after which we left *Duval* there, and when we got home, we sent some blacks to seek for him, and bring his packs.

THE shore is very steep and craggy between the *Little-River* and *St. Peter's-Plains*. My companions found among the rock the purple-fish of Panama, and a variety of other shell-fish.

August 27, we rested the whole day. This stony soil is well enough adapted to the culture of cotton, the thread of which is but short. The coffee that grows here is of a good quality, but yields very little, as usual in dry places.

28th, We set out at 8 o'clock in the morning, and in the course of our journey forded the rivers *Dragon* and *Galet*, at the last of which the shore ceases to be steep ; and we had from thence the pleasure of walking upon a fine sand by the seaside, along a large plain, which leads as far as the bay of *Tamarinds*. It may be about a quarter of a league broad, and more than a league long. Nothing grows upon it : but I think cocoa-trees might be planted to advantage, as they thrive in a sandy soil. To the right, there is a stream of bad water, running the length of the whole wood.

In some parts, which the sea has left dry, we found some fosil madrepores, which prove that the

sea

sea once washed over this shore. We dined upon the right-side of Tamarind-bay, and then my companions left me, and returned back.

From Black-River, I had but a short league to M. Messin's, and therefore resolved to sleep there that night. I forded the bay of Tamarinds, and from thence kept along the shore with more difficulty and fatigue than I expected: being very steep and craggy all the way 'till we got to Black-River. Among these rocks I found many sorts of *crabs*, and the same kind of *boudins* that I have spoken of before.

The bottom of this bay is a sand, and a landing might be effected here, if the situation at the entrance did not subject those who attempted it to a cross-firing. A battery at the point of the sand, on the right shore of the Black-River, would be of great service.

The 29th and 30th, at low water I continued my walk along the shore: I found the great *conch*, and a fish called the *faux-amiral*.

The 31st, I set off at six this morning, and passed the Black-River at a ford, near the house; after this, attempting to cut a-cross a kind of island covered with wood and stones, I bewildered myself in the grass, and had some difficulty to find the path again; at last, however, I did, and it brought me to the sea-side again. All along this shore the oysters stick to the rocks in great numbers: *Duval*, my new servant, in walking a-cross one of the mouths of the Black-River, got a very deep cut in his foot, by one of their shells. We made a halt about eight o'clock in the morning, and I gave him
some

some eau-de-vie for *Côte* and himself to drink, and to bathe his wound. As they were heavily laden, I thought it proper to make two halts in a day, to confine my walks to the morning and evening, and to give them all the refreshment I could. This little indulgence gave them strength and spirits,—they would have followed me to the end of the world.

Between the two mouths of the Black-River, a stag, pursued by hounds and hunters, came strait towards me. The poor beast wept and panted: as I could not save it, and was unwilling to kill it, I fired one of my charges in the air. He then took to the water, and was overtaken and killed by the dogs. Pliny observes, that this animal, when pressed by the hounds, will fly for protection to a man. I stopped at the first rivulet I came to, after having passed the Black-River; it runs into the sea opposite to a little island, called *Tamarina's-isle*, which is not described upon the chart; one may get to it on foot at low water, as also to the little island, called *Morne*, where vessels sometimes perform quarantine.

I had every thing necessary for dinner, but something to eat. Seeing a pirogue of a Malabar fisherman pass along the coast, I asked them if they had any fish on board; they sent me a very fine mullet, but would not let me pay any thing for it. I made my kitchen at the foot of a *talamaque-tree*; I lit a fire, while one of my negroes went in search of wood, and the other of water, that where I was being brackish. I made a hearty dinner of the fish, upon which I also regaled my servants.

I observed some pieces of the rocks to be ferruginous, and abounding in ore. There is a ridge of rocks, extending from the Black-River, as far as

the

the promontory of Brabant, which is the moſt leeward point of the iſland. There is but one place to land at behind the little iſland, called *Tamarind's-iſland*.

At two in the afternoon I ſet out again, but walked with more circumſpection than before. I had now twenty leagues to go through a deſart part of the iſland, where there are no more than two inhabitants; except the Maron negroes, who harbour thereabouts. I ordered my men to keep cloſe; and my dog, who uſed always to run before, now kept very near me, and at the leaſt noiſe pricked up his ears and ſtopped: he ſeemed ſenſible that we were not among men. Thus we continued our walk in good order, following the ſhore, which forms an infinite number of ſmall bays. To the left we had the woods, where the moſt profound ſolitude reigns. Behind theſe, runs a tract of hills, the tops only of which we could ſee; the ſoil here is but poor, notwithſtanding which, by the *polchers*, a ſpecies of tree, brought from India, and ſome other ſigns, it was evident that a ſettlement had been attempted. I had the precaution to take ſome bottles of water with me, and 'twas well. I did ſo, for the rivulets marked in the plan, were entirely dried up.

The continual bleeding of my negro's wound, made me very uneaſy: I walked very ſlowly, and at four o'clock made another halt. As night approached, I would not attempt to go round the promontory, but cut a-croſs the wood, over the iſthmus which joins it to the other mountains. This iſthmus is a hill of a middling height. Upon this eminence I met a black belonging to M. le Normand, whoſe houſe I was going to, and from which I was not above a quarter of a league. This man went

went on before, while I stopped, and looked with delight upon the prospect of the two seas. A house built here would be in a charming situation, if any fresh water were near. As I descended the hill, a black came and brought me a jug of water, and told me, that I was impatiently expected at the house. I got there. It was a long building of pallisadoes, covered with the leaves of the *latanier*. Eight negroes belonged to the plantation, and there were nine persons in family; the master, the mistress, five children, a young lady related to the family, and a friend. The master was abroad: all this I learnt from the negro as I went along.

THERE was but one large room, and of this the whole house consisted; in the middle was the kitchen; at one end, they kept their stores, and here also lay the servants; at the other was the bed where lay the master and his wife; it was covered with a cloth by way of tester, upon which was a hen sitting upon eggs;—under the bed were some ducks;— pigeons harboured among the leaves of the roof;— and at the door were three great dogs.

ALL the implements both of the husbandry and housewifery were hung up against the walls. What was my surprise at finding the mistress of this wretched dwelling, to be a very handsome genteel woman. Both she and her husband were of good families in France. They had come here several years since, to seek their fortune; and had quitted their relations, their friends, and their country, to pass their days in this desart, where nothing is to be seen but the sea, and the frightful cliffs of the promontory of Brabant; but the air of contentment and good-nature about this young mother of a family, seemed to make every body happy who came near her.

her. She gave fuck to her youngeft child, while the four others ftood round her, playful and contented.

Supper time being come, every thing the houfe afforded was ferved up with the utmoft propriety. —This meal appeared a very agreeable one to me. I could not help being ftruck with the fight of the pigeons fluttering about the table, the goat-kids and the children at play together, and fuch a variety of animals in perfect agreement with this amiable family, and with each other. Their peaceful fports, the folitude of the place, the murmuring noife of the fea, all combined to prefent to my imagination, a picture of thofe times when the children of Noah, defcended upon a new earth, began afrefh to partake of the domeftic enjoyments they had fo long been ftrangers to.

After fupper, I was fhewn to my lodging-room, which was a little hut, newly built of wood, at about two hundred paces from the houfe. The door was not yet put up; but I clofed the opening with the boards of which it was made. I laid my arms in readinefs, the Maron negroes being very numerous in this part. A few years ago, about forty of them, retired to the promontory, and began to make plantations. An attempt was made to take them; but fooner than fuffer this, they all threw themfelves into the fea.

September 1, the mafter of the houfe having returned home in the night, perfuaded me to defer my journey till afternoon; promifing to accompany me part of the way. It was no more than three fhort leagues to *Belle-ombre*, the laft plantation, or houfe that I fhould find. Madame de Normand
herfelf,

herself, prepared a remedy to apply to the wound of my poor negro. She made over the fire a kind of Samaritan's Balsam, with turpentine, sugar, wine, and oil. His wound being dressed, I sent him on before with his comrade. At three o'clock, I took leave of this hospitable house, and of the amiable and excellent mistress of it. Her husband and I set out. He was a very robust man; and his arms, legs, and face were exceedingly sun-burnt. He worked himself in the plantation, as well as in cutting down and clearing away trees. Nothing gave him concern, he said, but the ill health his wife brought upon herself by bringing up her children; and that she had lately added to the fatigue, by taking upon her the charge of an orphan. He told me only his grievances, for he could not but perceive how sensible I was of the happiness he enjoyed.

We crossed a rivulet near the house, and walked upon the green sod as far as point *Corail*. Here the sea runs up into the island, between two chains of perpendicular mountains: we followed this chain thro' broken and rugged paths, and sometimes swinging by the rocks. Our greatest difficulty was on the side of the bay, in doubling what they call the Cape. I saw several negroes passing it; they scrambled along the side of the rock, and had they made one false step, must have fallen into the sea. In bad weather this passage is impracticable, the sea beating in, and breaking among the rocks in a most frightful manner. In a calm, small vessels can come into the bay, at the end of which they load with wood. Luckily for us, the King's *Senau* the *Desire*, was then in the bay, and we borrowed her boat to cross it. M. le Normande went over with me, and we then took leave of each other, and parted.

AFTER

After three hours walking over a green fod, I reached the other fide of Point *St. Martin*. Sometimes I walked upon the fand, and fometimes upon the turf, which grew in thick tufts like mofs. Here I found a pirogue, in which M. Etiene, partner in the plantation of Belle-ombre waited for my coming. We foon got to his houfe, which was fituated at the entrance of the river *Cureniers*, on the left fhore of which they were building a fhip of two hundred tons.

All the way from M. le Normand's, the coolnefs of the air and the verdure of the ground is delightful. 'Tis a favannah, without rock, lying between the fea and woods, which have a beautiful appearance.

Before I paffed the Cape, I obferved a large fhelf of coral, above fifteen feet high. 'Tis a kind of breaker, which the fea has abandoned ; at the foot of it, there is a long piece of fenny-ground, which might be eafily converted into a bafon for fmall veffels.

September 2, my negro being almoft cured of his wound, by the remedy Madame de Normand had applied to it, I fixed my departure for that afternoon. In the morning I went out in the pirogue between the breakers and the coaft. The water was clear to the very bottom ; and one might fee a foreft of madrepores of five or fix feet high, like trees, fome of them with flowers growing upon them. Different forts of fifh, and of all colours, fwam about among their branches ; in fome parts were numbers of beautiful fhell-fifh, and in others tunny-fifh, equally beautiful, which meandered about, as the motion of the pirogue difturbed and frighted them. I might have made a valuable collection, but I had no
diver

# VOYAGE to the ISLE OF FRANCE.

tiiver here, nor any proper iron pincers to raife up the plants from this maritime garden, or to root up thefe trees of ftone. However, I brought away with me fome of the rock called, the Ear of Midas, the Golden Cloth, &c. &c.

Two officers of the *D*-*fire* dined with us, who, with Monfieur Etiene, agreed to accompany me as far as the arm of the fea *de la Savanne*, three leagues off. Nobody lives there, but there are fome huts made of ftraw; we had fent the negroes forward in the morning; and after dinner I followed them by myfelf.

I ARRIVED at *Poft Jacotet*; a part where the fea runs up into the land, forming a circular bay, in the middle of which is a fmall triangular ifland; this creek is furrounded by a rifing ground, that gives it the appearance of a bafon. It is open only at the entrance, where the fea-water enters; and at the other end receives a number of rivulets, that run over a fine fand, from a piece of frefh-water above, in which were plenty of fifh. Round this piece of water are feveral little hills, rifing one above another in the form of an amphitheatre, and crowned with clumps of trees, fome fhaped like pyramids or yews, and others like an umbrella,—behind, and far above all thefe, were the tow'ring tops of a wood of palm-trees, whofe bending branches looked like fo many plumes of feathers. This huge mafs of verdure, rifes out of the middle of the green turf, and is joined to the foreft, and to a branch of the mountain leading to the Black-River. The murmuring of the fprings, the beautiful greennefs of the waves, the conftant, but gentle whiftling of the winds, the fmoothnefs of the plain, with the pleafing umbrage of the high lands, and grateful fmell of the *veloutiers*, diffufed
around

around me peace and happiness. I regretted my being alone;—a variety of projects suggested themselves to my imagination; and I would have given up all the universe beside, might I but with some chosen and beloved objects, have spent my days to come in this delightful place.

I QUITTED this pleasing prospect with reluctance. Before I had gone two hundred yards from it, there met me a troop of negroes armed with fusils; upon their nearer approach, I perceived them to be a party sent out by the police of the island; they stopped when they came up to me. One of them had got in the shell of a gourd, two puppies just whelped; another of them led a woman tied by the neck with a cord made of rushes; this was the booty they had taken from a camp of Maron negroes, which they had routed. They had killed one man, whose *grisgris* they shewed me,—'twas a kind of talisman made like a rosary. The poor negro-woman, seemed overwhelmed with grief. I asked her some questions, but she did not answer me. She carried upon her back a bag made of *vacoa*, I opened it, and was shocked beyond measure at finding in it the head of a man. The country before me seemed no longer beautiful in my eyes, but was converted to a scene of horrors, from which I fled with precipitation.

MY companions met me again as I was with some difficulty going down a declivity, towards the arm of the sea *de la Savanna*; it was now night, and we seated ourselves under some trees at the bottom of the bay; where we supped by the light of flambeaux.

OUR conversation turned upon the subject of the Maron negroes, for they as well as I, had met the party
with

with the poor woman, who was carrying, perhaps, the head of her lover! M. Etiene told us, there were troops of them, of two or three hundred in number in the environs of *Belle-ombre*, and that they elected a chief, difobedience to whofe orders, was punifhed with death. They are forbidden to take any thing from the houfes in the neighbourhood, or to go to the fide of the frequented rivers to feek for fifh or other food. In the night they go down to the fea-fide and fifh; and in the day-time drive the deer or ftags to the interior parts of the woods, with dogs trained to great perfection for this purpofe. When there is but one woman in a party, fhe is referved for the chief; but if there are many, they are in common. The children that are born, are immediately killed, left their cries fhould difcover their retreat. The whole morning is fpent in cafting lots to prefage the deftiny of the enfuing day.

He told us, that being a hunting one day laft year, he met a run-away negroe, whom he purfued and prefented his gun at,—it miffed fire thrice. He was then going to knock him down with the but-end, but was prevented by two negroe-women, who came out of the wood, and weeping, threw themfelves at his feet. The black feized the opportunity and efcaped. He brought the two generous creatures home with him; he had fhewn us one of them in the morning,

I HAD obferved, that by clearing away fome of the beds of coral, *Poft-Jacotet*, the chearful place I have juft defcribed, might be made a very good harbour for fmall veffels. The arm of the fea *de la Savanna* would alfo ferve to load, or land goods from barges. This part in general, is by far the moft beautiful of the whole ifland; but it remains uncultivated,

tivated; a communication with Port-Louis being difficult, on account of the mountains between them; and the wind being so seldom fair for doubling *Brabant* promontory in returning from the Port.

SEPTEMBER 3, M. Etienne, and M. de Chezemure, Captain of the Desire, accompanied me as far as the left-hand shore of *la Savanne*; which is much steeper than the other ; in this place, their dogs put up a stag ; and here I took leave of them, to go alone the twelve leagues that remained, through a desolate and uninhabited country. I observed as I went along; that the meadows were much larger, and the woods thicker and better grown. The mountains run a long way into the land, and the summits only of the distant ones were to be seen.

I EVERY now and then came to a ravin. I forded three different rivers in the course of two hours walking, and the second, called the river *Anguilles*, with some difficulty ; its bottom being covered with rocks, and the current very rapid. It flows from springs of a ferruginous quality, which cover the water with an oil, the colour of a pigeon's breast.

IN the way, I saw a sparrow-hawk, which makes great havock among the poultry. It was perched upon the trunk of a *latanier*. I presented at him, within a gun's length; both my primes flashed in the pan, without either gun's going off. The bird kept his place, and there I left him. This accident made me look very carefully to my arms, in case of an attack from the negroes.

ON the left-hand side of the third river, and near the sea, I made a halt upon a level part of the rocks, under the shade of a *veloutier*. My blacks made me
a kind

a kind of tent, by throwing my cloak over some branches. Here I dined; and they catched me some perch and conchs,—and ears of Midas.

Two hours after dinner, I went on again, my guns, and people in good order: there was no need to fear a surprize, the plain being entirely open, and the woods at a great distance. As the path was a fine smooth sand,—that I might walk the more at ease, and not have the trouble of taking off my shoes and stockings at every ford, I determined to walk barefoot, as the hunters did in the morning. This is not only the most natural, but the safest way of going here, the foot seizing or griping the angles of the rocks like a hand. The blacks are so expert by constant use, that they can pick up a pin from the ground with their toes. 'Tis not therefore in vain, that Nature has divided this part into toes, and them again into articulations.

HAVING pulled off my shoes and stockings while I made these reflections, I walked on and forded the first river; but in coming out of the water, I received a violent stroke of the sun upon my legs; which immediately became red and enflamed. In crossing a second, I cut one of my heels, and one toe, and felt the wounds exceedingly painful, when I put my foot in the water. I gave up my project, lamenting that want of custom had deprived me of one of the advantages a man might enjoy here.

I CAME to the side of the river *Jacotet*, and crossed it upon the back of my negroe, at about cannon-shot distance from its mouth. The water makes a great noise in running over the rocks, and is so transparent, that I could distinguish the black snails that stuck to the bottom. I must own I shuddered at passing this stream.

stream. It being near sun-set, I determined to go no farther, but walked over the stones along its brink, to get to a shed which I perceived on one of the points of the mouth, and which I found it impossible to reach, the rocks were so very rugged. I returned, and again took the path, which led me to the top of the slope at the foot of which the river runs. On my left-hand, in a recess, I saw a little clump of branches of trees and liannes, but could not penetrate it. A thought struck me, to cut a way into it with a hatchet, and lay down as in a nest, thus assuring myself of a place to sleep in. But some drops of rain falling, a roof, though ever so bad a one, appeared to be the better shelter. I went down the recess towards the sea, and was very happy to find on my right-hand, the shed I had seen from the opposite shore. 'Twas nothing but a mere roof of leaves of *latanier*, built out from the rock; on my right, was the passage I had in vain attempted, and on the left, that I had descended by,—and before me was the sea.

EVERY thing seemed equally fitted for my safety and convenience: They made me up a bed of dry leaves, upon which I lay down. My two paniers were laid one on the right, the other on the left side of me, one of my blacks at each entrance, my pistols under my head, my gun at my side, and my dog at my feet.

THESE dispositions were scarcely made, before a shivering seized me. This was the consequence of the stroke of the sun, which is generally succeeded by a fever.

MY legs became very much enflamed and painful. They made me some lemonade, and by the light of a candle which they lit, I made notes of my
observ-

observations during this journey, and corrected some errors in the chart.

The whole coast, from the æstuary *la Sevanne*, is steep and inaccessible. The rivers that empty themselves here have steep banks.—It would be impossible for cavalry to get along at all, and the march of an enemy might be impeded with great ease, every river being a ditch of a depth absolutely frightful. As to the country, 'tis by far the most beautiful in the island.

At midnight the fever left me, and I fell asleep. At half past three o'clock, my dog waked me, by running from under the shed, and barking as loud as he could. I called to *Côte*, who rose; we went out, but could see nothing but a starry sky. My black returned in a few minutes, and said, he had heard some body whistle twice, as if in the wood. I ordered them to light a fire and keep watch, and placed *Côte*, armed with my sabre, as a centinel.

The sea came up almost as far as my cottage. The noise of its breaking among the rocks, added to the darkness of the night, inclined me to rest, but my apprehensions would not suffer me. I was five leagues from any house, and if the fever should again attack me, no assistance could be had. I had no fears about the Maron negroes; my servants were both resolute men, and my situation was such as would enable me to stand a siege. All things considered, I thought myself very happy that I did not take up my lodging in the thicket.

At day break, I gave a glass of eau-de-vie to my body-guards, and renewed my journey. Their burdens

burdens were much lightened, by the conſtant conſumption of our proviſions.

SEPTEMBER 4, It was half paſt five when I ſet off, reſolving not to ſtop 'till I got to a houſe. We preſently came to the ſide of a ſmall river, and a little farther on to a rivulet almoſt dried up. After an hour's walk, the beautiful turf I had walked on from the promontory of *Brabant* ended, and the ſoil became ſtony and covered with rocks, as in the other parts of the iſland. The graſs here is of a finer verdure, and of a large blade,—very proper for paſture.

I FORDED an arm of the ſea called *du Challon* over a ſand-bank. The deſcription of it in the plan is not a good one. The ſea runs deep into the land, through a narrow channel, a-croſs which gratings might be put, and there would then be a fine reſervoir for fiſh. On the left ſhore there was a ſhed, in which I reſted myſelf.

ABOUT half a league from thence the path divides, I took that to the left, which leads into the woods; it conducted me to a wide road, marked with a track of wheels,—an appearance that pleaſed me very much, as it was a ſign of my being near a houſe of ſome note, and the print of a horſes hoof was at that time a much more deſirable ſight than the foot-ſtep of a man. We ſoon arrived at a houſe, but the maſter was out; I therefore went back, and ſtruck into a path, that led through the woods to the plantation of M. Delaunay. I got here in good time, for my legs were ſo terribly inflamed, that I could ſcarcely walk. He lent me a horſe to carry me two leagues off to a plantation occupied by ſome prieſts.

I crossed fucceffively the rivers de la *Chaux*, and des *Crecles*, three quarters of a league from the laft, I croffed one of the bays to the fouth-eaft of the Port in a pirogue.

The fides of this bay are covered with mangliers. The views here are delightful, the country being hilly, and covered with plantations, interfperfed with a great number of clumps of orange-trees. It was fix o'clock when I arrived at the houfe of the prieft, who had the management of the plantation. My legs were bathed with elder-flower water, and I flept with great comfort.

Septembes 5, I was now but one league from the Great Port. The good Prieft lent me a horfe, and I got to the town about ten o'clock; it confifts of about a dozen houfes. The moft remarkable buildings are, a large mill nearly fallen to ruins, and the Governor's houfe in little better condition. Behind the town is a high mountain, and before it the fea, which forms a bay two leagues deep, including the rocks at its entrance, and four leagues long from point *Cecos* to point *Diable*. I alighted at the houfe of the curate.

September 6, 7, and 8, I was charmed with my hoft, and with the country I had feen; but neither he, nor his parifhioners drank any thing except water. It is frequently a month's voyage from hence to Port-Louis, and the inhabitants are upon thefe occafions in abfolute want of every article that comes from Europe. I gave part of my provifions to M. Delfolie, my hoft, who was a good fort of man.

The south-east port was formerly inhabited by the Dutch, one of whose ancient buildings is now used as a chapel. There are two ways to enter the Port, one at point *Diable*, for small vessels; the other, which is much wider, is by the side of an island towards the middle. At each of these places is a battery, and at the bottom of the bay, is a third called the Queen's battery.

If my indisposition would have permitted me, I should have examined the variety of strange bodies thrown a-shore by the sea, in order to have formed some opinion of the lands to windward of the island; but I could not undergo the fatigue, for my legs were very painful, and the skin peeled off entirely.

The following is all the information I could get:

Whales frequently come into the south-east port, where it would be very easy and safe to harpoon them. Fish is very plentiful upon this coast, especially shell-fish, of the most beautiful kinds. They gave me some oysters of a violet colour, from the mouth of the river *la Chaux*, and a species of cristalization from the neigbouring river, *Sorbes*.

I saw for three nights, a comet, which first appeared a fortnight before; the nucleus was pale and nebulous, its tail white and very long, the rays diverged but little. I drew the position of it in the sky, which was a little below the three Kings. Its course was eastward, and consequently its tail in a westerly direction. At half past two on the morning of the 6th, its elevation was about 50 deg. above the horizon,—my observation could not be very accurate for want of the proper instruments.

The

The air of this place was cool and refreshing, and the country beautiful and fertile: but the inhabitants are so few, that during a whole day, I saw but two negroes pass through the street.

September 9, I now found myself able to continue my journey, especially as the part I went through was inhabited. I determirned to stop for the night at four leagues distance from the mouth of the Great River, which is something broader than that of the same name, near Port-Louis.

We set out at six in the morning, and followed the course of the shore, which is broken in several places by bays, on the sides of which grow *mangliers* in abundance. It is not impossible but that the seeds may have been brought by the sea from some land to windward. We went along the side of a range of high mountains to our left,—they were covered with wood. The country is divided into small hills, on which grows a very fine grass; the provender of cattle, bred here in great numbers; 'tis a pleasant part of the island, but very fatiguing to travel over.

After walking about two hours, we saw upon an eminence a fine house built of stone. Here I stopped to refresh myself; it belonged to a wealthy inhabitant, whose name was V***. He was abroad.—His wife was a raw-boned Creole, who according to the custom of the country went barefoot. I found her in a room, with five or six girls about her, and as many mastiff dogs, who immediately attacked my dog, and were very near strangling him. She turned them all out of the room, and placed at the door to keep them out a negroe wench, who had nothing on but a ragged petticoat. I begged leave to stay in her house during the heat of the day. The first compliments were

were scarcely ended, before one of the dogs found means to get in among us again, and the uproar was renewed. Madame de la V―― held in her hand the prickly tail of a dried thornback, with which she gave the poor negroe a cut a-cross the bare shoulders, (which were marked immediately with a long wheal) and then she gave a back stroke to the dog, who ran howling away.

This Lady told me, she had narrowly escaped being drowned in going in a pirogue to harpoon turtles among the rocks. She seemed to value herself much upon going to hunt the Maron negroes in the woods; but she told me, the Governor had deprived her of her favourite sport, which was stag-hunting, and added, "I should have been "better pleased, if he had stuck a dagger in my "heart."

At four in the afternoon I left this negroe-hunting Bellona; and took a path, which went a-cross point *Diable*, so called, by the first navigators on this coast; because it is said, that their compass varied without their being able to account why it did so. We crossed the mouth of the Great River in a canoe,—it is navigable for nothing larger, on account of a sand-bank which runs a-cross it, and a cataract formed by it, about a quarter of a league from hence.

There is an earth redoubt on the left shore, at the beginning of the road that leads to *Flacq*, and along which we went, the rocks being so rugged upon the shore in this part, as to render it impassable. Here we once more entered the woods, which are very fine, and abound in orange-trees. A quarter of a league from hence I came to a house,—the

master

master of it was not at home; I stopped notwithstanding.

I HAD walked two hours and a half in the morning, and as much in the afternoon.

SEPTEMBER 10, we kept the road to Flacq, 'till we got about a quarter of a league beyond the river *Seche*, which we forded as we had done the rest: then taking a path on the right-hand, I came to the seashore at *Eaudouce* bay, where there was a post of thirty men.

WE now went again along the shore, it being very passable. Côte carried me over an arm of the sea, which was rather deep. The sand is almost every where covered with rocks, except a long meadow of dog's tooth-grass, of the same sort I had seen at Belleombre. All this part is dry and barren; the woods are low and thin, and extend as far as the mountains which are seen at a distance: this plain, over which are three roads, is not good for much, it reaches as far as a settlement called *Quatre Cocos*. There is no other water, but a brackish well, dug in the rocks, full of veins of iron ore.

AFTER dinner, a path on our left-hand, led us into the woods, which were very stony. We came to the brink of the river *Flacq*, at about a quarter of a league from the mouth, and crossed it upon planks. In going along the side of this river, I passed several plantations, of which there are many hereabouts, and came down to a store-house on the left, where there is a post, commanded by M. Gautier, the Captain of a company.—He desired me to lodge there that night.

SEPTEMBER 11, I laid by all day. This part, which is called *Le Flacq*, is the best cultivated in the island; rice grows in great plenty. There is a creek in the rocks, by which barges can come and load with the greatest convenience.

SEPTEMBER 12, my host accompanied me part of the way; we went in a pirogue to post *Fayette*, as far as which, the coast is entirely covered with rocks and mangroves. Near the landing place, we saw the trace of a turtle in the sand; this induced us to land in search of it, but we found nothing but its nest. We forded the bay *des Aigrettes*, which is a large arm of the sea. I was upon the shoulders of *Côte*, when the sea became so deep towards the middle of the passage, that I feared he would not be able to keep his feet; the water came up to his neck, and wetted me very much. A little farther on, we came to another æstuary, called the *bay de Requins*. I observed many parts of the rock pierced with a number of round holes, of about a foot diameter. Some of them were as deep as my cane,—and I imagined that the lava of some volcano, having formerly flowed through the wood, had consumed the trunks of the trees, and left the print of the place they had grown in.

FROM the post of *Fayette* to the river *du Rempart*, the meadow is continued. This part is also well cultivated, and here we dined. I then crossed the river, and went on alone, 'till I came to the river *des Citroniers*. The sun was just setting, when I perceived an inhabitant at a little distance, who invited me very kindly to his house.—— his name was Le Sieur Goule.

SEPTEMBER 13, In the morning he offered me his horse to go to the town, which was but five leagues off.

off. I would willingly have gone round the whole iſland, but there remained ſtill four leagues of the way totally without inhabitants, or water; beſides, from point *des Canoniers*, to the Port was a part of the coaſt that I already knew.

I ACCEPTED the offer my hoſt had made me, and left this quarter, which is called *La Poudre d'or*, on account, ſay they, of the colour of the ſand, which however, appeared to me to be white, as in other places. I croſſed the river, (which is called by the ſame name as the quarter) and then entered a large wood, the ſoil of which is good, but without water. In the quarter of Pamplemouſſe, which was the next I came to, the lands ſeem quite exhauſted, the inhabitants having cultivated them for thirty years, without ever laying dung upon them \*. I forded this river, and the rivers *Seche*, and *de Lataniers*, and in the evening arrived at the Port.

THE moſt fertile ſoils I had ſeen on my tour were all ſtony, except ſome parts of Pamplemouſſe.

I DID not find one monument worthy of remark. There are three churches in the iſland; one at Port-Louis, the ſecond at the ſouth-eaſt port, and the third, and handſomeſt at Pamplemouſſe; the two others being ſmaller than the churches of a little country village. They had built one at Port-Louis, upon a very handſome plan, but the roof being too much raiſed, the walls were inſufficient to bear its weight, and reſiſt the force of the hurricanes. What remains of it is now uſed as a ſtore-houſe, of which there are but

---

\* The author calls it *fumer*,—ſmoking them. Saturn was called *Stercutius* by the ancients, for having taught them this method of improving their lands. *T.*

few in the ifland, and the greater part of thofe built of wood, a material by no means proper for public buildings, efpecially here, where the ftrongeft beams will only laft forty years, if the worms do not deftroy them fooner; befides, ftone is found every where in great abundance, and the ifland is furrounded with coral, for lime. The greateft difficulty is in laying the foundations, for which, the rocks muft be blown up with gunpowder; and yet, all things confidered, I do not think, that a building in ftone would coft one third more than one of wood. The latter is foon built, and as foon decays. Thofe who are too eager for enjoyment, never enjoy any thing to perfection.

The ifland is reckoned to be about forty five leagues in circumference. It is watered by a number of rivulets, which run in deep channels from the center of the ifland into the fea. Although we were now in the dry feafon, I croffed above four and twenty, flowing with frefh and wholefome water. I fuppofe that about half this ifland lays fallow, one quarter of it confifts of plantations, and the remainder of pafture grounds, of various kinds.

## LETTER XVIII.

Of the COMMERCE, AGRICULTURE, and DEFENCE of the ISLE OF FRANCE.

ONE letter will not suffice to relate all that may be said upon these three subjects,—which are boundless. To begin with the first, I do not know a corner of the earth whose wants are supplied from so many, or so distant parts. Their dishes and plates come from China; their linen and clothes from India; their slaves and cattle from Madagascar; their provisions, or part of them, from the Cape of Good-Hope; their money from Cadiz, and their government and laws from France. M. de la Bourdonnais wished to have made it the staple of the trade to India— a second Batavia.

WITH the view of great genius, he had also the weakness of a man: place him but upon a point, and he will make the centre of all things.

ALL staples augment the expences of trade, and should never be established but when absolutely necessary. No nation has any staple between the Indies and Europe, but where the trade is immediately concerned. Batavia is a spice island.

THE Isle of France is looked upon, as a fortress which assures to us our possessions in India; with
equal

equal reafon Bourdeaux might be deemed the citidel of our American colonies. The Ifle of France is fifteen hundred leagues from Pondicherry. Suppofe a garrifon ever fo numerous were to be maintained here, yet, a fquadron muft rendezvous in a port, where the worms will totally deftroy a fhip in three years. Neither pitch, tar, cordage, or maft timber are found here; nor is the wood of a proper fort for any other branch of building.

We muft afterwards run the rifk of a fea-engagement. If beaten, we cannot fuccour the place; if victorious,—our foldiers, carried fuddenly from a temperate to a very fultry climate, will be unable to endure the fatigue of the fervice.

If half the money had been expended upon fome part of the malabar coaft, or at the mouth of the Ganges, in lieu of the Ifle of France, we might have had a refpectable fortrefs in India itfelf, and the troops would have been feafoned to the climate; nor would the Englifh in this cafe have been mafters of Bengal. From them we may learn how to form a a fettlement, and protect it when formed. They have an army of three or four thoufand Europeans upon the very banks of the Ganges; befides a number of diftant iflands under their dominion: they have nothing now to do but to eftablifh themfelves on the weftern fide of Madagafcar: but in all their enterprizes, they never while purfuing the means, lofe fight of the end. A flock of fheep would be in a dangerous fituation, were the dogs, their protectors, at fifteen hundred leagues diftance from them.

Wherefore then do we continue to keep this Ifle of France? To fupply us with coffee, and as a port for our fhips to put into upon occafion.

This

THIS country which produces little elfe than a fmall quantity of coffee, has wants, enough, to engage all its attention to them alone, this muft be entirely fupplied from France for fome time, or the colony will never arrive at a ftate to be of the leaft real ufe to the mother country. Our commodities, our cloths, our linnens, our manufactures are in plenty; and the cotton-works of Normandy are far better than thofe of India with which they clothe the flaves. No money but our own fhould circulate here. A paper currency is fet on foot but is of no great credit; at the beft rate of exchange, thirty three, and frequently fifty per cent is loft by it.—Indeed it is impoffible that this paper money can lofe lefs;—it is payable in France fix months after fight, it is fix months upon the voyage thither, and fix months on the return; this is eighteen months. Ready money is reckoned here, to produce thirty three per cent in eighteen months, if employed in the maritime trade; and therefore who ever gives paper for piaftres, juftly looks upon himfelf as running rifks of more forts than one.

WHATEVER is bought for the king, is fold to him at one third lefs than its real worth. The corn of the inhabitants,—all buildings erected for him,— ftores, and expeditions of every fort. You may have a ftorehoufe built for 20,000 francs, ready money; * if you pay in paper, the price is 10,000 crowns—and upon a matter of this kind, there never is any difpute.

ALL payments however are made in this paper money. 'Twas once thought it never would have gone

* A franc or livre is 10d. ¼ Englifh.

out of the ifland; but now not only this goes, but the piaftres alfo, and never to return; the colony would elfe be in want of every thing.

Of all the places to which it trades, the only one that is indifpenfably neceffary at prefent to its exiftance, is Madagafcar, for flaves and cattle. Thefe iflanders were formerly content with the wretched fufils that were offered them in barter, but they muft now have piaftres, and thofe milled at the edges— All the world is rifing into perfection.

Further, if there is the moft diftant profpect of this ifland being a flourifhing feat of trade, the port muft be cleared out without delay, there being now feven or eight hulks of fhips each forming an ifland, which is every day increafed by the madrepores growing round them.

No perfon fhould be allowed to poffefs lands fituated conveniently for the port, but what fhould pay for them accordingly. Nor fhould any perfon procure for himfelf grants of evtenfive and the fineft lands in the ifland, to fell them again to others. This abufe is exprefsly prohibited by the laws: but the laws here are not put in execution.

The breeding of the beafts of burthen fhould be attended to, and efpecially of affes, fo ufeful in a mountainous country: an afs will carry twice the load that a negroe can ftand under. The black is of a little higher price, but the afs is the ftrongeft and the happieft of the two.

They have made many laws relative to the planting bufinefs. No people in the world know their own intereft better than the inhabitants of the Ifle of France, nor what is beft fuited to the foil they poffefs. There

There are a number of soldiers here who are entirely useless,—these men might have lands allotted for cultivation, and assistance for clearing them, and might marry the free negroes. Were a plan of this kind adopted, in ten years the whole island would turn to profit in one way or another; and we should have an established nursery for sailors and soldiers to serve in India. This idea is so very simple, that I do not at all wonder it has been rejected as contemptible.

I leave to others the proposing of means for alleviating the severities of the bondage of the poor negroes;—some abuses are too enormous to admit of mediation.

If you talk upon the mode of defence proper for this island, a sea officer, will tell you a squadron should be kept here constantly; an engineer would have it fortified; a brigadier is persuaded that a few regiments would best answer the purpose; and the inhabitants think the island will of itself, defend itself. The three first of these objects depend upon the will of the administration and may partly be dispensed with, altho' in some respects necessary. I shall enlarge upon the last, as I wish you to be acquainted with some of the œconomical views of the people here.

I observed, in my tour round the island, that it was almost entirely encircled at some distance from the shore, by a belt of rocks: that in those parts where the belt was not continued, the coast is formed of rocks high and inaccessible. This disposition, so excellent for its defence, could not fail to astonish me; but it is nevertheless certain, the island would be totally inaccessible

inaccessible, but for some clefts in the rocks which afford a passage; of these I counted eleven. They are formed by the currents of the river.

In the securing of these passes then, consists the defence of the island from without—some of them might be shut up by means of floating chains, and others by batteries raised upon the shore.

As that part between the rocks and the shore is navigable for boats, small armed sloops might be used with good effect, when the pass is not within cannon-shot of the coast.

Behind the rocks, the shore is very accessible; the landing being upon a level. These parts however might be rendered impracticable by art, as those of the bays of the South East port are by nature. Nothing need be done but to plant *Mangliers*, a sort of trees which growing far out into the sea form forests absolutely impenetrable. This expedient is so very easy, that nobody has yet thought of it.

If in those parts of the coast where the surf runs high, some of the rocks are found to be accessible, these being no where of much extent, might be defended by raising a wall or line; by keeping chevaux de frise to throw into the water, or by *Raquettes* which will grow in the driest places; (but the *Manglier* will grow if there is ever so little sand;) by trees, prickly shrubs, &c. They have besides, this advantage, they cost but little; and time, the destroyer of every other fortification, increases and strengthens that I am recommending. So much for the defence against the attacks by sea.

I consider this island as a circle, and the rivers flowing from the centre, as so many Radii of it.
The

The shores might be cut either perpendicularly, or with a talus, or raquettes and bambos might be planted upon the sides towards the town, and the opposite shore laid open for three hundred toises. By this means the ground between every two rivulets is rendered a strongly fortified place, and the channel of each rivulet a very dangerous ditch. Every attempt to pass, on whatever side it is made, must be perceived by the inhabitants, who would be enabled thereby to act for their defence accordingly; nor could any enemy arrive at the town but through a thousand difficulties and obstructions. This system of defence might be adopted in all small islands, whose waters constantly flow from the centre to the circumference.

BETWEEN the two wings of the mountains which encompass the town and the port, there is need but of little fortification, except that part towards the sea. Upon the isle of *Tonneliers* should be built a fort, with batteries placed in a kind of covered ways to enfilade each other. These should be mounted with a number of mortars,—so terrible to shipping. To the right and left as far as the ends of the promontories, the land should be protected by strong and respectable lines. Nature has already done her part towards the defence of the right side,—the river *Latanier* running the length of the whole front.

A deep valley is formed at the back of the town by the mountains, and includes a vast extent of ground, whereon all the inhabitants of the island and their slaves might be assembled. The other side of these mountains is inaccessible, or might be easily made so, at a trifling expence.

THIS place has besides, a peculiar advantage; for in the very highest part of the moun
tain

tain, at the place called *Le Pouce*, there is found a large piece of land, planted with trees, among which run two or three rivulets of very fine fresh water. There is no ascending thither from the town, but by a very intricate path. It has been attempted by force of mines, to make a wide road of communication with the interior part of the island; but the back of the mountains are of so prodigious a height and steepness, that scarce any thing except a negroe or a monkey can scramble over them. Four hundred men in this post, if furnished with provisions, could never be driven from it; and there is space enough for the whole garrison.

If to these natural means of defence, we add those which should be furnished by government,—a squadron, and proper troops, an enemy would have the following obstacles to surmount.

I—He would be obliged to hazard the event of an engagement by sea.

II—Supposing the enemy victorious, our squadron might retard his descent, by making him bear to the windward of the island in the course of the engagement.

III—The difficulties of a disembarkation would remain to be encountered with. The coast can be attacked only at particular points, and no where upon a front of any extent.

IV—The passage over each rivulet would be attended with an engagement to his manifest disadvantage; if by the method I have proposed, the one side of the rivulet should be laid quite open.

V.

V—He muſt form the ſiege of the town on a ſide where there is but little room : muſt ſuſtain the fire from the promontories which command this place ; and open his trenches among rocks.

VI— Should the garriſon be driven out of the town, they might retire to the height abovementioned,—a ſecure retreat, well provided with water, and where they might be conſtantly ſupplied with ſuccours from the interior part of the iſland.

This would be a proper time for me to ſpeak of the defence of the neighbouring iſland of Bourbon; but I am yet a ſtranger to it. I know only that a landing is impracticable ; that it is well peopled, and grows more corn than it can conſume; yet does every one contend that the fate of Bourbon depends upon that of the Iſle of France. Is this, * becauſe the military cheſt is kept here ?

* The author has ſuppreſſed ſome obſervations relative to the Iſle of France, leſt what he propoſed as a means of its defence, might be of advantage to an enemy about to attack it. This ought to have occurred to thoſe who have publiſhed plans and charts of our colonies, of which our enemies have more than once availed themſelves to our diſadvantage. The Dutch will permit no plans of their iſlands to be engraved. Manuſcript ones are given to each Maſter of a veſſel, who at his return delivers them again into the proper office at their admiralty.

End of the First Part.

# A VOYAGE, &c.

## LETTER XIX.

### DEPARTURE FOR FRANCE—ARRIVAL AT BOURBON—HURRICANE.

HAVING obtained permiſſion to return to France, I prepared to embark on board L'Indien, a ſhip of 64 guns.

I gave *Duval*, the ſlave that bore your name his freedom; but lent him to a good man of the country, until he had diſcharged a debt he owed to the adminiſtration. Had he ſpoken French, I would have brought him to Europe. His tears teſtified his regret at parting with me, of which he ſeemed more ſenſible than of the pleaſures of liberty. I propoſed to have bought the freedom of *Cote* alſo, if he would have attached himſelf to my fortune, but he declared there was a girl in the iſland whom he could not part with. The ſituation of the King's ſlaves is very eaſy. Here he found himſelf happy, which was more than I could promiſe he ſhould be if he went with me. I ſhould moſt gladly have brought back my Favourite to his own country, but ſome months before I left the iſland my poor dog was taken from me,—in loſing him I loſt a faithful friend that I frequently regret.

Some days before I departed, I revisited Autouru, the islander of Taïti, who had been brought thus far on his way home from Europe.* On his passage from his own country to France, he was open, gay, and a little of the libertine—on his return, I observed he was reserved and polite,—he had studied the graces. He was enchanted with the Opera at Paris, and imitated the airs and dances he had heard and seen there. He had a watch, upon which he described the hours by the several employments of each,—He shewed the hour of rising, of eating, of going to the opera, of walking, &c. &c.—†This man was very intelligent, and expressed by signs whatsoever he pleased. ‡Although the men of Taïti pass for having had no communication with other nations before the arrival of Monsieur Bougainville, I observed, however, one word in their language and a custom which they have in common with other people; *Mattè*, in the language of Taïti, means to kill. The *Mattè* of Spain, and the *Mat* of Persia bears the same signification.§ They are also used to paint their skins, as was done by many people of the old and new world. They knew what iron is, though they have none of it—they call it *aurou*, and ask for it with eagerness. But all these analogies tend little to the tracing of the ori-

* He was brought from Otaheitie by Monsieur Bougainville in 1769—and staid eleven months in Paris. *T*.

† Aotouru by the accounts of several Englishmen who saw him in France, was very far from the intelligent man described by our author.—*T*.

‡ Aotouru himself told Monsieur Bougainville that an English ship was at Otaheitie, near a twelvemonth before his arrival there—and Monsieur Bougainville as plainly, as illiberally insinuates, that the English introduced the venereal disease among those islanders. *T*.

§ The author might have added the Italian *ammazare*, to *kill*. *T*.

ginal

ginal of a nation. Follies, wants, and evils of human nature appear naturalized among all people. A more certain mode of diftinction is the knowledge of their languages. All nations in Europe eat bread; but the Ruffians call it *Gleba*, the Germans *Broth*, the Latins *Panis*, the inhabitants of lower Britainy, *Bara*.

*Autouru* feemed chagrined at his long ftay in the Ifle of France. He walked, but always alone. I perceived him one day in a profound meditation, looking at a black flave at the door of the prifon, round whofe neck they were rivetting a large chain. It appeared a ftrange fpectacle to him, that a man of his colour fhould be thus treated by white people, who had loaded him with benefits and prefents when at Paris. But he knew not, that by their paffions, men are carried acrofs the feas, and that the morality by which they are influenced in Europe, within the tropics, actuates them no longer.*

I embarked on the 9th of November 1770, many Malayans accompanied me to the fea-fide, and with tears defired my fpeedy return. Thefe good people never lofe the hope of feeing again thofe who have

* To corroborate this opinion of the author's, I beg leave to infert an extract from the hiftory of the conqueft of New Spain, publifhed at Madrid in the year 1632 by Caftillo,— " We bought three fhips of the governor of Cuba,—who propo- " fed that we fhould pay him for them with flaves, which we " were to bring from the fmall iflands between Cuba and Hon- " duras—We rejected this propofal, telling him, that neither " God, nor the King had ordained thefe people, (by nature " free,) to be enflaved."—Caftillo afterwards engaged with Cortes, and accompanied him in his expeditions to Mexico, during which there is no doubt but he got rid of thofe fcruples which occafioned the above recited anfwer to the governor of Cuba. *T.*

done them service. I recognized among them a master carpenter who had bought my books of geometry, although he could scarcely read. He was the only man in the island who would have them.

We were detained in the road eleven days by a calm. The evening of the 20th we set sail, and at three in the afternoon of the 21st anchored in the road of St. Dennis, at Bourbon.

This island is 40 leagues to the leeward of the Isle of France. 'Tis one days sail only to Bourbon, but a month is frequently spent in returning. It appears afar off, like a part of a sphere, with very high mountains, the land of which is cultivated to the height of 800 toises,—They reckon 1600 perpendicular toises to the summit of the three *Salasses*, which are three inaccessible pikes.

The shore here is very steep; the seas roll with a great surf, preventing all but pirogues from approaching the land without being dashed to pieces. At St. Denis a draw-bridge is contrived for the unlading of sloops, which projects more than fourscore feet over the sea, and is sustained by iron chains. At the end of this bridge there is a rope ladder, up which those who would land, must climb. There is this one place only in the whole island, where any body can land, without first jumping into the sea.

As the Indien was to stay here three weeks to lade coffee, several of the passengers proposed passing some days on the island, and even waiting at St. Paul, seven leagues to leeward, 'till the ship should go thither to compleat her cargo.

PROVISIONS

Provisions being short on board, I with the Captain and several officers of other vessels, joined with them in this plan.

The 25th in the afternoon I embarked alone in a little yawl, and notwithstanding the breakers ran very violently, by keeping the boats head to the sea, I disembarked at the bridge. We were an hour and an half making this trip, which was not half a league.

I waited upon the commanding officer. He told me there was no inn at St. Denis, nor in any part of the island, and that strangers lodged with such of the inhabitants as they had concerns with. Night came on and having no traffick here, I prepared to return aboard, when this officer offered me a bed.

I next payed my respects to M. de Cremon, commissaire ordonateur who invited me to his house while I staid on shore. This was the more agreeable to me as I wished to see the volcano of Bourbon, to which I knew M. de Cremon had once made an excursion.

But I did not find an opportunity,—the way is very difficult—few of the inhabitants know it, and the journey would require an absence of seven or eight days.

From the 26th to the 30th the swell was so great that few of the boats used in the harbour came to land. Our Captain availed himself of a fortunate minute to get on board his ship, whither his affairs called him, but the bad weather prevented his relanding.

This breeze, which always comes from the S. W. rifes at 6 in the morning and ends at 10 at night. While I ftaid, it blew with equal violence day and night.

The firft of December the wind fell, but there rofe from the open fea a monftrous gale, which blew upon the fhore with fuch violence that the centinel on the bridge was obliged to quit his poft.

The top of the mountains is covered with clouds, very thick and motionlefs. The wind continued to blow from the S. W. but the fea ran from the W. Three large waves beat fucceffively over each other and appeared along the coaft like three ranges of little hills. From the upper part of them iffued feveral jets déau which fell down again in white furf, and rufhed violently upon the fhore forming an arch, which rolling as it were round itfelf, foamed to a height more than fifty feet perpendicular.

The air was fo heavy that we breathed with difficulty, the fky was dark, clouds of fea-fowls came from the main and took refuge on the land. The birds and animals on fhore feemed difturbed. Even men were feized with an inward horror at feeing a dreadful tempeft in the midft of a calm.

On the morning of the 2d the wind fell entirely, and the fwell increafed—The rolling waves were more numerous and came from a greater diftance. The fhore, beaten by the fea, was covered with a white mofs like fnow, which heaped together like packs of wool. The veffels in the harbour rode very hard at anchor. There was now no doubt but that the hurricane approached. The pirogues which were on the Galet were drawn a great way upon land, and every one haftened to fecure his houfe with cords and ropes.

There

## VOYAGE to the ISLE OF FRANCE. 189

THERE lay at anchor L'Indien, Le Penthievre, L'Alliance, Le Grand Bourbon, Le Gerion, a Gaulette and a little boat. The fhore was lined with people, drawn thither by the fpectacle the fea prefented, and the danger of the fhips.

ABOUT noon the fky loured prodigioufly and the wind began to frefhen from the S. E. We began to fear that it would turn and blow from the W. and run the veffels afhore. From the battery, the fignal was given them to depart, by hoifting the flag, and firing two guns with fhot in them. Immediately they cut their cables and fet fail. The Penthievre not able to fhip her boat, left it behind. L'Indien being anchored farther at fea, went before the wind with her four principal fails. The reft got out as faft as they could.. Some blacks who were on board a fhallop took refuge on board the L'Amitie. The little boat and the Gaulette were already in the rolling waves, in which they were every now and then loft to the eye; they feemed fearful of putting to fea, but at length, they alfo hoifted fail, exciting uneafinefs and prayers for their fafety, in all who beheld them. At two hours end the whole of this fleet difappeared in the N, W. being invelop'd in a gloomy horizon.

ABOUT 3 in the afternoon the hurricane announced itfelf by a moft tremendous noife; the wind blew from all quarters fucceffively. The fea—beaten— and agitated to the greateft degree—threw upon the land, clouds of foam, fand, fhells and ftones. Some boats refitting at fifty paces from the water-fide were buried under the furge. The wind carried away a fheet of lead from the roof of the church, and the colonade from the governors houfe. The hurricane lafted all night and till 3 in the morning.

ON

On the 6th, the two firſt ſhips that returned to anchor were the little boat and the Gaulette; they brought a letter from the Penthievre which had loſt her top-gallant-maſt. Themſelves had met with no accident—The loweſt ſtations are often the leaſt liable to misfortune.

The 8th, the Gerion appeared—ſhe had been driven ſo near the Iſle of France that ſhe put into the harbour; where ſhe learnt that the Garronne Pink, foundered while at anchor.

By about the 18th we had tidings of all the ſhips, except the Amitié and the Indien. The ſize and ſtrength of the Indien ſeemed to ſecure her againſt all events, and we did not doubt but that ſhe would continue her voyage to the Cape of Good Hope, there, take in proviſions, and go from thence to France. Beſides I knew this to be the Captain's intention.

The 19th in the morning, a ſignal was made that a ſhip was in ſight; it was the Normande, Pink; ſhe paſſed by St. Denis, and anchored at St. Paul. She came from the Iſle of France and was going to the Cape for proviſions. This opportunity was too favourable a one to be neglected by me and an officer with me. Monſieur and Madamoiſelle Cremon provided us with beds and linen for the voyage, we got horſes and guides to go to St. Paul, and were accompanied thither by a relation of Monſieur Cremon.

My effects being yet on board the Indien, I was deſtitute of every thing except linen, which I had brought on ſhore with me.

We ſet out on the 20th at eleven in the morning, we had ſeven leagues to go. The Pink was to ſail in the evening, and therefore having no time to loſe, we took leave of our hoſts. Our

Our horſes began forthwith to climb the mountain of St. Denis, by zig-zag paths, paved with ſharp ſtones. They were very ſtrong, and ſure footed, and, according to the cuſtom of the country, they were unſhod.

At two leagues and a half from St. Denis we found under ſome citron trees at the brink of a rivulet, a dinner, which M. de Cremon had cauſed to be provided for us.

After dinner, we deſcended and came to the *Grand Chaloupe*. 'Tis a frightful valley formed by two mountains that are very ſteep. We walked part of the way which the rain had rendered dangerous, and at the bottom we found ourſelves between the two mountains, in the ſtrangeſt ſolitude I had ever ſeen; we were in a manner between two walls, the heavens only being over our heads: we croſſed the rivulet and came at length to the ſhore oppoſite to the *Chaloupe*: at the bottom of this abyſs, there reigns an eternal calm, however the winds blew on the mountains.

At two leagues from St. Paul we entered into a large plain of ſand extending as far as the town, which is built like St. Denis. There are large lawns encompaſſed with hedges in regular rows, and in the middle is the houſe were the family lives. Theſe towns have the air of large villages.

St. Paul is ſituated by the ſide of a great lake of freſh water, of which a port might I apprehend be made.

It was night e'er our arrival there; we were much fatigued, and knew neither where to lodge, nor where to get bread, there being no baker at St. Paul.

My

My firſt care was to ſpeak with the Captain of the Normande whom I luckily found on ſhore. He told us he would not venture to take us on board without an order from the Governor of the Iſle of France, who was then at St. Denis, and that he ſhould not fail till next morning.

I immediately wrote to the Governor and to Madamoiſelle Cremon. I gave my two letters to a black, promiſing to reward him if he returned by eight o'clock next morning. It was then ten at night and he had fourteen leagues to travel on foot.

I found out my comrades, who were ſupping at the ſtore keepers. They lodged us in a houſe belonging to the King, unfurniſhed, except with chairs, of which we made beds. We were up betimes. At nine o'clock the anſwers to my letters were brought by a black whom my meſſenger had ſent in his room. What was our aſtoniſhment when we read that the Governor had left the maſter to his diſcretion.

At laſt after many negotiations and after having given him bills of payment for our paſſage he agreed to take us, and the departure of the ſhip was deferred till next day.

The following account is all I could collect relative to Bourbon. It is well known that the firſt inhabitants were pirates, who cohabited with negroe women from Madagaſcar. They fixed here firſt about the year 1657. The India company had alſo at Bourbon a factory, and a governor who lived with them in great circumſpection. The Viceroy of *Goa* came one day to anchor in the road of St. Denis and was to dine with the Governor. He had ſcarcely

ſet

set his foot on shore before a pirate ship of fifty guns anchored along side his vessel and took her. The Captain landed forthwith, and demanded to dine at the Governor's. He seated himself at table between him, and the Portugueze Viceroy, to whom he declared, that he was his prisoner. Wine and good cheer having put the seaman in good humour, Monsieur Desforges (the Governor) asked him at how much he rated the Viceroy's ransom. " I must have (said the Pirate) a thousand piasters." That's too little (said Monsieur Desforges,) for a brave fellow like you, to receive from a great Lord like him,— ask enough, or ask nothing." " Well, well, then I ask nothing, (replied the generous Corsair)—let him be free."

The Viceroy reimbarked instantly, and set sail, happy at having escaped on such good terms. This piece of service of the Governor was recompensed shortly after by the court of Portugal, who presented his son with the order of Christ.

The Pirate afterwards settled on the island, and was hanged, a considerable time after an amnesty had been published in favour of his companions, and in which he had failed to get himself included. This injustice was the work of a * *Conseiller*, who was desirous of appropriating his spoils to his own use. But this last villain, a little while after, came to nearly as wretched an end, although the justice of men did not reach him.

It is not long, since the last of these pirates whose name was *Adam*, died, aged 104 years.

* In the French courts of judicature, the judges are called *Conseillers* (Counsellors), and the Barristers, are called *Avocats* Advocates. *T.*

WHEN more peaceable occupations had softened their manners, there remained among them a spirit only of independance and of liberty, which corrected itself still more in the society of many worthy people who established in Bourbon for the purpose of cultivation. Sixty thousand blacks are reckoned to live in Bourbon and only five thousand inhabitants. This island is thrice as populous as the Isle of France, on which it depends for its export traffick. It is also much better cultivated, having produced twenty thousand quintals of corn and as much of coffee, besides rice and other provisions for home consumption. Herds of oxen are not scarce there. The King pays * fifteen livres per Cwt. of corn, and the inhabitants sell † a quintal of coffee for forty-five livres in piastres, and seventy livres in paper.

THE principal place in Bourbon is St. Denis, the residence of the governor and council. Nothing worth remark is to be seen here except a redoubt built of stone, but situated too far from the sea,—a battery before the governor's house, and the drawbridge before-mentioned. Near the town is a large plain called Le Champ de Lorraine.

THE soil seemed to be more sandy at Bourbon than at the Isle of France: it is mixed at some distance from land, with the same kind of small pebbles with which the sea shore is covered,—a proof that the sea has withdrawn itself, or that the island is risen out of the ocean. This I think might be the case, if we may judge from the mountains, which are full of chasms, and very rugged and broken in their interior parts. When we speculate upon nature, opposite opinions always pre-

* About thirteen shillings sterling.
† A quintal is equal to a cwt. English.

sent

sent themselves with a nearly equal appearance of probability.—The same effects frequently result from different causes. This observation might be extended very far, and should induce us to be very moderate in our decisions.

A man of eighty years of age assured me that he had been one of those who took possession of the Isle of France when the Dutch abandoned it. Twelve Frenchmen were detached for that purpose, who landed in the morning, and in the afternoon of the same day, an English ship anchored there, for the same purpose.

The manners of the first inhabitants of Bourbon were very simple, the greater number of the houses were not made to shut,—a lock was a curiosity. Some people even put their money in a tortoise-shell over their door. They dressed in blue cloth, went bare-footed, and lived upon rice and coffee; they imported but little from Europe, content to live without luxury so they lived without want. They joined to this moderation the virtues which ever attend it: good faith in commerce, and generosity in their proceedings. As soon as a stranger appeared, the inhabitants came to him, and as a stranger offered him their houses.

The last war in the Indies has made a change in their manners. The volunteers of Bourbon distinguished themselves in it by their bravery; but the stuffs of Asia and the military distinctions of France, thereby got footing in their island. The children, richer than their parents require to be treated with more consideration. They have now no enjoyment of an unnoticed good-fortune, but seek in Europe, pleasures and honours, in exchange for domestic happiness, and the quiet of a country life. The attention of the fathers being chiefly fixed upon their sons, they send them to France, from whence they seldom return. Hence it is, that in this island there are more than five hundred marriageable girls, who are likely to die without husbands.

We went on board the Normande on the 21st in the evening. We found a case of wines, of liquors, coffee, &c. which Monsieur and Mademoiselle Cremon had caused to be put on board for our use. We were received at their house with the hospitality of the ancient inhabitants of Bourbon, and the politeness of Parisians,

I am, &c.

Bourbon, *December* 21, 1770.

## LETTER XX.

### DEPARTURE FROM BOURBON, ARRIVAL AT THE CAPE.

WE left the bay of St. Paul at ten o'clock at night. The sea here is calmer, and the anchorage safer than at St. Denis, the road of which is spoiled by a vast number of anchors left there by ships. Their cables cut presently. Yet the seamen prefer St. Denis.

When the wind blows into the bay of St. Paul, there is no getting out of it, and if a vessel should run on shore, she must certainly be lost; the sea breaking upon a very high sand.

On the 23d we lost sight of Bourbon. The services we had received from Monsieur and Mademoiselle de Cremon while we staid, the fair winds, a good table, and the company of Monsieur de Rosbos our captain condoled us for our disappointment in not finding the Indienne.

WE pitied the passengers on board of her, who had to undergo at once, very bad weather, and want of provisions.

They reckon ninety leagues from Bourbon to the Cape. On the 6th of January 1771, in the morning we saw Point Natal ten leagues a head of us. In three days we hoped to be on board the Indienne. We went before the wind all the way till Monday. It fell calm in the evening, and was fultry hot. At midnight it light'ned prodigiously, and the horizon was every where covered with large and heavy black clouds. The sea shone with the fishes which played round our ship.

At three in the morning a contrary wind blew from the W. with such violence that it obliged us to make for the Cape under our mizen. The tempest drove on board of us a little bird like a titmouse. The coming of land birds on board of ships is always a sign of bad weather, as it proves that the violence of the storm extends far over the land.

On the third day of the storm we perceived that our mizen-mast was sprung four feet above the yard—we reefed the sails, strengthened the mast with ropes and splints of wood, and stood for the Cape under a mainsail.

The sea was tremendous and hid the horizon from us. We were much surprized to see within cannon-shot a Dutch vessel steering as we did. It was impossible to speak with her; the fifth day the wind abated. The mizen-mast was examined, and found absolutely broken through. This accident caused us to redouble our efforts to reach the Cape.

The bad weather occasioned us to lose way, which the calm now prevented our recovering.

On

ON the twelfth we again saw the Dutch ship, and spoke to her. She very warily came up to us with her matches alight, and her guns run out: she came from Batavia, and was going to the Cape.

AT length on the sixteenth of January we saw the Cape, over our starboard quarter. We beat about all night. On the seventeenth in the morning a violent gale blew. The air was darkened with a thick fog, which totally hid the land. We were near missing the entrance of the bay when we perceived in a part which cleared up for a moment, a corner of the table mountain. We directly loughed up, and about noon found ourselves near the coast, which is very high. It is entirely bare of trees; the higher part rises to a point, formed by the declivities of parallel rocks; it resembles the walls of an old fortification with their talus.

WE came under the land. At night we found ourselves behind the lion mountain, which at a distance appears like a lion couchant. The head is formed by a great rock, and detached from the body, which is composed of the ridges of different hills. From the head of the lion, they give signals to ships.

HERE the wind failed us, being sheltered from it by the lion. We were forced, in order to enter the bay, to pass between the island of Roben, which we saw before us on our left, and a neck of land called the point, which is found at the foot of the lion. We were within two cannon-shot, and our impatience redoubled. From hence we could perceive the ships in the road, and the Indienne could not be the least remarkable among them.

At laſt the tide making, we ſaw, from the tops, twelve veſſels ſucceſſively appear, which were lying at anchor. But none of them had French colours. It was the Dutch fleet.

We caſt anchor at the mouth of the bay. At three in the afternoon, the Commandant of the bay came on board, and aſſured us that the Indienne had not appeared.

At the bottom of the bay we ſaw the table mountain, which is the higeſt land on this coaſt. Its top is level, and ſteep on all ſides, like an altar: the city is at the foot of it, upon the edge of the bay. There frequently gathers upon the table, a thick fog, heaped up as it were, and white as ſnow. When this happens, the Dutch ſay, the cloth is laid.

The Commandant of the bay hoiſts his flag, as a ſignal for the veſſels to be upon their guard, and a prohibition for the ſloops to put to ſea. From this cloth deſcend whirlwinds mingled with fog like long flakes of wool. The earth is covered with clouds of ſand, and ſhips are often forced to ſet ſail. This gale ſeldom riſes in this ſeaſon but at about ten in the morning, and laſts till evening. Sailors are very fond of the land at the Cape, but are afraid of the road, which is moſt dangerous from April to September.

In 1722 the whole India fleet periſhed at anchor, except two ſhips. Since that time no Dutch ſhip is allowed to anchor there after the ſixth of March. They go to Falſe-bay, where they are under ſhelter.

An attempt was made to have formed the road into a harbour with only one opening, by joining the point *aupendus* to the iſle of Roben; but it did not ſucceed.

I hoped to have landed that evening, but was prevented by a breeze from off the land.

EARLY in the morning the Normande anchored nearer to the town.—It is compofed of white ftones in ftrait rows, which at a diftance look like houfes built with cards.

AT fun rife, three fhallops very prettily painted came on board us. They were fent by the town's-people, who invited us to land and lodge among them. I went on board a fhallop of a German's, who affured me that for my money I fhould be well accommodated at Monfieur Nedling's.

IN our way acrofs the road, I reflected upon the fingular fituation I was in; to find myfelf, without clothes, money, or acquaintance, among Hollanders, at the very extremity of Africa. But my reflections were interrupted by a fpectacle quite new to me. We paffed by a number of fea-calves, lying at their eafe upon floats of fea-weed, like the long horns with which fhepherds call their flocks together: Penguins fwam quietly within reach of our oars; fea fowls came and perched upon the fhallop, and on my landing upon the fand I even faw two pelicans at play with a large maftiff, and taking his head into their great beak.

I conceived a good opinion of a land, in which hofpitality and good will fhewed themfelves fo confpicuoufly even among the brute creation.

CAPE OF GOOD-HOPE, *January* 10, 1771.

## LETTER XXI.

### Of the CAPE, our excursion to CONSTANCE and the TABLE MOUNTAIN.

THE streets at the Cape are very strait, some of them are watered with canals and most of them planted with chesnut trees. It was very pleasing to see them covered with leaves in the month of January. The front of the houses were shaded with their foliage, and at the two sides of the doors were seats of brick or turf, on many of which sat ladies with clear and ruddy complexions. I was rejoiced, at once more seeing the countenances and the architecture of Europeans.

I walked through some part of the place, with my guide, to Madame Nedling's, a fat Dutchwoman, who was very sprightly. She was drinking tea among seven or eight officers of the fleet, who were smoaking their pipes. She shewed me a very neat apartment and assured me that every thing in her house was at my service.

WHEN a man has seen one Dutch town he has seen them all: 'tis the same here,—the order of each house is alike. The custom of Madame Nedling's was this, there was always company in the parlour, and a table covered with peaches, melons, apricots, raisins, pears, cheese, fresh butter, wine, pipes and tobacco.

and tobacco. At eight o'clock tea and coffee is ready for breakfaſt. At noon they have game and fiſh in plenty for dinner—at four they drink coffee and tea, at eight they have a ſupper as plentiful as their dinner,—Theſe good people are eating from morning till night.

The expence of boarding in this manner, was formerly no more than half a piaſtre, or fifty French ſols (a trifle more than two ſhillings) per day, but ſome French officers of the marine, in order to diſtinguiſh themſelves from other nations, raiſed the price to a piaſtre, which is now common'y paid.

This price is enormous, when we conſider the great plenty of proviſions;—it is true, that more elegance is to be found here than in our beſt taverns. The ſervants of the houſe are at your command; you may invite whom you pleaſe, and may paſs ſome days at your landlord's country-houſe, and have the uſe of his carriage, without any additional expence.

After dinner I went to ſee Monſieur Tolbac, the Governor, a man of eighty years of age, whoſe merit procured him this government fifty years ago. He invited me to dinner the next day. I had apprized him of my ſituation, of which he ſeemed very ſenſible.

I then walked in the Company's garden; it is divided into four quarters, and watered by a rivulet. Each quarter is bordered by a row of cheſnut-trees, twenty feet high. Theſe pallifadoes ſhelter the plants from the wind, which always blows hard; they have even had the precaution to defend the young trees of the avenues, by a ſcreen of reeds.

I SAW

I saw in this garden the plants of Asia and Africa, but particularly the trees of Europe, covered with fruits at a season when I had never before seen leaves on them.

I recollected that an Officer in the King's service, named the Viscount du Chaila, had at my leaving the Isle of France, given me a letter for Monsieur du Berg, Secretary of the Council. This letter was in my pocket, having had no time to put it among my other papers on board the Indienne, I therefore waited on Monsieur de Berg, and delivered it to him.

He received me very cordially, and as he made me an offer of his purse, I made use of his credit for such things as I absolutely wanted. I asked him if I could not procure a passage on board an India ship, six of which were then going away, and the other six were to go in the beginning of March.

He assured me it was impossible,—that the Dutch India Company had absolutely forbidden it. Indeed the Governor had told me as much, I was therefore reduced to the necessity of staying at the Cape till some other opportunity offered of getting away.

An unforeseen accident had brought me thither, and I hoped for another that should carry me away again.

However, the society of a good tempered and happy set of people, added to the plenty of every sort of provisions, made my confinement very supportable.

Monsieur de Berg's son invited me to go to Constance, a famous plantation of vineyards, situated

about

about four leagues off. We slept at his country-house, behind the table-mountain, at two short leagues distance from the town. We walked thither through a beautiful avenue of chesnut-trees. We saw there—vineyards, ripe for vintage—orchards, chesnut-groves, and a very great abundance of fruits and vegetables.

The next day we continued our route to Constance; it is a little hill, rising to the north (which is here the side of the sun at noon). On our approach, we passed through a wood of silver trees. (*Arbres d'Argent*;) They resemble the pine-tree, have a leaf like the willow, and are covered with a white down, which is very shining.

This forest seemed to be all of silver. When the wind blew them about and the sun shone, each leaf glittered like a plate of metal. We walked through these groves, so rich and so delightful, in order to look at the vines, which though less splendid in appearance, are of far greater utility.

A broad avenue of old chesnut-trees conducted us to the vineyard of Constance. Over the front of the house we saw a vile painting of a strapping girl, and ugly enough, reclining on a pillar. I took it for a Dutch allegorical figure of chastity: but they told me it was the portrait of a Madam Constantia, daughter of a Governor of the Cape. He caused this house to be built with deep ditches round it like a fortification. He proposed to raise it a story or two higher, but was prevented by orders from Europe.

We found the master of the house smoking his pipe in his night-gown. He carried us into his cellar, and made us taste his wine. It was in little casks called *alverames*, containing about ninety pints, ranged

ranged very regularly under ground. There were thirty of them. This vineyard, in common years, produces two hundred. He fells the red wine at thirty-five piaftres per alverame, and the white for thirty. The eftate is his own, conditionally, that he fhall referve fome wine yearly for the Company, who pay him for it. This he told us himfelf.

Having tafted his wine, we went into his vineyard. The tafte of the mufcadine grapes was perfectly like that of the wine. The vines are not upon efpalieres, and the grapes are but a little way from the ground. They let them ripen till the fruit is about half preferved by the fun. We tafted another fort of raifins, which are very fweet, but not mufcadine. They make a wine of them which is of an extravagant price, but is a very fine cordial.

The Conftance wine, derives its quality from the particular nature of the foil. They have planted the fame ftocks, and treated them in the fame manner at a place called Lower-Conftance, a quarter of a league from hence but they have degenerated; as I perceived when I tafted them. The price, as well as the tafte is very inferior, it being fold for twelve piaftres the *alverame*; there are fome knaves at the Cape, who fometimes are too fharp for ftrangers in this particular.

Near the vineyard is a garden of immenfe extent, I faw in it, moft of our fruit-trees, in hedges and efpaliers, loaded with fruit. They are rather inferior to ours, except the grape, which I prefer. The olives here are not pleafant.

When we returned from our walk, we found a plentiful breakfaft; our landlady overwhelmed us
with

with kindnefs; fhe defcended from a French refugee*, and feemed in raptures at the fight of one of her countrymen. Her hufband and fhe fhewed me a large hollow chefnut-tree, before the door of the houfe 'in which they fometimes dined. Their union was like that of *Baucis* and *Philemon*, nor were they lefs happy,—except that the hufband had the gout, and the wife cried when any body fpoke of France.

From Conftance to the Cape you travel through an uncultivated plain, covered with fhrubs and plants. We ftopped at Neuhafen, one of the Company's gardens; 'tis laid out as thofe in the town are, but is more fertile. All this part, is not expofed to the wind, like the territory of the Cape where fo much duft is blown up, that moft of the houfes have double fafhes to the windows, to fecure them. In the evening we arrived at the town.

Some days after, my landlord, Monfieur Nedling, invited me to his country-houfe, near that of Monfieur de Berg. We fet out in his voiture, *(whether coach or cart does not appear)* drawn by fix horfes. We paffed many days there in the moft delightful tranquillity. The ground was ftrewed with peaches, pears, and oranges, which nobody gathered; the walks were fhaded with moft beautiful trees. I meafured a chefnut-tree, which was eleven feet in circumference; it is faid to be the moft ancient tree in the whole country.

The 3d of February my hoft propofed to fome Hollanders, to go upon Tableberg, a fteep moun-

* The Abbé de la Caille fays, that the French tongue was no longer fpoken among the defcendants of the Refugees,—except by the few then alive, who were the immediate children of thofe who left France, between the years 1680, and 1690. T.

tain, at whose foot, the town appears to stand. I was of the party. We set out at two o'clock in the morning, on foot. The moon shone very bright. We left on our right a rivulet, which runs from the mountain, and directed our course to an opening in the middle, and which appeared from the town like a chasm in an old wall. On our way we heard some wolves howl, and fired several guns to disperse them. The way is rugged to the foot of the mountain, but from thence upwards, is much more so. The seeming apertute in the table, is an oblique separation, of more than musquet-shot wide at its lower entrance; above, it is not more than two toises. This cavity is like a very steep stair-case, filled with sand and loose pieces of rocks. We climbed it, having to the right and left, precipices two hundred feet high. Great massy pieces of stone project, and are ready to roll down.—The water drops from the cracks of the rocks, and nourishes a variety of aromatic plants. We heard during this excursion, the howlings of bavians, a sort of large monkeys, resembling bears.

AFTER three days and a half's fatigue, we reached the top of the table. The sun rose over the sea, and its rays enlightened on our right-hand, the steep summits of the tiger, and of four other chains of mountains, the most distant of which seemed the highest. On our left, and a little behind us, we saw, as upon a plan, the Isle of Penguins, then Constance, False-Bay, and the Lion-Mountain: before us was the Isle of Roben. The town was at our feet. We distinguished even the smallest streets of it. The vast squares of the Company's garden, with its avenues of chesnuts, and its lofty espaliers, appeared but as a parterre, with borders of box; the citadel as a little pentagon, the size of one's hand, and the India ships, as walnut-shells. I felt a kind

of

of pride at the thoughts of my elevated station, 'till I saw eagles hovering above me, so high, that they were nearly out of sight.

AFTER all, it would have been impossible to have thought, but with contempt of such trifling objects, and especially of men who appeared to us like ants, if we had not felt the same wants as ever. We were cold and hungry. A fire was kindled, and we breakfasted. After breakfast, our Dutchmen hoisted a cloth at the end of a stick, as a signal of our arrival: but in about half an hour they took it down, left it should be mistaken for a French flag. The summit of Tableberg, is a plain flat rock, which I take to be about half a league long, and about a quarter broad. 'Tis a species of white quarry, covered here and there, with about an inch or two's depth of black mould, mixed with sand and white gravel. We found some little pools of water, formed by the clouds, which frequently are stopped here.

THE strata of this mountain are parallel; I could find no fosils there. The lower rock is a kind of brown free-stone, which turns to sand if exposed to the air. Some pieces of it resemble pieces of bread, with their crust. Although the soil of the summit has so very little depth, it grows a prodigious number of plants.

I GATHERED six species of the *immortals*, some small myrtles, a filex, which smells like tea, a flower like the imperial, of a fine purple-colour, and many others whose names I did not know. I found there, a plant, whose flower is red, but without smell; by its appearance, one would have thought it a tuberose. Each stalk has two or three leaves turned up together, and holding a little water. The most singular of all, because unlike to any vegetable I had ever seen,—is a flower, round like a rose, of the size of a shilling, and entirely flat. This flower glitters with the utmost brilliancy—It has neither stalk nor leaf—It grows very thick upon the gravel, to which it is held by imperceptible fibres. When taken up into the hand, nothing can be perceived but a slimy substance.

Here are five entire plants, which seem to affect in this configuration, a resemblance to only one part of what is common to other plants. First the Nostoc, which is only a sap, as it were; secondly a chevelu, (a small root or fibre issuing from another root) which grows upon the tops of nettles; thirdly, a lichen, or moss, resembling a leaf; fourthly, the ingulated flower of the table-hill; fifthly, the trufle of Europe, which is a fruit. I might add, the root of the groffe (or groffo) of the isle of France, if it was not an instance by itself.

I am much inclined to believe, that nature has adopted this plan among animals.—I know many, marine ones, especially, which in form resemble the members only of other animals.

In my walk, I reached the extremity of the table, from whence I hailed the appearance of the Atlantic Ocean, for having doubled the Cape of Good Hope, you are no longer in the Indian ocean. I did homage to the memory of Vasco de Gama, who dared first to go round this promontory of tempests. All maritime nations should have combined to erect a statue of him at this place, before which I would most willingly have made a libation of Constance wine, in honour of his heroic perseverance. It is however doubtful, whether Gama was the first who opened a commerce with the Indies

by

by the Cape of Good Hope. Pliny fays, that Hanno went round from the fea of Spain as far as Arabia, as may be feen, fays he further, by the memoirs he has left of that voyage in writing. Cornelius Nepos * declares, he had feen a Captain of a fhip, who flying from the anger of King Lathyrus, went from the Red Sea to Spain. And long before this, even Cælius Antipater, affirmed, that he had known a Spanifh merchant who traded by fea to Æthiopia.

However this be,—the Cape, fo terrible to mariners for its tempeftuous fea, is a vaft mountain,— fituated fixteen leagues from hence; it gives its name to this town, notwithftanding fo far off.——It terminates the moft fouthern part of Africa. In treaties, it is looked upon as a point, beyond which, naval captures are lawful many months after the Princes have been at peace in Europe.

Peace has frequently been feen here on the right, and war on the left hand between flags of the fame nations; but it has been more often feen, that they have maintained a good underftanding in thefe roads, when difcord has reigned in every place elfe through-

* Neco, King of Egypt, fent out fome Phœnicians fhips with orders to go down the Red-Sea, and having gone round thence to the north-fea—to return home through the Pillars of Hercules. —They landed in Africa, fowed corn, waited the harveft, and then again embarked,—they did the like the year fo lowing, and in the courfe of the third year landed in Egypt, having paffed, as directed, between the Herculean columns, and through the Mediterranean fea.—— Herodotus, from whom this account is taken, fays, "On their return they related, what, if others give " credit to, I confefs I cannot, viz. *that*, in their way round " Africa, the fun was on their right-hand." T. *See* Herod. 4: book, *for the account of this expedition, and of another undertaken by command of Xerxes.*

out the two hemispheres. I could not but behold with admiration, this happy shore, which war has never yet made desolate; and which is inhabited by a people, useful to the whole world, from the resources of its œconomy, and the extent of its commerce. The dispositions of men are not entirely dependent upon the climate they live in; nor is this wise and peaceable nation indebted for their manners to the soil of their country. Piracy, and civil wars agitate the Regencies of Algiers, Morocco, and Tripoli; but at the other extremity of Africa, the Dutch have established a settlement blessed with agriculture and concord.

I BEGUILED my walk by these pleasing reflections, so rarely to be made in any other part of the world; but the heat of the sun obliged me to seek for a shelter. There is none but at the entrance of the ravin. Here I found my companions reposing by the side of a spring. As they began to grow tired, they determined upon returning. It was high noon.—We descended, some by sitting down and suffering themselves to slide,—others, upon their hands and knees. The rocks and sand gave way when we trod upon them. The sun was nearly vertical, and the rays reflected from the collateral rocks, made the heat almost insupportable. We frequently quitted the path, and fled to the shade of some point of the rock to take breath. My knees failed; and I had a violent thirst upon me: towards the evening we arrived at the town. Madame Nedling expected us, and had prepared refreshments against our return. We had lemonade, with nutmeg and wine in it. Of this we drank without danger, and went to bed. No excursion had ever proved so entertaining to me, nor was rest ever before so welcome.

- CAPE OF GOOD-HOPE, *Feb.* 6, 1771.

## LETTER XXII.

Qualities of the AIR and SOIL of the CAPE OF GOOD-HOPE.

PLANTS, INSECTS, and ANIMALS.

THE air of the Cape is very healthy. It is refreshed by the south-east winds, which are so cold, even in the midst of summer, that cloth is worn here all the year round. Its latitude is, notwithstanding thirty-three degrees south. But I am persuaded that the south pole is much colder than the north.

THERE are but few disorders incident to the people of the Cape. The scurvy is soon cured, altho' there are no sea turtles. But the small-pox on the other hand, makes most dreadful ravages,—many of the inhabitants are deeply scarred with it. It is reported to have been introduced here by a ship from Denmark. Most of the Hotentots who caught it, died. Since which time, they are reduced to a very small number, and they seldom come down to the town.

THE soil of the Cape is a sandy gravel, mingled with a white earth. I don't know whether precious minerals are a part of its productions. The Dutch

Dutch formerly had gold mines at Lagoa, in the ſtreights of Moſambique, and had alſo a ſettlement there, but were forced to abandon it, on account of the badneſs of the air *.

I have ſeen at the houſe of the Fort-Major, a ſulphureous earth, in which were pieces of wood, reduced to a cinder; alſo true *gypſum*, and black cubes of all ſizes, united as it were by amalgamation, without having loſt their ſhape. Theſe laſt are believed to be iron ore.

I saw no tree peculiar to the country but the tree of gold, and tree of ſilver, the wood of which is only fit to burn. The former differs from the latter in nothing but the colour of its leaf, which is yellow. There are ſaid to be foreſts of theſe within land; but in this part, the ground is covered with a variety of flowering, and other ſhrubs. This confirms my opinion, that they flouriſh only in a temperate air, their calice being formed to imbibe no more than a moderate heat.

Among the plants which ſeemed moſt worthy of notice; excluſive of thoſe already mentioned, are, a red flower, which reſembles a tufted butterfly, with legs, four wings, and a tail. A ſpecies of hyacinth, with a long ſtalk, all the flowers of which are formed at the top, like the buds of the *imperial:* another bulbous flower, growing in the marſhes; it is like a large red tulip, in the center of which is a multitude of ſmall flowers.

A shrub, whoſe flower reſembles a large artichoak, of a fleſh colour. Another common ſhrub, of which

* Bad indeed is that air which will drive a Dutchman from a gold mine. *T.*

they make beautiful hedges: It bears clusters of papilionaceous flowers of a rose-colour. They are succeeded by leguminous grains.

I BROUGHT some of them to plant in France, which stood the winter in 1771, and vegetated in the King's garden in 1772.

AMONG the insects I have seen here, is a beautiful red grashopper, speckled with black; some very fine butterflies, and another very singular insect;— 'tis a little brown scarabæus, and runs very fast; when attempted to be taken, it emits with noise a wind, followed by a little smoak; if the finger is touched by this vapour, a brown stain ensues, which lasts some days. He repeats this operation many times successively. The inhabitants call it the cannonier.

THE Humming-Bird is not uncommon here. I saw one of the size of a walnut, of a changeable green colour on the belly. It had a collar of red feathers, which shone upon his stomach like rubies; its wings were brown, like a sparrow's, and appeared upon his beautiful plumage like a surtout. His beak was black, of a good length, and being curved, was of a proper shape to seek for honey in the bosom of flowers. It had a long and taper tongue. It lived several days. I saw it eat flies, and drink sugared water. But as it was attempting to bathe in the cup set for that purpose, its feathers adhered together, and the same night the musquitos devoured it.

I HAVE seen some birds of the colour of fire, with a belly and head like black velvet; they become brown in the winter. Some of them change colour thrice a year. There is also a bird of Paradise, but not so beautiful as those I saw in Asia. I did not see one of these alive. The *Gara'ner's Friend*, and a kind of *Tarins* are frequently found in gardens. I wished to have taken a *Gard'ner's Friend* to Europe,— it would have been of great service there. I observed it to be constantly employed in catching caterpillars, and hooking them upon the thorns on the bushes.

HERE are eagles, and another bird very near of the same species. It is called the *Secretary*, having round its neck a row of long quills, fit for writing with. It has this particularity, that it cannot stand upright on its legs, which are long, and covered with scales. It lives upon serpents only. The length of its claws renders it very capable of seizing them, and this ruff of feathers round its neck, protects it from their bites. This bird also ought to be naturalized amongst us. The ostrich is very common here; they offered me young ones at a crown each. I have eaten of their eggs, which are far inferior to those of pullets. The *Casuar* is found here, and is covered with coarse hair instead of feathers. There is a prodigious number of sea birds, of the names and natures of which, I am entirely ignorant. The eggs laid by penguins are thought much of, but I did not think them extraordinary. They have this singular quality, that the white being boiled, continues always transparent.

THE sea abounds in fish, which I thought better than that of the Islands, but inferior to that of Europe. We find on the shore some shells, the paper-nautilus, the medusa's-head, some *lepas*, and very beautiful lithophytes, which when arranged upon paper, represent trees, brown, saffron, and purple. They are sold to travellers. I saw a fish here, of the size and shape of the blade of a flemish knife.

It

## VOYAGE to the ISLE OF FRANCE. 217

It was filvered over and marked naturally on each fide with the impreffion of two fingers; here are fea-calves, whales, fea-cows, cod, and a great variety of other common fifh, of which I fhall not fpeak, my obfervations having been but few, and my knowledge of ichthyology, but flight.

THERE is very common here, a fpecies of mountain turtle, with yellow fhells, marked with black; they are fit for no ufe whatever. There are porcupines, and marmots, which differ from ours in form; ftags and deer are in plenty, as alfo wild affes, zebras, &c. An Englifh engineer, fome years ago killed here a giraffe, or cameleopard, an animal fixteen feet high, that browzes on the leaves of trees.

THE *lavian*, is a large monkey, made like a bear. The nature of the monkey feems to have an analogy with that of every clafs of animals. I remember to have feen a fapajou, which had the head and mane of a lion. That of Madagafcar, called maki, refembles a leveret, and the orang-outang is like a man.

EVERY day fhewed me fome animals unknown in Europe,—they feem to have taken refuge in thofe parts of the globe leaft frequented by men, whofe neighbourhood is always fatal to them. The fame may be faid of the plants, the fpecies of which are the moft various, the lefs cultivated the ground. M. de Tolbac informed me, that he had fent to Monfieur Linnæus of Sweden, fome plants from the Cape, fo different from plants known in Europe, that this great Naturalift wrote to him : " *You have conferred* " *upon me the greateft pleafure ; but you have thrown* " *my whole fyftem into diforder.*"

THE

The horses of the Cape are good, and the asses beautiful. The oxen have a large swelling or excrescence on their necks, formed of fat, and some small vessels interspersed. At first sight, this excrescence seems monstrous; but one may soon perceive that it is a reservoir; with which nature, for its support, has furnished this animal, destined to live in the scorching plains of Africa. In the dry season, the beast grows thin, and the swelling diminishes; but recovers itself, and the wen is recruited with supplies when it feeds on green herbs. Other animals under this climate, have the same advantages. The camel has a bunch, the dromedary has two, in the form of a saddle. The sheep has a large tail, made en capuchon, or poake, which is but a hump of suet, of several pounds weight.

They have taught the oxen here to run almost with the carts they are harnessed to.

Beef and mutton are so plentiful, that the heads and feet are thrown away; which draws the wolves of a night into the very town. I frequently hear them howling in the environs. Pliny observes, that the European lions found in Romania, are more active and stronger than those of Afric, and the wolves of Africa and Egypt, he adds, are but small, and not very strong. In fact, the wolves of the Cape are much less dangerous than ours. I might add, that this superiority extends even to the men of our continent. We have more spirit and courage than the Asiatics and Negroes; but methinks it would be a commendation more worthy of us, could it be said, we surpassed them in justice, benevolence, and the other social virtues.

The

The tiger is more dangerous than the wolf; he is cunning as a cat, but wants courage. The dogs attack him fearlesly.

It is not the same with the lion.—As soon as they hear his roar, terror seizes them. If they see him, they stand, but will not approach him. The hunters shoot him with guns of a large bore *. I have handled

* Our author not having mentioned the elephant,—which is commonly found and frequently hunted at the Cape,—I will insert an abstract from the Abbé de la Caille, which I hope will be pleasing to the reader.———" The hunters always seek for the ele-
" phant in the neighbourhood of rivers—and attack him in the
" following manner: Three cavaliers well mounted go out toge-
" ther—two of them remain at a proper distance in the plain, and
" the third waits the coming of the beast to quench his thirst at
" the river,—of which the third cavalier gives notice by a signal
" to his companions,—and then pierces him with a stroke of a
" launce, while drinking.——The animal, enraged at the wound,
" pursues the cavalier, who retires to the plain. One of his
" companions hastens to his aid, and attacking the elephant,
" wounds him a second time. The beast forgetting his first assail-
" ant, pursues the last.—The third cavalier then advances, and
" wounds him also.—— The creature now disregards the second,
" in like manner as he did the first—and follows the third, upon
" whom he seems desirous of wreaking his fury———In the mean
" time he loses blood very fast, and not the less for the violence of
" his rage,—and he sometimes dies exhausted before his first ene-
" my returns to the charge—this, however, is not usually the
" case, and he is then again attacked by the first man, and so on
" by the second and third—till he expires."——I have here described the chase only of the elephant—The inhabitants have many ways of taking him alive,—sometimes by a female put in a park, fenced in for the purpose, and sometimes in toils, of which ther are various kinds.

The Abbé then relates a tragical event which happened while he was at the Cape:——" Three brothers, who had been long used to this exercise, were about to return to Holland, but determined to add one more to their many triumphs.—The first brother pierced the beast and escaped;—the second wounded him, but in flying, his horses fore-feet sunk into a mole-hill—and could not recover before the elephant came up.——The furious beast handled one of them, but few, except peasants of the country can use them.

Lions are not found within sixty leagues of the Cape; this animal inhabits the forests within land; his roaring, at a distance, sounds like the grumbling of distant thunder. He seldom attacks man,—he neither seeks, nor avoids him; but if wounded by a hunter, he will select that man among all the rest, and spring upon him with an implacable fury. The Company allow privileges and rewards for the encouragement of lion hunting.

I was told the following circumstance by the Governor, M. Berg, the Fort-major, and the principal inhabitants, who vouched the truth of it:

At about sixty leagues from the Cape, in the uncultivated lands, there is found a prodigious quantity of small Cabris, (goats). I saw some of them in the Company's menageries; they have two small horns on their heads; their hair is fallow coloured spotted with white. These creatures feed in such vast numbers, that those who go first in the route they take, devour all the pasture, and become very fat, insomuch that their followers, finding no food, grow

beast seized the cavalier with his trunk, tore him from his horse, and whirled him upon the ground,—he then took up the horse also with his trunk, and threw him several yards into the air,——this done, he returned to the poor man, who lay unable to rise from the earth, and having again seized him, cast him with all his might into the air and held out his teeth to catch him as he came down—the unhappy wretch falling from a prodigious height, upon one of the teeth, it pierced him through the body and he lay there impaled. The savage beast persisted in holding him for some time in this condition, and seemed to exult over him, by advancing him towards his companions, who though they saw his distress, and heard the agonizing cries he uttered, were unable to assist him. I.

very

very lean. Thus they continue their march in vast herds, until stopped by some chain of mountains; they then turn back, and those in the rear, finding in their turn fresh herbage, recover their good plight, while those who were leaders before, lose their flesh, and become lean. Attempts have been made to form them into herds, but they cannot be tamed sufficiently for that purpose. These innumerable armies are constantly followed by troops of lions and tigers, as if nature in creating the former, had decreed a certain subsistance to the latter. It is scarcely to be doubted, from what was declared to me by the above men, that there are lions innumerable in the interior parts of Africa: the account of the Hollanders tallies with history in this respect. Polybius says, that being in Africa with Scipio, he saw several lions placed on crosses, to deter others from approaching the villages. Pompey, according to Pliny, did at one time turn six hundred lions into the amphitheatre, among which there were three hundred and fifteen males. There seems to be a physical cause in the natural system for Africa's being the practical residence of the brute creation. It is to be presumed, that want of water has prevented the increase of the human species, and their forming themselves into great nations here, as they have done in Asia. Vast in extent as this coast is, the rivers are but few, and these small. The animals of Africa can feed a long time without water. I have observed on board of ships, that the African sheep drink but once a week, altho' their provender is dried herbs.

The Dutch have establishments for 300 leagues along the coast, and for 150 upon the straits of Mosambique; they have scarce any at above 50 leagues within land. It is pretended that this colony can put under arms four or five thousand white men, but it would

would be difficult to get them together. Their numbers would be very soon increased, if the free exercise of religion were permitted. Holland perhaps, upon its own account, fears the aggrandizing of this colony, preferable in every respect to the mother country. The air is pure and temperate; all manner of provisions abound; a quintal of corn costs there no more than one hundred sous, ten pounds of mutton and twelve sous. A legre of wine, containing two hogsheads and a half, for one hundred and fifty livres *. They exact considerable duties upon these articles when sold to strangers; but an inhabitant buys at a much cheaper rate.

Other articles of the trade of this country, are the skins of sheep, oxen, sea-calves, and tigers; aloes, salt provisions, butter, dry fruits, and all sorts of eatables ‡. They have tried in vain to grow coffee and sugar, the vegetables of Asia will not thrive here. The chesnut-tree grows very fast, but being very soft, is not fit for buildings. Firs do not thrive.

* About Six Pounds Ten Shillings sterling.

‡ In 1771, the Dutch East-India ships homeward bound, being at the Cape and not freigted, took on board in bulk, some corn, (the produce of the country) and brought it to Holland. The wheat is a beautiful berry, thin skinned, white, quite dry, and clean, and in weight exceeds the best English or Zealand, as 140 to 132.——The rye is superior to any of Northern growth.——My information of its proportional weight, is not so accurate, as that of the wheat; but it was sold at ten or twelve per cent. above the best rye of Prussia.——The barley is thin, and much inferior to our Norfolk.——'Tis more like the Zealand barley.—— The Dutch incline to cultivate this new branch of trade, which promises much benefit.—They sell it in small lots at public auction. In 1774, the wheat sold at two hundred and thirty guilders, which is about sixty-four shillings a quarter, Winchester————The heat of the climate at the Cape so effectually dries the grain, that it may be brought in bulk, though the voyage is so long a one, without apprehension of danger from its effervescing. T.

The

The pine rises to a moderate height. This country might from its situation, have been the mart for the commerce of Asia; but the north of Europe monopolizes all maritime affairs. The harbour is by no means safe, and the entrance of it always dangerous. I have seen at this season, which is the finest of the year, many vessels forced to hoist sail and go to sea. After all, the people should be thankful to Providence, for having given them every requisite, to supply the real wants of Europeans, without having added those things that serve only to gratify their passions.

*Cape of Good-Hope, Feb.* 10, 1771.

## LETTER XXIII.

### SLAVES, HOTTENTOTS, HOLLANDERS.

THE plenty of this country difuses itself even amongthe slaves. They have bread and greens at discretion. A sheep is allowed weekly for two negroes. They do not work on Sundays. They lay upon beds with matrasses and coverlids. Both men and women are clad with warm clothes. I speak on this subject from experience, having been told by several blacks that their French masters had sold them to the Dutch by way of punishing them, but, that in fact, they had thereby done them a service. A slave costs as much again here as in the Isle of France. Man is therefore doubly valuable in this place. The situation of these negroes would be preferable to that of the peasants of Europe, if there were any compensation for the loss of liberty.

The good treatment they meet with, has a great influence upon their behaviour; their zeal, activity, and fidelity, are amazingly great. Yet these are the very same islanders of Madagascar, who are so inattentive to their master when in our colonies.

The Dutch bring slaves from Batavia also. They are Malays a nation of Asia, very populous; but little known in Europe. Their language and customs are peculiar to themselves. They are more ugly than

than negroes, and refemble them in feature. Their ftature is lower, their colour *d'ur noin cendré*, * their hair long, but thin. Thefe Malays are fubject to the moft violent paffions.

The Hottentots are the natural inhabitants of the place, they are free—They are not robbers—they do not fell their children, nor do they attempt to enflave each other. Among them adultery is punifhed with death—the culprit is ftoned. Some of them let themfelves as houfhold fervants for a piaftre a year, and ferve the inhabitants with fo much affection as to hazard their lives for them. They are conftantly armed with a demi-lance or dart.

The government at the Cape feem to make a point of protecting the Hottentots. When they lodge a complaint againft an European, they are favourably heard: it being prefumed that the party known to have the feweft defires and feweft wants is the moft likely to be in the right.

I have feen many of them come into the town, driving waggons drawn by eight pairs of oxen. They have whips of a great length which they ufe with both hands. The driver, from his feat, flogs with equal addrefs the fore or wheel horfes.

The Hottentots are a paftoral people, and are all upon a footing; but in each village, they chufe from

* I do not know how to tranflate thefe words, unlefs by thofe made ufe of by a young Midfhipman, who was caft away with Captain Barton in the Litchfield during the laft war. In defcribing the complexion of the Emperor of Morocco; the young failor obferves, that they do his Imperial Majefty's complexion manifeft injuftice, who fay that he is a negroe, for that he is only of a dark chefnut complexion, *T*.

among themselves, two men to whom they give the title of Captain or Corporal, these manage their commercial business with the company. They sell their flocks very cheap,—so cheap even, as three or four sheep for a roll of tobacco. Although they have such numbers of cattle, they generally wait till they die by accident or old age before they eat them.

Those whom I saw had a sheep-skin over their shoulders, with a cap and belt of the same stuff. They shewed me how they lay to rest, which was naked at their length upon the ground, and their cloak serving to cover them.

They are not so black as the negroes—like them hovever they have a flat nose, wide mouth and thick lips. Their hair is shorter and more curly, like wool*. I have observed a something very particular in their speech,—every word is preceded by a clack of the tongue, the reason without doubt of their being called the Choccoquas; which name they have in some old maps by Monsieur de L'Isle. One would really think they continually repeated choccoq.

As to the apron of the Hottentot women, 'tis a story which every body affirmed to be false; 'tis drawn from Kolben's voyage, which is full of such ridiculous fables.

* Many different accounts are given of the stature of the Hottentots—Our author is silent on this subject—The A. de la Caille says he measured one, who was 6 feet 7 inches ¾ high, and corpulent in proportion—this man came into the town with many others, and does not appear to have been selected for his extraordinary stature—we may therefore suppose these people to be in general larger than Europeans. Had he been remarkable for his size, the Abbè would doubtless have spoken of him accordingly. *T.—The French foot is to that of England as* 1000 *to* 1068.

Pliny's

Pliny's remark is more to be depended on, that animals are lefs fagacious, in proportion as their blood is thicker. The ftrongeft animals by his account have the thickeft blood, and the more cunning the thinneft. I have myfelf remarked that on bleeding a Negroe, his blood curdled very quickly. To this caufe I fhould readily attribute the fuperiority of white people over the blacks.

Besides their flaves, and the Hottentots, the Dutch retain indented fervants. They are Europeans, to whom the Company advance money, and whom the inhabitants take home with them, having firft paid the government their difburfements.

They are chiefly employd to fuperintend houfhold matters. They are diligent enough at firft, but good living makes them idle.

The people at the Cape do not game, nor do they vifit much. The women look after their fervants and houfes, the furniture of which is always in the niceft order. The hufband manages the bufinefs abroad. In the evening the family affembles, they walk, and take the air as foon as the breeze is at an end. The fame bufinefs and the fame pleafures are repeated each day.

The utmoft harmony prevails among relations. My hoftefs's brother was a Peafant of the Cape who came feventy leagues from hence. This man hardly ever fpoke, and was continually fitting and fmoaking his pipe. He had a little boy with him of ten years old who conftantly ftood by him. The father put his hand to his cheek and careffed him without opening his lips; the child, as filent as the father preffed his great hands in his own, looking up to him with eyes expreffive of the moft filial tendernefs. This little boy wore the country habit,—he had a coufin in the houfe of his own age who was very genteely dreffed; thefe children ufed to walk out together with the greateft intimacy. The little citizen did not look with contempt upon the Peafant,—he was his coufin.

Madamoifelle Berg, though but fixteen years old, manages without affiftance a very refpectable family. She receives ftrangers,—attends to the fervants,—and maintains the moft perfect order in the houfe, and with a countenance always at eafe. Her youth,—her beauty—her accomplifhments, and character gain her the efteem of every body : yet I never obferved her pay any regard to the compliments addreffed to her. I told her one day, fhe had a great many friends; "I have one great one," faid fhe,—that is my *father*.

It was this magiftrates delight when he came home from bufinefs to feat himfelf among his children. They jumped round his neck,—the little ones embraced his knees ; they appealed to him in their little difputes—while the eldeft daughter, excufing fome —approving others—and fmiling upon all, redoubled the joy of the truly parental heart of her father. Methought I faw the Antiope of Idomeneus.

This people, content with domeftic happinefs, the fure confequence of a virtuous life, do not yet feek after it, in romances, or upon the theatre. There are no public exhibitions at the Cape, nor are they wifhed for. In his own houfe each man views the moft pleafing—the moft affecting of all fpectacles, fervants, happy:—children, well brought up:—and wives, faithful and affectionate. Thefe are the delights which the tales of fiction cannot afford. They

are

are a penſive ſet of people, who chuſe rather to feel —than to converſe, or to argue. Perhaps the want of ſubjeƈt, is the cauſe of their taciturnity. But of what conſequence is the mind's being vacant, ſo the heart be full, and aƈtuated by the tender emotions of nature, unexcited by artifice, or unconſtrained by unreaſonable decorum and unnatural reſerve.

As ſoon as the girls of the Cape are in love, they avow it ingenuouſly. They call it a natural ſentiment, a gentle paſſion, upon which depends the felicity of their lives, and compenſates the pains and danger of their becoming mothers; but they themſelves—will themſelves make choice of the man to whom they make their vows of conſtancy.

They make no myſtery of their paſſion;—as they feel it—ſo they expreſs it. Are you beloved? You are accepted, entertained, and publickly diſtinguiſhed. I was a witneſs to a parting ſcene between Mademoiſelle Nedling and her lover. In tears, and with ſighs ſhe prepared the preſents which were to be the pledges of her affeƈtion—in which employment ſhe neither ſought for witneſſes, not did ſhe ſhun them.

This mutual inclination is generally produƈtive of a happy marriage. The young men are equally frank in their proceedings. They return from Europe to fulfil their engagements; and bring with them the merit of the dangers through which they have paſſed, and of a love unaltered by an abſence from its objeƈt. Eſteem and affeƈtion are united, and maintain or life that deſire of pleaſing which elſewhere ſhews itſelf more towards other objeƈts, than towards that to which it is properly due.

As happily as they live here, blessed with simplicity of manners, and a country so rich and plentiful — yet, every thing which comes from Holland is received among them with transport. Their houses are papered with views of Amsterdam, of its public places, and environs. They look upon Holland as their country, and even strangers in their service speak of it in that light only. I asked a Swede in the company's service, how long the fleet would be on its return to Holland — "we shall be at least three months, replied he, before we get home."

They have a handsome church, wherein divine service is performed with great decency. I don't know whether the Dutch think religion an addition to their happiness, but there are men here whose ancestors have sacrificed every thing that they held most dear to the exercise of it. I speak of the French Refugees. At some leagues distance from the Cape they have a settlement, which is called La Petite Rochelle. They are quite in raptures at the sight of a Frenchman, they bring him home to their houses, and present him to their wives and children, as a man, happy, in having seen the country of their forefathers, and in a prospect of returning to it again. France is continually the subject of discourse, they admire it, they praise it; yet do they complain of it, as of a mother whose severity towards them had been too extreme. Thus do they break in upon their enjoyment of the country they now live in — by lamenting their exile from that which they have never seen.

The Magistrates of the Cape especially the Governor are treated with the utmost deference. His house is distinguished only from others, by the sentinel at the door, and by the custom of sounding a trumpet when he sits down to dinner. This piece of respect

respect is annexed to his place. No other pomp attends his person. He goes out without retinue, and is easy of access. His house stands by the side of a canal shaded with chesnut trees planted before his door. In it, are the pictures of Ruyter, Van Trump, and some other illustrious persons of Holland. It is small and plain, and suited to the very few people who have affairs to solicit with him; but the governor himself is so respected and beloved, that the inhabitants do not even pass his door without shewing some mark or other of their respect.

He gives no public entertainments, but his purse is always open for the service of worthy and indigent people. They need pay no court to him. If they seek for justice, they obtain it of the council;—if succour, this he takes upon himself, as a duty,—injustice only can be solicited, but it constantly meets with the merited success.

He has much time upon his hands, which he employs for the preservation of peace and concord, being persuaded of their tendency to the well being of all societies. He is not of opinion that the power of the chief magistrate depends upon discord, and dissension among individuals. I have heard him say that the best policy was to deal justly and honestly with every man. He frequently invites strangers to his table. Although more than eighty years old his conversation is lively; he is acquainted with most of our works of genius, and is fond of them. Of all the Frenchmen he has seen, he chiefly regrets the Abbé de la Caille, for whom he built an Observatory here. He esteemed him for his learning, his modesty, his disinterestedness, and social qualities. I know nothing more of this learned man than by his works;

but in mentioning the respect paid by strangers to his memory, I feel a satisfaction at finishing my account of this estimable body of people with their eulogium of one of my countrymen*.

# LETTER XXIV.

## CONTINUATION of my JOURNAL to the CAPE.

I WAS invited by Monsieur Serrurier, first minister of the church to go to see the library. The building is handsome and fit for the purpose. I could not help remarking a number of books of theology, which have never yet occasioned any controversies, and indeed the Dutch never look in them. At the end of the company's garden, there is a menagerie containing a great number of birds. The pelicans that I saw upon the beach on my arrival had been boarders in this place; but they were driven away, because they eat the young ducks. In the day time they went into the road to seek for fish, and at night returned to roost on shore.

* The late Dr. Goldsmith frequently spoke of this chapter, as a master-piece of good sense, and well directed attention and sensibility. *T.*

# VOYAGE to the ISLE OF FRANCE. 233

On the 10th of February a fignal was made that a French ſhip appeared: 'twas the *Alliance,* that had been forced from Bourbon by the hurricane. She had loſt her mizen maſt in the ſtorm. She could give us no tidings of the Indienne. Having taken in proviſions, ſhe continued her voyage to America without repairing the loſs of her maſt. The Dutch have a number of them in ſtore, which they keep buried in the ſand: but they ſell them very dear. A new mizen maſt for the *Normande* coſt 1000 crowns.

On the 11th the *Digue,* a pink of the King's that left the Iſle of France a month before, came into the Cape to get proviſions. I knew the captain, Monſieur le Fér. He told me he ſhould anchor here for a few days only; and then ſteer for the weſtward. Deſpairing to ſee the *Indienne* and my effects any more, and thinking this opportunity a favourable one, I reſolved to embrace it.

I acquainted Monſieur Berg, and Monſieur Tolbac, with my determination; both of them again offered me their purſes. Supping one evening at the governor's and talking of Conſtance wine, Monſieur de Tolbac aſked me if I would not carry ſome of it with me to Europe. I very naturally anſwered that the diſorder in my finances by the accident that had happened, prevented my making a little purchaſe of it, which I meant to have done, as a Preſent for a lady to whom I had a particular attachmen. He told me he would relieve me from this embarraſſment by giving me if I thought proper an alverame of red or of white wine, or of both. I anſwered him that one would ſuffice, and that I would preſent it in his name to the perſon for whom I intended it. "*No, ſaid he, 'tis to you I give it, as a remembrance of me, and all the acknomledgement I aſk, is, that you will*
                                                          *write*

*write to me when you get to France."* He sent me the wine next morning. Monsieur Berg to whom I had frequently mentioned the civilities I had received from Monsieur and Mademoiselle Cremon, told me, he would take upon himself the making my acknowledgements to them, and that he would send them as from me two dozen of Constance wine.

In a situation, where I was in absolute want of every thing, I was not a little happy at meeting among strangers, with men of so obliging and benevolent a disposition.

I agreed with the captain of the *Digue*, to pay him 600 livres for my passage to France. He was to sail in a few days. I was very cautious of using Monsieur de Berg's credit. I made up one single suit of clothes only and a little linen. This was the whole equipage of an officer returning from the East-Indies. I had not only lost all my effects, but found myself 140 livres in debt.

I had but just settled my affairs here, when the *African* came to an anchor at the Cape; she came to take in provisions; she left the Isle of France about the middle of January, and brought the following account of the *Indienne*.

This unfortunate vessel had lost all her masts in the storm; and after having kept the sea for more than a month returned at length to the Isle of France in so bad a condition, that she had been since disarmed. The seas she shipp'd had spoilt part of her cargo, and had filled the powder room with water, insomuch that the trunks of the passengers were afloat. Monsieur Moncherat, a good man I knew there, had looked

over

over my luggage, and wrote me word, that but little damage had been done to any thing, except to the things in my cabbin.

They told us of an odd accident that happened on board the *Indienne*. Among the transports who were sent to the Isle of France, there was one of a good family, named \*\*\*. He had assassinated his brother-in-law in France. On the voyage he quarrelled with the supercargo, and when they landed, he stabbed him without ceremony, and broke the blade of his sword in his body. He fled to the woods, but was found, and committed to prison. He was tried and condemned, but while under sentence of death, there was a hole made in the wall of his prison, through which he escaped.

This event happened two months before my departure.

During the tempest the Indienne was exposed to, the mizen mast was carried away, and fell into the sea. While they were hastily cutting away the rigging, they saw in the middle of the waves, a sailor hanging by the round of the floationg mast. He cried out, save me, save me, I am \*\*\*. It was really this unhappy wretch. At the return of the *Indienne* to the Isle of France, they suffered him once more to escape. When Monsieur de Tolbac heard this anecdote, he only said, *He that's born to be hanged will never be drowned.*

They had heard nothing of the *Alliance*, which probably was lost.

It was very fortunate for me, to receive my effects on the eve of my departure, and to be no longer on board

board the *Indienne*, which was likely to be detained some time at the Isle of France.

The *Digue* did not fail till the second of March. I paid all my expences with bills of exchange upon the Treasurer for the Colonies, at six months, by which I lost twenty-two per cent. discount.

I took leave of the Governor, and of Monsieur Berg, who gave me several natural curiosities. I had presented him with some of mine. Mademoiselle Berg, gave me three perroquets from Madagascar; they had grey heads, and were of the size of sparrows. My landlady furnished me with fruits, and weeping, wished me, as did her family, a good voyage.

It was with concern that I left these good people, and their gardens of European fruit-trees, which, though in the month of march, were loaded with fruit. I rejoiced in the thoughts, however, of finding them in blossom in Europe, and of enjoying in one year two summers and no winter : but what far exceeded the delights of a beautiful country and mild season, I was about to revisit my native country, and the friends I left in it.

LET-

# LETTER XXV.

## DEPARTURE FROM THE CAPE.

Description of the Island of Ascension.

THE 2d of March at two in the afternoon, we set sail in company with six of the fleet from Batavia. The other six went fifteen days before. We went out by the second opening of the bay, leaving Roben's Island on the left. We soon out-sailed the Dutch ships. They kept company to the latitude of the *Azores*, where two ships of war waited, to convoy them to Holland.

Mariners reckon the Cape to be a third part of the way from the Isle of France to Europe : another third they call, to the line : and the last, from thence home.

Eight days after our departure, while we were sitting upon deck after dinner, in the most perfect security, we saw a great flame issue from the kitchen-chimney, which rose several yards above deck. Every body ran forward. It was no more than a panic : an awkward cook had thrown some fat upon the hearth. It was mentioned by some of the officers upon this subject, that a few years ago, in a ship

ship called the ———, the fire had catched the mast, and that all the rigging forward being on fire, the officers and crew were in distraction, and came in a tumult to tell the Captain, who coming out of the cabbin, said very coolly, " My good friends, this is " nothing, only bear away, and put before the " wind."

In fact, the flames driven by the wind, ceased when all the sails were burnt. The man thus endowed with sang-froid, was Monsieur de Surville, an officer of great merit in the Company's service.

We had the wind S. W. constantly, and a fine sea, till we got to the Island of Ascension. The 20th of March we were near its latitude, ( 8 deg. S.) but we had taken it too much Eastward. We were obliged to run down the longitude, our intention being to anchor there; and catch some turtle.

The 22d in the morning we had sight of it.— This island is seen ten leagues off, although scarce a league and half over. One can distinguish a pointed hill, called the Green-Mountain. The rest of the island is formed of small black and red hills, and the pieces of rocks near the sea were quite white with the dung of birds.

The nearer you approach, the more horrid the landscape appears. We coasted along shore, in order to anchor in the North-west. At the foot of these black hills, we perceived an appearance like the ruins of an immense city. They were sunken rocks, which have proceeded from an ancient volcano; they are scattered all over the plain, and as far as the sea, in strange shapes. The shore hereabouts is composed of them. Some are formed like

pyramids,

# VOYAGE to the ISLE OF FRANCE.

pyramids, others like grottos; half finished arches, the waves break against which; one while they flow over them, and in running down again, cover them with a kind of table-cloth of foam; sometimes finding flat pieces raised high, and full of holes, they beat against them underneath, and throw up long jets deau of various forms.

THESE black and white shores were almost covered with sea-fowl. A number of frigate-birds hovered about our rigging, where they were taken by the seamen. We anchored in the evening at the entrance of the Great-Bay, I went into the boat with the men who were to catch turtle. The landing-place is at the foot of a mass of rocks, which is seen from the anchorage at the extremity of the bay on the right-side. We got out upon a large sand, which is white, mixed with grains of red, green, and other colours, like that kind of aniseed called *mignonette*. Some paces from hence we found a little grotto, and in it a bottle, in which the ships who touch there put letters. They break the bottle, and having read the letters, put them into another.

WE went forward about fifty paces, taking to the left, behind the rock, to a little plain, where the ground broke to pieces under our feet, as if it had been a covering of snow. I tasted some of it; it was salt, which I thought very strange, there being no appearance of the sea's coming so far.

THEY brought up wood, the kettle, and the sail of the boat, upon which our men lay down in expectation of night. 'Tis about eight in the evening only that the turtles come on shore. The people were laying here at their ease, when one of them jumping up; called out in a great fright, *a dead man, here's a dead a dead man.*—The matter was, by a little crofs, placed on a fmall hill of fand, we perceived that fome perfon had been buried there. The man had lain down upon this place without thinking; but not one of them would ftay here a moment after this difcovery; and we were obliged to comply with their whim; and remove about a hundred yards farther.

The moon rifing, began to diffufe a light over this folitude, which, unlike agreeable views, that are rendered more ftriking by the light of the moon, appeared but the more horrible, and difmal. We were at the foot of the black-hill, at the top of which we could fee a large crofs, put up, as we fuppofed by fome failors who had been there. Before us, the plain was covered with rocks, from which rofe an infinite number of points about the height of a man.

The moon caufed a fparkling on the top of thefe points which were whitened by the dung of the birds that had refted there. Thefe white heads upon black bodies, the one of which were upright, the other floping, appeared like ghofts wandering over the tombs. The moft profound filence reigned in this difmal region; a filence, now and then only interrupted and rendered more horrid, by the roaring of the fea on the beach, or the cry of a ftray frigate-bird frighted at the fight of men.

We were at the edge of the bay waiting for turtles. We lay upon our bellies as ftill as poffible, this animal flying at the leaft noife. At laft we faw three come out of the water; they appeared like black clouds, creeping along the fand. We ran to the firft, but our impatience occafioned our lofing it. She went down the cliff again, and fwam away. The fecond was advanced farther, and could not efcape not efcape, but was thrown upon its back. In the courfe of the night, and in the fame valley, we turned above fifty, fome of which weighed above 5 cwt;

The fhore was dug in holes, where they had lain fo many even as three hundred eggs, and had covered them with fand, in which they were to be hatched by the fun.

The failors killed a turtle and made foup of it; after which, I laid me down in the grotto, where the letters are depofited, that I might enjoy the fhelter of the rock, the diftant noife of the fea, and the foftnefs of the fand. I ordered a failor to fetch me my wrapping-gown; but he dared not go by himfelf paft the place, where the man had been buried. No beings, certainly, can be at once fo intrepid, and fo daftardly fuperftitious as feamen are.

I flept very comfortably. On awaking, I found a fcorpion and fome crabs at the entrance of my cave. I faw no other herbs here, than a fpecies of milk-thiftle, or celandine. Its juice was milky, and very bitter. The herbage, and the animals were worthy of the country they were in.

I went up the fide of one of the hills, the earth of which refounded under my feet. It was a perfect cinder, of a reddifh colour, and falt. From hence, perhaps, proceeds the little covering of falt upon the fhore, where we fpent the night. A booby came and pitched on the ground a little way from me. I prefented the end of my cane to him, and he took it in his bill, without attempting to fly away.

R            These

These birds will suffer a man to take them up in his hand, as will every other species unused to the society of mankind; a proof, this, that there is a sort of good-will and confidence, natural to all animals towards those creatures, which they do not think mischievous *. Birds have no fear of oxen.

Our sailors killed a number of frigate-birds, for the sake of a piece of fat that is round their necks. They think it specific in the gout, because this bird is so swift: but nature, which has annexed this evil to our intemperance, has not placed the remedy for it in our cruelty.

About ten in the morning, the shallop came to fetch the turtles on board. As the surf ran high, she anchored at a distance, and drew them on board with a rope.

This business employed us all day. In the evening, the turtles that were not worth taking, were thrown into the sea again. When they have been long on their backs, their eyes grow red as a cherry, and stand out of their head. There were many on the shore that had been left by other ships, to die in this situation,—a negligence that was unpardonable.

* Possibly a good argument might be deduced from this circumstance, in refutation of the opinion of Hobbes, that if in a supposed state of nature, an human being, should accidentally meet for the first time, another of the species, they would mutually run away. *T.*

## LETTER XXVI.

CONJECTURES upon the Antiquity of the Isle of Ascension, the Isle of France, the Cape of Good-Hope, and of Europe.

WHILE our sailors were getting the turtles on board, I sat me down in a chasm or cavern of the rocks, with which the country is covered: a variety of reflections suggested themselves to my imagination at the sight of so horrible a disorder.

If these, thought I, were the ruins of a great city, what memoirs should we have had of those, by whom it was built, and by whom it was destroyed? In Europe there is not a single column.

Wherefore do we, so well informed in other matters, remain in total ignorance of whence we came, and where we are? All the learned are agreed as to the origin and the duration of Babylon, now desolate and uninhabited; but by no means concur in opinion concerning the nature and antiquity of the globe, the country of all mankind. Some maintain it to have been produced by fire, and others, by water; these, by the laws of motion; and others by those of chrystallization. The people of the western world believe it to be six thousand years old only,—while those of the East say that it is from all eternity.

It is probable that one fyftem only would be a-dopted, if all the world were like this ifland. Thefe pumice-ftones, thefe hillocks of cinders, and thefe broken rocks, which have bubbled up a kind of metallic drofs, evidently prove it to have been the work of a volcano;—but how many years have elapfed fince the eruption to which it owes its origin?

Methinks, if this had happened a very long time ago, thefe hills of afhes would have loft their pyramidical form, and have been rendered flat by the heavy rains, and the heat of the fun. The angles and out-lines of the rocks would not be fo fharp and pointed,—it being one property of the atmofphere to deftroy the projecting parts of every Body; ftatues of marble carved by the artifts of ancient Greece, by being expofed to the air for a feries of years, no longer retain their original form; but are again reduced to mere fhapelefs blocks.

Might not then a judgment be formed of the antiquity of a Body by the degree of decay it has fuffered, in like manner as the antiquity of a medal is determined by its ruft? Is not an old rock as much a medal of earth, engraved by time?

Moreover, were this ifland very ancient indeed, thefe blocks of ftone upon the furface of the ground, would have e'er now been buried in it, from their own exceffive weight; this effect of a heavy body, though flow, is yet fure. The piles of fhot, and the cannon, ranged upon the floor of an arfenal, in the courfe of a few years bury themfelves therein. The greater part of the monuments of Greece and Italy, have funk deeper than their furbafes—and fome have entirely difappeared.

If

IF then I could know *in how long a time a Body of a known form and weight, would be in burying itself in a foil of a certain known refiftance*, I fhould have an hypothefis, whereby I might difcover what I am in fearch of. The calculation would be eafy, were the data once known: in the mean time there is great reafon to believe this ifland but of a modern date.

I AM partly of the fame opinion, with refpect to the antiquity of the Ifle of France ; but as its piqued mountains are already tabulated on the tops, its rocks a third or fourth part only funk in the earth,—and their angles but a little blunted, I am rather induced to believe it fome ages more ancient than the other.

THE Cape of Good-Hope appears to be of far greater antiquity. The rocks broken from the tops of the mountains are entirely buried in the earth, where they are found by digging. The foot of each mountain has a large and high Talus, formed of the broken pieces of the upper parts. Thefe have been feparated from their original fituation by the continued action of the atmofphere upon them ; in confirmation of this conjecture, they are in far the greateft quantity in thofe parts where the winds are ufed to blow. I particularly noticed this at the table-mountain, the part of which, oppofite to the fouth-eaft wind, has a much more extenfive Talus, than that part next the town.

I HAVE alfo remarked upon the table-mountain, fome ftones ftanding by themfelves, the fize of a tun or large cafk, the angles of which, are blunted. The pieces broken off from them have now no longer the fharp edges they feem formerly to have had ; and are of no harder confiftence than a white and fmoothly polifhed gravel, like almonds. Thefe ftones are very hard, and in colour and grain, like plates of China, that have been much used.

The decay of these bodies are evidences of their great antiquity. In many places the rock is quite bare, nor is the bed of vegetable earth above two inches deep any where. It cannot then have been many ages since vegetables first grew there, although they are now common.

We cannot, however, form any judgment from hence, because the summit of the mountain being neither of sand nor of porous stone, but of a sort of flint, white, polished, and very hard; the seeds of plants brought hither by the winds, may have remained a long time before they could be able to germinate.

The vegetative bed is much deeper on the plains, but from hence neither, can we decide as to the antiquity of the soil,—for where this bed is of a considerable depth, it may have been increased by the floods from the mountains after hard rains, or have been driven or washed farther off, in parts where it is thin.

If there were in Europe an high mountain standing by itself, with a flat summit as that of the Table, and not covered as that is, with a matter unfit for vegetation, a comparison might be made between the thickness of its vegetative bed, and that of any newly formed land alike insulated, for example, with the crust of earth which covers some of those islands formed in the course of the last century at the mouth of the Loire.

'Till

'Till the contrary is proved by experiment, I will then prefume that Europe is more ancient than the Cape of Good-Hope,—becaufe the fummits of the mountains are not fo fteep,—their fides incline more gradually, and the angular pieces of thofe rocks yet uncovered with earth, are blunted and round.

I do not hereby mean fuch rocks as appear on the fides of mountains, which the fea, torrents, or the falling of rivers have rendered fteep, nor the ftones which the rain has left bare, by wafhing away the earth which covered them; and much lefs, thofe flints in the fields, which the plough covers one year and uncovers the next: but thofe only, which by their weight and fituation, are fubject to the laws of gravity. I faw none of this laft fort in the plains of Ruffia and Poland. Finland is paved with rocks, but of a totally different fhape; 'tis a feries of fmall hills and vallies of folid rock, and may be called a petrified earth. Neverthelefs as fir-trees grow on the tops of thofe hills, it fhould feem that they have been a long time in the air, which has decompofed them.——It appears even that in a climate lefs cold than the one I fpeak of, this diffolution would be very confiderably accelerated; but that the fnow covering the furface for fix months in the year, and the ground being hardened by the froft, the effect of their weight is retarded.

The kind of rocks moft proper for thefe experiments, is fuch as are found in the neigbourhood of Fontainbleau. It is a free-ftone, in huge maffes detached from each other, the edges of all which the hand of time has rounded off. Some of them are half,—fome two thirds buried in the earth, and others lay on the furface in heaps, as if brought thither for the purpose of building.—These last, are probably the summits of mountains, which have not yet entirely disappeared.—Each century, has perhaps, seen them farther and deeper immersed, and two thousand years ago, it is not unlikely, but that they were as lofty mountains as many at this day. The force with which the elements act, and the intrinsic gravity tends to preserve the globular form of the earth. In time, the mountains of Europe will be far less steep than they now are,—in time, the sea will have dissolved the rocks by which its bounds are limited, and upon which it is continually breaking, in like manner as it has already destroyed those once famous ones of Scylla and Charibdis.

BEWILDERED in these reflections,—I took from my pocket a book of ancient history, and opened a place wherein, speaking of some families of Europe, the author says, *so great is their antiquity, that their origin seems lost in the night of time*, as if their ancestors had been born before the sun. In another place, he speaks of the people of the North, as the fabricators of human nature, *Officina Gentium*; " as a torrent of " barbarians, which the North could no longer " contain."

I HAVE lived some time in the North, and have travelled through more than eight hundred leagues of it, but I do not recollect to have seen there one single monument of antiquity. Yet, we see durable traces of all populous nations every where else, and from the lowly steeple in a country village, to the pyramids of Egypt, every land where mankind have inhabited, bears testimony to their industry. The plains of Greece and of Italy are covered with antique ruins, why are they not likewise seen in Russia and Poland

Poland?—becaufe mankind can only increafe according to the growth of the fruits of the earth where they inhabit,—and becaufe the North of Europe lay barren and uncultivated, while the South was covered with harvefts of corn, vineyards, and olive trees. The people of the South, in their abundance, raifed altars to every Good.—Ceres, Pomona, Bacchus, Flora, Pales, the Zephyrs, the Nymphs, were Pleafures, therefore they were Deities.—The Virgins offered pigeons to the God of Love, and garlands to the Graces, praying to Lucina to blefs them with good hufbands, who fhould be faithful and affectionate. Religion was congenial with nature, and, as acknowledgement was in every heart, the earth under this aufpicious fky, was covered with altars. They rofe in every orchard to the Deity of gardens; to Neptune on the fea-fhore, and in every bower to Cupid: The Nayads had their grottos,—the Mufes, porticos,—Minerva, peryftiles—An obelifk to Diana, appeared in every copfe, and the temple of Venus raifed its cupola over the trees of every foreft.

But no fooner was an inhabitant driven from this delightful climate, to feek a new eftablifhment in the North; no fooner had he, with his unfortunate family found himfelf within the frigid zone—Heavens! what could equal the horror which feized him on the approach of winter! The fun fcarcely prefented his red and gloomy difk above the horizon, the winds roaring through the woods, and fplitting the trunks of the fir-tree and the oak,— the fountains congealed, and the courfe of rivers ftayed by the freezing hand of Winter. Deep fnows covering with a fpotlefs robe the meadows, woods, and lakes alike. The plants, the flowers, the fountains,—every thing by which human life can

can receive comfort, or even support—dead. He can scarcely breathe, nor dares he touch any object that presents itself to his eyes—for death is in the air, and every thing he sees, furnishes him with new cause of sorrow. When this unhappy creature hears the cries of his helpless infants, beholds their tears freezing on their livid cheeks, and their arms stretched out to him for the help he has not to afford them, discoloured, and perhaps mortifying.— How horrible must be his ideas of the land he is come into—Can he hope for a posterity from nature, or to reap harvests of grain from fields of adamant.—His hand must tremble at opening a soil replete with death to his inhabitants.— Nothing remains but to participate his misery with his flocks: with them to brouze on the moss and bark of trees, and continue to wander over a land, where a state of repose can be purchased only with life. How then can he think of building?—A den or cavern dug in a rock is his temporary protection from the cold; and if from the bosom of these snows, a monument of any kind should arise—what other can it be than a tomb?

It is probable that the North of Europe was unpeopled till the Southern parts were nearly abandoned. The Greeks, harrassed by their successive tyrants, preferred the sweets of liberty to those of their native climate, which they therefore deserted, and carried with them into Hungary, Bohemia, Poland and Russia, those arts by means of which, man alone, of all animals, can triumph over the elements, and bid defiance to the inclemencies of every climate. From the Morea to Archangel, an extent of five hundred leagues, no language is spoken but the Sclavonic, the words and even letters of which derive from the Greek.

The

THE Northern nations are therefore of Greek defcent,—they, however, again funk into a ftate of barbarifm; but are now once more emerging from it, under the influence of a legiflature more mild than that of former times. Peter the Great, has laid the foundation of their modern grandeur, and in our time, they live under the government of an Emprefs who gives them laws worthy of Areopagus.

## LETTER XXVII.

OBSERVATIONS upon the ISLAND of ASCENSION. DEPARTURE. Arrival in FRANCE.

I WAS totally abforbed in my reflections upon this ifland—Pleafing objects are for our enjoyment, calamitous ones for our reflection. The happy man reafons but feldom—the afflicted mind meditates, and in meditation often finds relief from the evils which deprefs it. So true is it that nature hath made pleafure the univerfal purfuit of man, and when his heart is incapable of it, fhe places its feat in his head.

ALTHOUGH the ifland of Afcenfion may be faid to be without earth and without water, it does not occupy a place upon the globe to no purpofe. The turtle has made choice of this coaft to lay its eggs, which it does for three months in the year. 'Tis a folitary animal that flies frequented fhores. A veffel's anchoring here for twenty four hours will drive them from the bay for feveral days, and if a gun be fired, they will not return in many weeks. The frigate and booby are more familiar, being not fo much experienced; but thefe, upon fhores that are inhabited, keep upon the very fummits of the rocks, and will not fuffer themfelves to be approached. This ifland is their commonwealth,—the primitive manners are retained, and the fpecies multiply; for no tyrant can

take

take up his abode amongst them. Doubtless the common mother of all beings has ordained that barren rocks and sands should be in the ocean, desolate indeed, but protected by the jarring elements, as a refuge and asylum, where the animal world may enjoy what even among mankind are deemed her chiefest blessings, tranquillity and liberty.

FERTILE and pleasant countries are deprived of their natural freedom, which this island still retains. Surrounded by the Atlantic it has escaped that slavery, which is the bane and the disgrace of Africa and America. It is common to all nations, possessed by none, and is frequented by few but English and French ships which stop in their way from India to catch turtle. The Dutch being victualled at the Cape, seldom put in here.

THE air of Ascension is pure—I lay two nights together on the ground without covering; I have seen rain fall from the clouds whose course was stayed by the summit of the green mountain, which however did not appear to be much higher than Montmartre—This stopping of the clouds is occasioned by attraction, which is always more forcible at sea than within land.

IF a sailor is ill of the scurvy while here, they cover him with sand, and he quickly finds his complaint relieved. Although I was very well, I held my legs for some time in this dry bath, and felt for several days after an extraordinary quick circulation of blood, which I could not account for. But I suppose that this sand being composed of calcareous particles, attracts to the skin the humours of the body it incloses; like those absorbent stones

which

which are applied to a sting to extract the venom : it were to be wished that some able physician would make experiments in other disorders, of a remedy which instinct alone has taught to the scorbutic sailor.

We were to pass one more night ashore—At ten in the evening I bathed in a small bay, between the landing place and the main, surrounded with a semi-circular chain of rocks. At the end of this bay the sand is raised to a height of fifteen feet, and runs down to the sea in a slope. There are several rocks at the entrance, but they do not rise above the surface of the water. The sea when much agitated, breaks over them with a prodigious noise,—I was obliged to gripe fast by the rocks, as the billows beat over my head almost every minute.

The 24th in the morning, the bar was very high; the ship hoisted a flag as a signal for us to come off. It was impossible for the boat to land at the usual place; she had been taking in a dozen of turtles that had been reserved, and was then swinging by a grappling iron at half a musqet shot from where we stood. Some of the strongest among the sailors pulled off their clothes, and watching the moment of the surges leaving the shore, carried the luggage and passengers on board—running as fast as they could the whole way.

I told the officer who commanded, that I thought her very sufficiently loaden—twenty persons were on board her, and as many remained on shore—but being desirous of saving the trouble of a second trip; they continued to go on board. In the mean time, a monstrous surge raising up the barge, broke the grappling, and threw her on the shore—eight or ten men up to the middle in the sea expected to be

dashed

dafhed to pieces—Had fhe brought up fideways, fhe had been loft, but luckily fhe was thrown in ftern-foremoft. Two or three waves fucceedingr lifted her almoft upright, by which means fhe fhipped a good deal of water aft—The people on board in their fright jumped into the water, and were near drowning—But at length the united efforts of us all, fet her once more afloat.

On her return for us who remained, fhe narrowly efcaped the like accident, and happy for us that fhe did fo, for we were not hands enough to have got her off—The fhip muft have failed—and we had been left on an ifland whereon we could have found neither provifions, wood, nor water. And yet it is faid there are fome little ponds of frefh water at the foot of the green mountain—and a few goats, who finding no herbage but dog's tooth, are half ftarved. Cocoa trees were planted here, but would not grow.

The South Eaft part of Afcenfion is compofed of lava, and the North Eaft of hillocks of cinders; whence I conclude that the wind was to the S. E. when the volcano rofe from the fea—and that it blew gently, elfe the cinders would have been too much fcattered to have formed the promontories of hills they now compofe further that the internal heat (or combuftible matter) of volcanos is not kindled by the revolutions of the atmofphere, and that the commotions and tempefts of the earth, are independent of thofe of the air.

They fhould feem rather to depend upon the water;—of all the volcanos I have feen or know of, there are none but what are near the fea, or fome great lake—I made this obfervation fome time ago when

I

I was endeavouring to account for the caufe of their—and being confirmed by nature, my opinion is the more likely to be a juft one

We fet fail at five in the evening of the 24th of March. We lived upon turtle for near a month after—They were kept alive all time by laying them fometimes on the back and fometimes on the belly,—and by throwing fea-water over them feveral times a day.

Turtle is very nutritive, but one is foon tired of it—the flefh is very tough, and the eggs but of an indifferent tafte.

We repaffed the line, having calms fometimes, and fometimes ftorms. The currents run northward very perceptibly; they more than once, carried us ten leagues in four and twenly hours, when there was no wind—The 28th of April in lat. 32 N. we faw an eclipfe of the moon at about eleven o'clock at night: we had feveral days of calms; they are faid to be the intervals between the different winds which prevail in thefe latitudes. From 28 to 23 deg. N. the fea was covered with a marine plant, called *grappe de raifin* (clufter of grapes) it was full of fmall crabs and the fry of fifh. This perhaps is a means which nature makes ufe of to people the fhores of iflands with animals, which could not be tranfported thither by any other: the fifh frequenting near the coaft being never found in the main fea.

With great joy we faw the pole ftar again appear above the horizon—and the pleafure was heightened every night that it rofe; the fight of it made my evening walks very agreeable. One night at ten o'clock as I was walking upon the quarter deck, fomebody fpoke in much hafte and feeming fright to
the

the officer who had the watch: he bid the man light a candle, and follow him along the forecaftle. I took the fame way they did, and prefently we were not a little furprized to fee a cloud of thick and black fmoke iffue from the hatchway.—The failors of the watch were laid down very quietly upon one of the fails of the mizen maft, and when we called to them, were feized with terror. Two or three of the moft daring went down the hatchway with a lanthorn, crying out that we fhould all perifh. We looked about for buckets, but could not find even one. Some were for ringing the bell to call up the people, others for working the pump that was aft, to carry water below; every man propofed, but no man attended; the diforder cannot be defcribed.

At length being all ranged with our heads ftooping over the hatchway, we waited our deftiny. The fmoke increafed, and we even faw gleams of flame iffue from the crevices. Prefently however, a voice from below called out, that the fire had only catched fome wood put into the oven to dry.—This moment of inquietude appeared like a century. Hard fate of feamen! In the midft of fine weather, in the midft of the moft perfect fecurity, and in the very hour of return to our native country, one unfortunate accident had well nigh brought upon us the moft dreadful of all deaths.

The 16th—the failors were exercifed in firing at a mark, which was a bottle hung at the end of the yard; the guns were tried: We had five of them. This was done, that we might be prepared, in cafe we were attacked by the *Saltin's*\*—Fortunately we

---

\* There is no Englifh word for *Saltins*—but *Sallee* being about that latitude, I fuppofe the Author means the Rovers of that place. *T.*

met with none. Our small arms were in such bad condition that at the first firing one of them burst near me, and wounded the sailor that held it very dangerously.

The 17th, I perceived at noon day, upon the sea, a long band of a greenish cast, in direction from North to South—It was motionless, and extended near half a league. The vessel passed it at the South end. There was no swell upon it, or near it. The captain as well as the officers agreed that it must be a shoal or flat—it is not marked upon the chart. We were now as high as the Azores.

The 20th of May—we saw an English ship bound to America; they told us we were in 23 deg. longitude, which was 140 leagues farther to the westward than we imagined ourselves.

The 22d of May, in 45 deg. 45 min. N. we thought we saw a rock, over which the sea broke. The weather being calm, they hove out a boat. It was a shelf of surf formed by the bed of the sea—Two hours after, we found a mast furnished with rigging, which appeared as if cut away from an English ship in stress of weather. We took it on board joyfully, for we began to want firewood. and what was worse, provisions;—having made but one meal a day for eight days past.

The sky had for some time been clouded over in the middle of the day, so that we did not know in what latitude we were. The 28th, the wind blew so hard that the vessel could carry none but her lower sails. At eleven in the morning we perceived a small ship before us—we passed to leeward of her. There were seven men upon her deck, pumping with all
their

their might; the water ran out of all the scuppers. We neither of us made much way, and in tacking, sometimes passed so close, that I feared the next wave would have run us foul of each other. The Pilot in his red night cap, called out to us through a speaking trumpet, that he had not been four and twenty hours from Bourdeaux, and was bound to Ireland. We suspected him by his haste, and the bad condition of his vessel to be a smuggler,—it is customary at sea, as well as on land, to form our opinions of strangers by their appearance.

About ten o'clock, the wind subsided; the clouds seperated into two long ranges, between which the sun shone out. All the sails were now set, and men placed upon the main top to look out,—her head was kept to the North East, that we might have the better chance for seeing land before evening.

At four o'clock we saw a small smack, which we hailed, but she did not answer: she was driving before the wind. At five o'clock a man aloft, called out, *land, land, to leeward*—we immediately went upon deck—and many of the people ran up the shrouds, we presently distinguished rocks, that whitened as we approached—they were thought to be the mountains of Penmanmaur. We lay too during the night, and at break of day perceived the coast three leagues a head: but nobody knew what land it was. The wind was scant, and by no means suited to our impatience. At length we saw a boat, and hailing her, was answered, that she had a Pilot on board. Overjoyed at hearing the voice of a Frenchman just come from his native shore—the crew ran with eagerness to the ship's side to see the Pilot come aboard— *What cheer, Brother*, said the Captain, *what land is that?*

*that?* Belleifle, faid the Pilot—"*D'ye think we fhall have a breeze?*"—"*An'it pleafe God mafter, perhaps we may.*"

He had brought with him a large barley loaf, which having been baked in France, we very foon eat up for him.

The calm lafted all day; towards evening it frefhened, and in the morning we were along fide the Ifle of Grois and came to an anchor.

The cuftom-houfe officers came on board; and after them a croud of fifhermen.—We bought fome frefh fifh, determining to eat our laft meal together;—during which, we got up, we fat down again,—but we did not eat,—we could think of nothing, we could look at nothing, but the coaft of France.

The crew were overwhelmed at the thoughts of their return home, with a joy, that fhewed itfelf in the moft extravagant ways—I fpoke to feveral, but could not get an anfwer from one of them—I therefore agreed with a Fifherman to carry me and my baggage on fhore, and having taken a hearty and friendly leave of the Captain, went into the boat, and was foon landed—thanking God for having once more reftored me in fafety to my native country.

## LETTER XXVIII.

### On VOYAGES and VOYAGERS.

IT is customary to try in the beginning of a book to gain the good will of the reader, who very often does not read the preface at all; in my opinion 'tis much better to wait till the end—to the very moment when he is going to form his opinion; then it is impossible for him to escape without paying attention to the Authors excuses—the following are mine.

I have composed this work as well as I could, and nothing has been wanting to give it all the perfection I am capable of giving it—if it is ill executed—it is not therefore my fault; for one should be blamed for doing ill, but when we can do better,

If the style is faulty, I shall be very glad to see its errors pointed out; it shall be my task to correct them. During the ten years I have been absent from my country, I have almost forgotten my own language, and I have observed that it is often of greater use to speak well, than to think, or even to act well. My conjectures and my ideas of nature, are materials which I design for the construction of a considerable edifice; till I am able to elevate which, I submit them to criticism. Just censures are like thaws, which dissolve soft stones, but harden hewn ones. I shall trouble you with one more observation only, which I shall now make

make use of—twas said, "a Saint began with a single stone, what afterwards became a magnificent Abby—he atchieved this miracle by time and patience,—for my part 'tis no-wonder if I lost both the one and the other.

Having said enough of myself, let us go on to more important objects—'Tis rather singular that that there has not been one voyage published by those of our writers who have the greatest fame in literature and philosophy. We have no model of this so interesting species of writing and we shall long want one, since Monsieur de Voltaire, D'Alembert, Buffon, and Rousseau have given us none. Montaign * and Montesquieu have written their travels, but have not published them. It cannot be said that they thought those countries in Europe where they had been, sufficiently known; since they have made so many new observations on even our own manners which are so familiar to us. I believe this species of writing, so little attempted, abounds with difficulties. It is necessary that there should be an almost universal knowledge, a plan well arranged, warmth of style, and truth. One must speak of every thing.

If any subject is omitted, the work is imperfect—If all is said that can be said, one becomes diffuse and uninteresting.

We have notwithstanding some valuable writers of voyages; of whom Addison is in my opinion among the foremost—Unluckily he is not a Frenchman. Chardin is philosophic, but prolix. The Abbè de Choisi

---

* Since the Author wrote this letter, the manuscript of Monsieur Montaign's travels through Italy was found in an old chest, and was published at Paris in the course of last year. T.

saves

saves the reader the irksomness of a sea journal—he is agreeable, but that is all we can say of him. Tournefort describes learnedly the monuments and plants of Greece, but on such a subject as the ruins of Athens a man should write with more feeling. La Hontan speculates, and sometimes bewilders himself in the solitudes of Canada. Lery describes the manners of the Brasilians, as well as his own adventures, with a pleasing simplicity. From these different geniuses might be composed one excellent one—but every man has one peculiar to himself—for instance, the sailor who wrote in his journal that he " passed " by Teneriff at the distance of four leagues, the " inhabitants of which place seemed very affable."

Some Travellers speak on one subject only; this seeks after monuments, statues, inscriptions, medals, &c. If they meet with a man of extraordinary learning, they beg of him to write his name and some sentence in their *album*. Although this custom is a commendable one, I should prefer an enquiry after examples of probity, virtue and greatness of soul of the most eminent men of each place.—Had I written my voyages to the north, the world would have seen therein, the names of Olgorouki, the Palatine Xatorinski, Duval, &c. Remarkable buildings would not have been unnoticed, such as the Arsenal of Berlin, and the Royal Academy of Cadets at Petersburg : As to subjects of antiquity, I confess that they inspire me with none but the most gloomy ideas. A triumphal arch is to me a proof of the weakness of human nature and the uncertainty of its pursuits ; the column,—the statue remains,— but the conqueror to whose honour they were erected, is no more.

I prefer the tendril of a vine to a pyramid, and should with far greater pleasure import to France one nutritive plant, than the silver shield of Scipio.

In the same degree that the arts become naturalized among us—nature herself is estranged—We are even so artificial that we give to objects, merely natural, the appellation of *curiosities*, and seek for proofs of divinity among books, in which (those of revelation apart) but vague reflections and general indications of universal order are to be found. Yet would we shew the ingenuity of an artist, we should rather particularize the several parts of his work, than give a general definition only of it. Nature presents to us relations so very ingenious, intentions so beneficent, and scenes, which though mute, and I might even say imperceptible, are so expressive, that they must influence the most inattentive mind—and excite an exclamation of, *surely there is a* GOD.

The art of describing natural objects is so little known or used, that terms to express them are not yet invented. Attempt but the description of a mountain in such manner that it shall be recognized; when you have spoken of the base, the flanks, and the summit, you have said every thing. But what a variety is discernable in these forms, round, long, flat, hollow—'tis a mass of words without information. The difficulty is the same as to hills and vallies—If a man were to describe a palace, he could do it without being the least embarrassed—'Tis of some of the five orders of architecture—'tis subdivided into surbase, principal story, entablature; and in each of these, from the plinth to the cornish, there is not a single moulding without its proper name.

We

WE need not wonder then at the imperfect accounts travellers give of natural objects—In delineating a country, they tell you of towns, rivers, and mountains,—but the picture is as barren, and conveys as little idea to the imagination, as a mere geographical chart——Of Indoſtan or of Europe, 'tis all one. The phyſiognomy (if the expreſſion may be allowed) is not there. Do they ſpeak of a plant? they give a detail of the flowers, the leaves, the bark, the roots; but its port, its ſemblage,, elegance, or inelegance are not to be defined—The ſimilitude of an object depends upon the harmony, the unity, and connection of its ſeveral parts—for you may have the meaſure and proportion of all the muſcles in a man's body, but you will not therefore have his portrait.

IF travellers, who have treated of nature, are defective in point of expreſſion, they amply make up by the abundance of their conjectures. For a long time I was induced to believe, from the accounts I had read, that men might live in the woods in a ſtate of nature. I did not find one ſingle wild, and unknwon fruit, that was fit to eat in all the Iſle of France; and thoſe I taſted, I did ſo at the hazard of being poiſoned. Some few indeed were of a tolerable taſte, but of theſe 'twould have been hardly poſſible to collect enough for the breakfaſt of a monkey—there are indeed ſeveral noxious roots, that are bulbous and of a ſort called *Nymphea*, *(or Water Lilly)* but even theſe grow under water, where 'tis not likely our man in the ſtate of nature would ſeek for them. At the Cape I expected to have found mankind better ſupplied. I ſaw artichokes of a fine freſh colour growing upon buſhes; but they were ſo crabbed, they were not eatable. In the woods of France and Germany there is no other than the maſt of the beach and the fruit of
the

the chesnut—and these last but a short season. It is affirmed that in the golden age of the Gauls, our ancestors lived upon acorns; but the acorns of our oaks are too astringent, those of the green oak only being digestible. It is also rarely found in France, altho' very commonly in Italy.

The firs in the forests of the north yield a kind of apple, upon which the squirrels feed greedily, but I doubt they are not proper for the food of men. Nature would have dealt but hardly with the sovereign of the animal world, had she spread a plenteous table for every other race of beings, and left him destitute; but that he alone is endued with reason, and a disposition to society, without which the former would be but of little use to to him. From this one observation we may draw the following consequences—that the most stupid peasant is superior to the most intelligent animal—which no art could teach to till, to sow, and reap,—that man is born for society, and incapable of living without it—and that the community owes to each individual that subsistance, which community alone can provide, and without which the individual must perish.

Another fault of travellers—is, their placing happiness any where rather than in their native country. Their descriptions of foreign countries are so entirely agreeable, that they incline one ever after to be out of humour with ones own.

Nature seems in my opinion to have more equally distributed her good things, than we may at first apprehend. I know not whether to prefer a very hot, or a very cold climate. The latter is the more wholsome; moreover the cold is an inconvenience easily

to

to be remedied, whereas the heat, is hardly to be endured, and can never be avoided. For one six months I have seen the landschape about Petersburg perfectly white; for another six months I have seen the Isle of France totally black; add to this the destruction occasioned by the vermin and the hurricanes, and which then shall we chuse? It is true that in India the trees are in leaf all the year round, and bear fruit without being grafted—and that the birds are numerous and beautiful,—but all things considered I give France the preference, especially if the constant spectacles of misery be considered in the estimate—for the sight of one man in a state of wretchedness is sufficient to effectually destroy my happiness. Can one think without horror that Africa, America, and a great part of Asia are in slavery? In Indostan all directions to servants are delivered with a stroke of a rattan; insomuch, that the cane has obtained the title of King of the Indies; even in the boasted country of China, corporal punishments are inflicted for the most trifling offences. Among us,—culprits even, are treated with some degree of consideration as men. How desolate, how rigid soever the northern climates may be deemed—nature in its rudest state will still in some respect present me with a pleasing prospect. I have been witness of very affecting scenes even among the rugged rocks of Finland. I have seen there, summers finer and more serene than those of the tropics, days without night, lakes so covered with swans, ducks, woodcocks, plovers, &c. that one might say they had forsaken all other waters to come hither and build their nests. The sides of the rocks are frequently covered with moss of a shining purple, and the *Kloucva* * with

* A beautiful kind of creeper with a red flower.

its

its flowers of scarlet, and leaves of lively green, having spread abroad a carpet on the ground, meets with the stately fir, and round the dusky pyramid twines its fragrant branches, forming retreats alike adapted to love or to philosophy. In a deep valley, and on the margin of a meadow, stood the mansion of a gentleman of family, where repose was undisturbed, save by the sound of a torrent of water, which the eye saw with pleasure falling and foaming upon the black surface of a neighbouring rock. 'Tis true, that in winter the verdure and the birds disappear together. Wind, snow, hoar frost, and hail envelope and beat upon the house, while chearfulness and hospitality reign within. They will go fifteen leagues to visit each other, and the arrival of a friend proclaims a festival for a week: * they drink the healths of their guests, their ladies, and their great men, to the sound of horns and drums. The old men sit smoaking by the fire and relate the feats of their youth, while the young fellows in their boots, dance to the fife or tabor, round the Finland maid; who in her furred petticoat, appears like Minerva in the midst of the youths of Sparta.

If their manners are uncouth, their hearts are not without sensibility—They talk of love, of pleasure, of Paris; for Paris is the metropolis of the female sex. 'Tis thither that the women of Russia, Poland, and Italy come to learn the art of ruling the men,

* The women are of their parties, and 'tis but just that as they bear their husbands company in the wars, they should preside in their entertainments. Instances of conjugal affection among these people are frequent and extraordinary. The wives of some general officers I have known, have followed their husbands in the field from their first entering into the army. Note of the Author.

with

with ribbands and laces; 'tis there the fair Parisian exerts her power with humour ever gay, and graces ever new, and tyrannizes over her English lover, who throws at her feet, his gold, and harder to part with, his melancholy; while she, from the very bosom of art, laughing prepares, a garland which binds by its pleasures every people of Europe.

OF all cities I should prefer Paris, not for its diversions, but because its inhabitants are a good sort of people, and live in liberty. What are to me its splendid coaches, its Hotels, its crowded streets, its public shews, its banquets, visitings, and friendships as soon dissolved as made. These numerous pleasures are productive of only superficial happiness, and enjoyment. Life ought not to be a mere spectacle. 'Tis in the country only that a man enjoys the genuine feelings of his heart, and the pleasures of society with his wife, his children and friends. A country life is preferable in every respect to living in towns; the air is pure, the prospects enlivening, the walks fine, provisions at hand, and the manners of men, better, because more simple. The lover of liberty depends upon heaven alone: here the miser receives new presents hourly, the warrior gives himself up to the chace, the voluptuary places here his garden, and the philosopher may indulge his meditations without fear of interruption. Of animals, shew me one more useful than the ox, more noble than the horse, or more faithful than the dog.

OF all rural scenes, I prefer those of my own country; not on account of their superior beauty, but because I have been brought up there. In a man's native place there is a secret attraction, a something affecting, which is not the gift of fortune, nor can any other communicate it. Where are the games of our infant days?

days?—days when pleasure abounded without forethought and without alloy? What joy I have experienced at finding a bird's nest!—With what delight have I cherished and caressed a partridge—received the strokes of its bill—and felt under my hand the palpitation of its heart and the fluttering of its wings! Happy the man who revisits the scenes where every thing was beloved, every thing was amiable—the meadow he had ran races in! or the orchard he had ravaged! more happy he, who has never quitted you, paternal roof, sacred asylum! The wanderer returns indeed, but does not find his home;—of his friends, some are dead,—some gone away; his family is dispersed, his protectors——but life is no more than a short voyage; and the age of man like a winter's day. I will not however think upon its troubles, but call to mind the virtues, the good offices, and the constancy of my friends. Perhaps their names and my grateful acknowledgement may continue to live even in these letters—Perhaps they may sometime reach even to you, amiable inhabitants of the Cape! For thee unhappy African, who, on the rocks of Mauritius bewailest thy truly wretched lot; it is not for my feeble hand to alleviate thy griefs, or dry thy tears—but if I have induced thy tyrant master to look upon them, with regret, and upon himself, with remorse as the cause of them—I have nothing more to ask of India—I shall have made my fortune.

PARIS, *January* 1, 1773.

# LETTER XXIX.

## OF TREES.

AMONG the curiosities I have brought home, are some madrepores, which are very common in the seas of India, the Islands in general being encompassed with them. They grow under water, and form forests of several leagues extent, in which fishes swim about, as birds fly in the woods. The madrepores do not bear fruit, nor can they be included in the vegetable system; they are the work of an infinite number of small animals, who unite their efforts for the formation of these plants of the sea. The shrubs which I have sent with the madrepores, are called litophites, and are, as well as the corals, equally the work of small animals. This, which you may look upon as a mere conjecture, is confirmed by microscopical observation. The chymical experiments on this matter are rather uncertain, because the reasonings of chymistry are founded upon the dissolution of the subject. At length, however a conclusion is drawn from the regularity of these works, in favour of the opinion, that they are produced and effected, by beings actuated by a spirit of order and intelligence. After all, a shrub is not more difficult to make than an hexagonal cell of wax, as formed by bees. The dispute subsisted for some time; but all the world is now agreed *.

* All the spunges have the figure of plants, and are branched in so many different ways, that we could hardly believe them to be the work of marine insects,—their texture is so compact, and their fibres so delicate, that it is inconceivable how these animals can lodge in them. BOUGAINVILLE, on Nat. Hist. of Isle de Malouines. T.

But

In my opinion, that every flower is inhabited, I stand entirely alone. * Do not think I mean to adopt the Grecian fancy of the Hamadryads, that every Laurel had its Daphne, and that every one unfortunately killed by a Quoit, is the inhabitant of one sort of tree; or that all who die of self-love should be lodged in the Narcissus.—Could I absolutely confirm the truth of this system, I should not thereby prove the purpose of universal happiness to be advanced.—The legs and arms may be lopped off from the sisters of Phaeton, for a clown to make faggots of.—My inhabitants have no such fears;—but they are wise, and they are ingenious.

I am aware that the support of this opinion, will be more difficult, than of that with respect to the madrepores.—Men interest themselves little about what passes at the bottom of the sea, but 'tis widely different with flowers, which are objects generally known and used, and have a received opinion affixed to every thing relating to them. And yet I cannot see why our plants, which resemble the madrepores in every other respect, should not in their being inhabited also.

Every machine of a natural construction has an internal organization, which tends to a certain effect, by a certain means. For example; in the ear there is a thin elastic concave membrane called the tympanum, adapted to the reception of sounds; and in the eye, a sort of transparent and convex membrane, which collects the rays of light upon the retina. The ear is evidently contrived for the purpose of hearing,

* See an Essay on the subjects of chymistry which was published in 1771, by Dr. Watson, then Professor of Chymistry, but since, Reg. Prof. of Divinity of Cambridge. *T*.

us the eye for seeing: never will a blind man see by means of his ears, nor a deaf man hear with his eyes. If then a tree is a machine, one part of it must be appropriated for the bearing of flowers, another for the spreading of the roots, both of which would in that case, make their appearance, at the extremity of the plant assigned to them by nature:—but should we plant a willow at the water's edge, with the head downwards, the roots would in due time bear leaves. But we are not for this reason to expect an hydraulic machine to sprout from our planting a common pump in the ground; or that laying in a supine posture any animal incapable of turning himself, his claws or his legs, would in process of time grow out of his back.

CHANGE of position cannot affect the parts so as to cause either to perform the office of the other; in every machine which has been investigated, each part produces its proper effect, nor can it be instrumental to any other. The laws of nature are simple, universal, and constant.

I look upon a tree as a republic, and not as a machine. As soon as a branch of a willow is planted on the margin of a river, the little animals which were inclosed in it, betake themselves to those parts where their labours are most immediately necessary—All secondary considerations are laid aside. The leaves are deserted and fall off. Some employ themselves in closing the breach that has been made in their habitation, by surrounding and covering it with a bourrelet (or pad). Others have pushed forth in the earth, long subterraneous galleries, in search of provisions and materials for the use of the community. If they meet with a rock, they turn their course another way, perhaps surround it with their labours, to form a support for the fabrick they are constructing. In some species, as in the oak, they drive down a long pivot (or *tap root*) which supports the whole habitation; each nation has its different manners: Some build upon piles like the Venetians, others upon the surface of the earth, as the Savages raise their cabbins or huts.

WHEN the disorder is set to rights, they employ themselves in making magazines of provisions. Population among the little republicans is very rapid, because of the ease of subsisting. They live upon oils and volatile salts, with which the air and the earth abound. To obtain those of the air, they have recourse to the method practised by sailors when in want of fresh water, and as they spead out their sails in rainy weather,—these display leaves, as so many surfaces; which, that they may not be carried away by the wind are most ingeniously fastened by one point of support, at the extremity of a pliant and elastic tail or stem.

SOME of them ascend through the trunk with drops of liquor, others again descend by the bark with the superfluous aliment.

IF the leaves were formed by the sap, as may be imagined by some, the fruit and flowers might be so likewise: but, graft a wild stock; the fruits of the graft shall be good, while those of the stock shall not be changed in the least. If the sap which has ascended by the trunk of the graft, and has descended again by its bark, had partaken of any quality, it would have shewn itself in the fruits of the stock. But this does not appear, and why it does not is evident: The animals of the stock bring materials to close the orifice made for inserting the graft, which, on their arrival, the inhabitants of the graft receive

and

and fabricate of them excellent fruits: whilſt thoſe of the ſtock continue to form their uſual indifferent ones. The materials are the ſame, the ducts are in common, but the artificers are different. It may be aſked, how theſe beings are protected from an inclement winter. They, as other animals, have inſtinctive precautions for their ſafety; they invelop their houſes with coverings proportioned in number and texture to the climate they are deſigned by nature to inhabit. The trees of the North, as the fir, the birch, &c. have three ſeveral barks,—thoſe of hotter countries have a ſort of cuticles only, by which the ſap deſcends.

The ſagacity of theſe animals ſhews itſelf in another reſpect,—they proportion the height of their edifice to the ſize and extent of its baſe. In laying their foundations, they meet with a variety of obſtructions,—another tree,—rocks,—or an improper ſoil when they have reached a certain depth. In the air, they are not reſtrained, except by conſiderations of ſafety. We have a ſtrong proof of this in plants which twine and cling; for they ſpread themſelves to a very great extent without ſtopping. Some of the liannes have ſhoots ſo long, that it would be difficult to find the ends of them. The beans which climb, riſe to an extreme height, while the marſh bean ſcarcely attains to three feet—theſe are notwithſtanding equally long lived. We ſee alſo, that trees growing on mountains, are low in ſtature: thoſe of the ſame ſpecies in deep and ſheltered vallies, that have no fear of the winds, riſe with more boldneſs to a far greater height; and I am perſuaded, that if an elm in the courſe of its growth, were to paſs through a number of terraſſes, its inhabitants would with courage lay a ſeparate foundation in each, and raiſe the head to a height that would be prodigious.

The Chinese make a curious experiment, which will confirm what I have juſt advanced. They chooſe upon an orange-tree, a branch with its fruit, which they bind hard with a braſs wire, and cover this ligature with wet earth, upon which is preſently formed a bourrelet (or pad) with roots,—they then cut off this little tree, and with its large fruit ſet it upon a table. Had it been left in its original ſituation, it would have formed a ſecond ſtage of orange-tree. Here then we have another proof that trees are not machines,—becauſe they can always grow, and have no determined ſize.

\* Monſieur Bougainville ſays, that in Otaheitee weeping willows are allow'd to be planted before the houſes of great men only,—and that it is known, that by bending the branches of this tree, and planting them in the ground, the ſhadow may extend as far, and in what direction you pleaſe.——Of this tree the dining-hall of the Kings of Otaheitee is formed. *T.*

# LETTER XXX.

## Of FLOWERS.

THERE are many productions of nature, of which our eyes will not enable us to form a judgment; are we therefore to doubt of their exiftence; fhall we fay that the animals of which I fpeak are void of the feveral fenfes of tafte, fight, or feeling: as well may we doubt that the Romans, who built the amphitheatre of Nimes, eat, drank, or flept, becaufe the Hiftorians, who tell us of this building, do not make particular mention of their doing fo. Your garden is watered daily, and you afk whether its inhabitants drink? You know that when plants deprived of air, decay almoft immediately; and you again afk, whether they breathe? Some flowers are known to clofe, and fhut up their leaves in the night; and others not only do fo, but even change their colours.—Among trees alfo, there are fome that clofe their leaves entirely in the evening, as the tamarind-tree. Can we then deny the influence of the light upon them, when its effects are fo evident.

THE movement and contraction of the fenfitive plant upon the approach of the hand towards it, has been attributed to the animal heat; but this cannot be the cafe, becaufe I have feen it equally to move and contract upon being touched with a ftick, stick, a stone being thrown towards it, and even by the wind *. Its powers of motion and contraction can proceed therefore from no other than an intrinsic cause.

Should it be objected, that these animals depart from the universal system of self-preservation; that all others employ themselves in labours useful to themselves, and these, in making flowers which answer no purpose but the pleasure and gratification of mankind, and which, after all the pains and trouble bestowed in their formation, can scarcely be said to exist for a day. A reply is ready from the continuation of the account of their proceedings: The mother-country, and speaking of *inhabitants*, the expression I think may be allowed) being now too populous, the next care is to send forth colonies.—The fine weather in the spring, is the time chosen for this purpose, and for providing sustenance for the emigrants.—Sugar, milk and honey are collected, and deposited in buildings constructed with admirable ingenuity. The heat and action of the sun is now of the greatest consequence, as well to bring to perfection the provisions, as to promote and accelerate the sponsalia.

It should seem, that this politic people, when they colonise, unite their colonists by ties the most forci-

* A new species of Sensitive Plant has been lately discovered in the marshy parts of North America, which has been transplanted to England, and grows there. It is called the *Dionæa Muscipula*, or *Venus Attrapemouche*. Its leaf is no sooner touched by a fly or other insect, than it folds itself over its prey, and remains in that compressed state till the captive is entirely consumed. It will close up equally if touched by a straw, hair, or pin. Experiment has not yet ascertained, whether this plant derives its nourishment from the flies it takes; but it seems very likely that it does so, and if this be the case, the *Attrapemouche* tends more than all hitherto known, of the different species of the Polypus, to confirm the analogy between animals and vegetables. *T.*

ble

ble, that nature knows or is capable of,—they adopt the meafure of government when eftablifhing our fettlements on the Miffiffippi, who fent out very few perfons, but fuch as were newly married.

THE males erect little hollow tubes, on the tops of which they form lodgements of golden duft, from whence they defcend to the bottom of the flowers, where the females expect them with impatience.

THE flower, appears to be the work of the female—It is hung with the moft beautiful fattins, purple—fky-blue black.—One may fancy it a bridal-chamber, whence are exhaled the moft flagrant perfumes.—Or it may be called a vaft temple, in which at once are celebrated an infinity of nuptial ceremonies—each leaf is a bed—each ftamina a bride—and many families inhabit under the fame roof.

SOMETIMES the females make their appearance by themfelves upon one tree, and the males upon another. Perhaps in thefe republics, the ftronger fex keeps the weaker one in fubjection, and will not admit them to affociate upon public occafions, altho' there is a neceffity for making ufe of them upon particular ones.—Like the Amazons of old, who were ferved by flaves of the male fex, but allied themfelves with none but free people.

IN the palm-tree, the female alone is employed in preparing the conjugal bed; which when perceived by the male, he fubmits himfelf to the difpofal of the winds, and is by them tranfported upon thefe beds, called by the botanifts, Prolific Duft.

I MAY feem on this occafion, to be tranfported by my imagination beyond the bounds of probable rea-

son;

son; let me therefore return to my subject and speak of the form and shape of flowers; which is always circular, whatever be the form of the fruit.—Their leaves, or coronets are disposed around as mirrors;—plain, spherical, or eliptic, so as properly to receive and reflect the heat to the focus of their curves, for the due formation of the embrio which contains the seed. The flowers that yield seed are single ones, because the placing of one mirror behind another, would have answered no end.

Among vegetables, the juices of which are viscous and less liable to ferment, such as bulbous and aquatic plants, my little geometricians construct reverberating machines, in the form of furnaces, which, are portions of cylinders, funnels, or bells,—observable in lillies, tulips, hyacinths, jonquils, lillies of the valley, narcissusses, &c.

Those that begin their labours early in the spring, adopt also this prudent mode of formation, witness the primrose, crocus, snow-drop, &c.

Those that build exposed to the air, and that grow but near to the ground—as the daisy and pissabed, form mirrors nearly plain. Those on the other hand, that are something more in the shade, as violets and strawberries, form mirrors that are more concave.

Those that attempt to transplant themselves in hot weather, contract the circumference of the flower, in order to diminish the effect; such are the blue-bell, and pink, &c. Others, as the pomegranate and wild poppy, rumple up their leaves to shelter the disk from the sun, the two great heat of its rays rendering such a protection necessary,—'tis the same in papillonaceous flowers, whose form is rather calculated to re-unite the direct rays of the sun, than to collect anew their reflected heat. ANOTHER

ANOTHER example of their attention, is, that the flowers of fummer which have large cups, are faftened to ligaments, by which they are rather fufpended than fupported; they quickly lofe their flowers: of this kind, are the wild poppy, the poppy, the flower of the pomegranate, &c.

THERE is another fpecies, of which the fun-flower is one, whofe leaves are difpofed as radii round the circumference; the flower is here placed upon a flexible knee, by means of which, the inhabitants are conftantly turning it towards the fun. One might fancy them fo many Academicians, directing a telefcope, or reflecting mirror towards that luminary.

THE fame prudent conduct is remarkable with refpect to the colours of flowers,—white and yellow being the moft adapted for collecting the reflected rays; the generality of fpring and autumnal flowers are of thofe or fuch like bright and clear teints; the degree of heat being fo fmall makes the ufe of active mirrors neceffary.

THE flowers of thefe two feafons which are of a deep red, as the anemony, piony, and fome fort of tulips, have their centers black, as moft proper to abforb the rays immediately. The fummer flowers are of deeper colours, and lefs adapted for reverberation. In this feafon we frequently fee blue and red, but black very rarely, becaufe it never reflects at all. Poppies which are of a deep brown, are, if expofed to the fun, burnt up before the flower is developed.

THE elevation of plants, their fize, their colour and the form in which they are cut or fcolloped, feem

all

all combined in a wonderful harmony—Confidered in this light, flowers inftead of being mere objects of pleafure, are fit fubjects of ftudy for the ableft geometricians.

Nature in all her difpofitions is equally bountiful and juft—Things for our ufe are furnifhed to us with fimplicity: for fuperfluity and enjoyment, with magnificence. Corn, olive trees and vines, are inftances of the former, flowers, and many other beautiful natural productions, of the latter.

The animals of India as they differ from ours in their wants, are equally different in their operations—in our climates, heat is neceffary: our animals therefore form the flowers before the leaves.—And farther north, they build a folid flower and cover it with fcales—thefe are ranged in a conoid form upon a fort of efpalier. The fir tree, and the birch would be parched up in hot countries, wherefore they never grow there.

The trees of India are full of fpreading leaves, under the fhade of which grow the flowers. Their circumference is never very compact, as may be feen in the orange or citron trees.

On trees that have but few leaves, as the agathis, the various forts of palms, the date, cocoa, and latanier,—the flowers grow in pendant clufters—In this inverted ftate, they are not liable to be fcorched by the fun, having no other heat than a reflected one. Trees of Europe bearing flowers in clufters, bear them upright, as the vine, lilach, &c.

To conclude—In Europe the flowers seem to seek for the sun; in India, to avoid and shun it, the greater number either growing close to the trunk of the tree, or else hang down in bunches as those above described.

## LETTER XXXI.

### OF FRUITS.

IT may be alledged as an argument against the system for which I contend, that my animalcules reasoning too much from consequences, seem therein even to be wiser than men. Wherefore is this but because the animal is endued with an instinct, equal in effect to that experience which man is ever arriving at, and never attains to. The spider, weaves as soon as it issues from the egg— The portion of intelligence afforded to each species is perfect from the beginning, and suffices for all the wants of the animal.—'Tis a general observation, that the smaller the animal, the greater its industry—Among birds, the swallow is more alert than the ostrich: of insects none is so small, nor is any so laborious as the ant—Activity and adroitness seem given to the weaker animals as a compensation for the want of strength—and mine being so much smaller than all these; I am justified in believing that they are also more intelligent.

A degree of heat being amaſſed, ſufficient to unite the families at the bottom of the calice or cup of the flower, the whole nation is employed in carrying thither honey and milk. This laſt is a ſuſtenance apparently deſigned for all animals when in their infant ſtate; even the yolk of an egg, if 'tis diſſolved in water, is converted to a conſiſtence like cream. The colony then takes up its reſidence in the part called the *Bourgeon*, (or bud). The proviſions are ranged around, under the appearance of milk, which is ſoon after changed to an oily, and more ſolid ſubſtance.

To protect this colony from accidents it might be liable to, it is, together with its proviſions, enveloped in a ſhell. This covering is ſometimes as hard as a ſtone; great care however is taken to leave an opening, as in nuts, or ſmall holes at the end, covered by a *valve*—by this outlet, the young family find egreſs. Not one ſingle grain is known, but what is in its organiſation, ſuited to this purpoſe.

Nor in advancing this, do I attribute to them a greater degree of intelligence, than is ſeen in other inſects.—The ſpider lays its eggs in a bag, which alſo has its orifice. The ſilk worm ſhuts itſelf up in a pod, of a texture wonderfully compact, except in that part towards the head, which is ſo contrived as to allow it to eſcape from its confinement at the proper time—this precaution is common to all vermicular inſects. But all animals that unite their labours, have infinitely more ingenuity in their proceedings, than thoſe which work individually—theſe, exceed in ingenuity all others—for, while they conſtruct the building, and collect proviſions for the ſupport of the infant colony, leſt the work ſhould be deſtroyed by the birds, or other animals, it is environed with a ſubſtance

stance of a nauseous taste, as the external coat of walnuts, which is bitter,—or fortified with prickly points, as the shell of the chesnut. These operations of my animalcules originate from the same cause, which directs the rabbit to dig itself a burrough in the earth; the lapwing to suspend its nest by a few threads; and the duckling to take to the water, before it has seen the drake swim upon the surface. Let us not wonder then that the rose bush is armed with prickles, and protected all over, by the same means, which the chesnut has provided for its fruit alone.

This defence is commonly seen among shrubs that grow on the borders of the woods, and are exposed to the ravages of beasts that feed there—The sea rush, the bramble, the black and red thorn, the gooseberry tree, and even the nettle and thistle, which grow by the way side, are furnished with prickly points for their defence. They are in fact to the woods, as frontier towns are to a province.

The colony once supplied with the necessary provisions, have various modes of transplanting, or transporting themselves—those suspended aloft in the air, have nothing to do but to suffer themselves to fall down—the fruit drops, and after having rebounded a few times, rests perhaps thirty paces from the parent tree. And here I must remark that those fruits which fall from a great height, are rounder and harder in proportion to their fall—The acorn, the mast of the fir tree, the chesnut, the common nut, the pine apple, are in their several ways protected from the violence of the stroke they receive in coming to the ground. Nature having pre-contrived when she raised them so far above the earth, that their return to it, should not be attended with ill consequences. On the

the other hand, the artificers of the linden tree, which grows in moift and fwampy grounds, know very well, that fhould they conftruct unweildy coverings, their weight would bury them in the fame place they fell. Wherefore, their feed is fixed to a long fibre or feather, with which it is let down by degrees, and carried away by the winds. The willow, which grows in the fame kind of foil, has its tufts of feathers as well as the reed. The feeds of the elm, are placed in the midft of a large follicle or purfe; by means of thefe, which ferve them as wings, they are tranfported to any diftance. By the conftruction of its feed, I fhould be induced to think the elm defigned for the inhabitant of the valley. We need no longer wonder that the cherry and peach tree rife but to a middling ftature. A full grown peach which fhould fall from the heiget of an elm, would not go far. How then, you will fay, do thofe that are mere fhrubs, fuch as the blue bell, artichoke, thiftle, &c. for they cannot roll away from where they lit. I anfwer, that thefe alfo affix their colonies to a kind of wings, and they are then tranfported by the wind. In autumn you may fee the air full of them. They are fufpended with equal induftry as ingenuity, and however far they travel, the feed always falls perpendicularly; and there are fome fort of peas with elaftic fhells, which when ripe, fhoot forth their feed to the diftance of ten or twelve feet. Do you now think that a plant is no more than an hydraulic machine?

Further, as the inhabitant of the chefnut, and other fruits which I have mentioned, protect themfelves from the attacks of the birds—fo the ftrawberry, and the rafberry, make their enemies fubfervient to their purpofes. The former, are warriors, the latter, politicians. They environ themfelves with a fubftance, alluring to the eye and grateful to the tafte.

taste. The birds feed upon this substance, and are nourished by it; and by a natural operation, sow the seeds again in the earth. They devour the fruit, but this does not damage the seed, which is too hard to be affected by their digestive powers. Many other fruits that have stones in them, are sown by the same means. This finesse is not peculiar to the animals of our hemisphere. The nutmeg, is a kind of peach, growing in Molucca; its nuts bring in a large revenue to the States of Holland; who, that they may reserve to themselves the benefits rising from it, have endeavoured to destroy and eradicate this tree, in the islands that do not belong to them; but their attempts are in vain: a particular species of sea fowl, sowing it, soon after they have eaten it. Thus weak is man, when he militates against nature: a whole nation could not extirpate one single vegetable.

The King of Prussia for the encouragement of population, once gave orders to cut down some forests, to provide lands for new married people. It was represented to him, that this measure would occasion a scarcity of timber; to which he made answer, " I had much rather have men in my dominions, than trees." Can it be supposed that the sovereign ruler of all things, would not rather chuse for his subjects, animate beings, than mere uninformed machines?

We have seen animalculæ moving in the juice of plants—and although they are too minute for us, their various operations are imperceptible to our organs, though assisted by the best microscopes: yet they as certainly labour, act in concert, and perform every thing else I have related of them, as the animal inhabitants of the Madrepores, and Litophites —for as these are the plants of the sea, the others are in like manner the Madrepores of the air.

You

You will say, they certainly differ in their construction, because the Madrepores do not bear fruit —but this is an opinion rather started, than to be received. For 'tis to be confidered, that they live in a fluid, where their fruits can neither fall nor roll; to what end then should they environ the colony with a cumberfome body; or with a lighter fubftance, like the wad which furrounds the feeds, which are to fall in the water.

It is certain however, that a milky juice has been feen in their flowers, like that in the feeds of our fruits, which milk is difperfed in the fea like the fpawn of fifh.

Arts and manners differ, in different elements; a failor and a citizen, are both of them men; but a fhip and a houfe, are by no means conftructed alike.

The little animals, builders of the plants in the air, live in an element which appears to be in perpetual motion,—the moft gentle zephyr, is to them a hurricane. They have taken the moft prudent precautions to fecure the foundations of their edifices, and to tranfport their families without rifk of their being damaged or fcattered abroad.

Those who build in the fea, live in a fluid, which is not altogether fo eafily put in motion; and when once agitated, moves in waves and large maffes. The drops are not fo active and penetrating as the globules, of which the air is formed, and which are inceffantly dilated, and contracted, by different degrees of heat or cold. They do not therefore require to be fo carefully inclofed, as thofe feeds, which are liable to be fo eafily diffipated. Their milk is befides of a more vifcous nature, not eafily diffolved.

If

If the animals of the water, had inhabited a still more solid element, for example, the earth; they would not have been exposed to any sort of agitation. And it is probable that they would then have had no occasion to put down roots, to raise a stem, spread out leaves, fashion flowers, or fabricate fruits, as do those that inhabit the air.

In confirmation of my assertion; the truffle has none of the parts abovementioned, nor has it any use, for them. To what end should there be flowers on a plant that never sees the sun, or roots to a vegetable not exposed to any shock? I have heard many people say, they cannot divine by what means the truffle is reproduced: its revivifcency is in my opinion, effected by the communication of its animalculæ with each other through the interior parts of the soil it grows in, where reigns a calm eternal and undisturbed.—The fluid being tranquil, the communication, cannot but be easy—no vessels are necessary, for the little inhabitants may swim along in safety. One would be almost sorry that the animals of so charming a fruit, should be so indolent, and of such apparent incapacity: but the endowments of every being, are proportioned to its necessities—and man, of all beings the most indigent, is at the same time the most intelligent. 'Tis to be wished indeed, that he were the happiest; and yet the inhabitants of the truffle, though less sensible than others, may perhaps be more contented

Having accounted I hope, for the ordinary causes of vegetation, if you are not yet satisfied, I will now speak of its extraordinary productions: and my best mode of doing this, will be by anticipating such objections as I think you may probably make to what has been already advanced; and the first is one, which you will say perhaps, all the laws of hydraulics cannot obviate.—That a young tree, full of sap, frequently fought after. Others have been mentioned, and very juftly condemned by Monfieur Voltaire, for having taken out the bowels of a living dog, to fhew the fpectators the lacteal veins. I would by no means encourage the practice of fuch barbarous experiments; but my fyftem does not affect the life of the animals, whofe exiftence it is meant to prove. For as they are too minute to become the objects of vifion, fo neither can they be affected by our powers of digeftion.

FINIS.

www.ingramcontent.com/pod-product-compliance
Lightning Source LLC
Chambersburg PA
CBHW022112230426
43672CB00008B/1356